The Architecture of Neoliberalism

The Architecture of Neoliberalism

How Contemporary Architecture Became an Instrument of Control and Compliance

Douglas Spencer

Bloomsbury Academic
An imprint of Bloomsbury Publishing Plc

B L O O M S B U R Y
LONDON • OXFORD • NEW YORK • NEW DELHI • SYDNEY

Bloomsbury Academic

An imprint of Bloomsbury Publishing Plc

50 Bedford Square
London
WC1B 3DP
UK

1385 Broadway
New York
NY 10018
USA

www.bloomsbury.com

BLOOMSBURY and the Diana logo are trademarks of Bloomsbury Publishing Plc

First published 2016
Reprinted 2017 (twice), 2018

© Douglas Spencer, 2016

British Library Cataloguing-in-Publication Data
A catalogue record for this book is available from the British Library.

ISBN: HB: 978-1-4725-8152-5
PB: 978-1-4725-8151-8
ePDF: 978-1-4725-8154-9
ePub: 978-1-4725-8153-2

Library of Congress Cataloging-in-Publication Data
A catalogue record for this book is available from the British Library.
Names: Spencer, Douglas, author.
Title: The architecture of neoliberalism: how contemporary architecture became an instrument of control and compliance / Douglas Spencer.
Description: New York: Bloomsbury Academic, 2016.
Identifiers: LCCN 2016009047| ISBN 9781472581525 (hardback) |
ISBN 9781472581518 (paperback) | ISBN 9781474299824 (xml)
Subjects: LCSH: Architecture and society. | Architecture–Political aspects.
| Neoliberalism. | BISAC: ARCHITECTURE / Criticism. | ARCHITECTURE /
History / Contemporary (1945-). | POLITICAL SCIENCE / Political Ideologies
/ Conservatism & Liberalism.
Classification: LCC NA2543.S6 S6427 2016 | DDC 720.1/03–dc23 LC record
available at http://lccn.loc.gov/2016009047

Cover design by Daniel Benneworth-Gray
Cover image: Zaha Hadid's London Aquatics Centre, 2014 © Douglas Spencer

Typeset by Deanta Global Publishing Services, Chennai, India
Printed and bound in Great Britain

For Becky,
a continuing source of inspiration

Contents

List of Illustrations

Acknowledgements

This work is the result of research and writing undertaken over a number of years. During that time I have had the opportunity to discuss this work with a number of people whose criticisms, comments, encouragement and support have proved invaluable to its development and realization. These include Tanis Hinchcliffe, Andrew Higgott, Ross Adams, Ivonne Santoyo-Orozco, Camilo Amaral, Libero Andreotti, Eva Castro, Alfredo Ramirez, Clara Oloriz Sanjuan, Tim Waterman, Ed Wall, Jon Goodbun, Marina Lathouri, Manuel Shvartzberg, Alexendra Vougia, Platon Issaias, Jack Self, Don Rawson, Helen Beesley and the students of MA History and Critical Thinking at the Architectural Association from 2012 to 2015. Thanks to Ana Abram, Savia Palate and Shengze Chen for the photographs. Thanks to James Thompson at Bloomsbury for his enthusiasm and support for this project, and for his patience. Special thanks are due to Nadir Lahiji and Ben Noys for taking the time to read and comment on draft chapters of the book. My most sincere gratitude and greatest respect are due to Murray Fraser and David Cunningham for the part they have played in standing up for, and nurturing and refining, my research with their tireless efforts and invaluable insights.

Preface

This book originated in a critique of what I have called, elsewhere, 'Deleuzism' in architecture. I was concerned, in this, with challenging the appropriation, by certain architects and architectural theorists, of the conceptual vocabulary of Deleuze and Guattari in order to present themselves as the advanced guard of a new and emancipatory direction for architecture. These claims were contested through close readings of the written discourse of this 'architectural Deleuzism', and through an analysis of its built projects that showed how these were, rather than liberatory, in fact instrumental to a neoliberal agenda of subjectification. This critique, and its methods, remains central to this book. Rather than focusing only upon the appropriation of the thought of Deleuze and Guattari, however, I also consider other factors through which architectural discourse and practice has rendered its services to neoliberalism as instruments of control and compliance. I address the development of a post-critical and 'projective' position in architecture, and the refashioning and repurposing of architectural theory through which this was accomplished. The uptake of universal models of self-organization, complexity and emergence in architecture is also reflected upon, particularly in light of their role in the construction of neoliberalism's own 'truth games'. The more recent turn to theories of affect in architectural discourse and its affirmations of an unmediated and post-linguistic experience of the built environment are also critically contested here.

In calling to account the claims of what Jeff Kipnis once designated as the 'new architecture', I have turned, as well, to a mode of analysis through which the development of both neoliberalism and the architectural positions that effectively further its causes can be understood in historical terms. To this end I have drawn upon an earlier period of theorizing, particularly where this was concerned, in certain works by Jean Baudrillard, Jean-François Lyotard and, especially, Michel Foucault, with what was at stake in the new modes of power whose outlines had first emerged in the 1970s. I have also returned to the thought of the so-called Frankfurt School, particularly that of Theodor Adorno, in order to mobilize his critique of affirmation and his perspectives on conceptual thought, experience, perception, aesthetics and mediation in relation to the latest turns within late capitalism.

I have tried, as well, to understand and represent here how neoliberalism operates as productive of models and means of power and control, particularly in relation to what I refer to, following Foucault, as the 'production of subjectivity'. Rather than presenting neoliberalism simply as some unrestrained, extreme expression of the essential and unchanging 'nature' of capitalism, I have sought to comprehend it as a school of economic thought that has consciously directed itself, through key individual thinkers, as a project to remake the mentality and behaviour of the subject in its own image, as in accord, that is, with a totalizing logic of economically opportunistic valorization. Foucault's lectures on the 'Birth of Biopolitics' have been fundamental to this task, as has the writing of those who have, more recently, responded to and built upon these, such as Christian Laval and Pierre Dardot, and Philip Mirowski. In addition to these secondary accounts of neoliberal thought, I have also addressed certain of its key texts directly, especially those written by its chief intellectual theorist, Friedrich Hayek. Through the analysis of these I have outlined some of the arguments through which the central tenets of neoliberalism have been contrived, particularly those concerning spontaneous orders, self-organization, complexity and cybernetics upon which much contemporary architecture also now grounds its own principles and practices.

The analysis of the key architectural projects contained in this book – works by Zaha Hadid Architects, Foreign Office Architects, Rem Koolhaas/OMA and others – draws, in part, upon methods practised by figures such as Siegfried Kracauer, Jean Baudrillard and Fredric Jameson. In their critical reflections on the phenomenal experiences of the built environment, these figures sought, in different ways, to grasp the mediation of larger forces at play in the material expressions of the architectural work. With the same goal in mind, I have drawn upon these practices, but I have also tried to understand the role of other agents of mediation in the process. In the analysis of the design of workspaces, of spaces of education, commerce and communication, the practices of neoliberal governmentality in which these are implicated are also considered in some depth. I also understand particular architects and theorists, in the arguments promoted and publicized in their writings, as instrumental to a neoliberal agenda, whether by design or in effect. The extensive analysis of some of their writings contained in this book should be understood, in this spirit, as a critique of arguments and positions, rather than as a criticism of the individuals who have signed their name to these. The focus on these individual figures, on both their discursive and their architectural practices, should also be understood as motivated by the fact of their prominence within architectural culture. This book pursues its critique of an architecture of neoliberalism through a contestation of its most visible manifestations. Certainly this architecture accounts only for a small fraction of the built environment, yet it exerts a broad influence on architectural practice, pedagogy and theory. For this reason it is deserving of precisely the kind of critical analysis it seeks to insure itself against through its own theoretical manoeuvres.

Introduction: Architecture, Neoliberalism and the Game of Truth

Swarm-modelled figures dispersed across smooth space. Steered between buildings. Channelled along elevated walkways. The architecture is fluid. Its forms materialize out of thin air or extrude themselves into existence. The pleats, grilles and apertures patterning their surfaces seemingly subject to the same unseen forces. There are no signs of labour. Threaded between the buildings and pathways, sometimes woven into the architectural envelope, are the green spaces that signal sustainability, deference to the laws of nature. The trajectory of the virtual camera as elegantly choreographed as that of the environment it records as it spirals around the site, tracking pathways, banking over structures and hovering, momentarily, over details. The scenography of contemporary architecture. The friction-free space supposed to liberate the subject from the strictures of both modernism and modernity, to reunite it with nature, to liberate its nomadic, social and creative dispositions, to re-enchant its sensory experience of the world, to conjoin it with a technology itself now operating in accord with the very laws of the material universe, with emergence, self-organization and complexity.

What is being played out in this scenography is the spatial complement of contemporary processes of neoliberalization. What was championed, only half-ironically, by Jeff Kipnis in 1993 as the 'New Architecture' – also known, variously, as projective, post-critical or Deleuzian, an architecture of folding, complexity or parametricism, the architecture of Greg Lynn, Zaha Hadid, Alejandro Zaera-Polo, Farshid Moussavi, Reiser + Umemoto, Lars Spuybroek, latterly Rem Koolhaas, to name some of its more prominent practitioners – is in thrall to the same notions of liberty as are propounded in neoliberal thought. Both parties profess their hatred of hierarchical planning and their enthusiasms for spontaneous ordering and self-organization. Both have drawn substantially upon systems theory and cybernetics in the development of their theories and practices. What they share, most of all, is a conception of the nature of the human subject, of its relations with the world around it, and of how it should be governed.

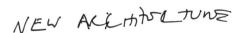

NEW ARCHITECTURE

This shared understanding of subjectivity has furnished architecture with the opportunity to design and build for the continued expansion of neoliberalism into the worlds of work, education, culture and consumption, both in the West and beyond, within the territories latterly exposed to its influence.

Michel Foucault examined the operative nature of the neoliberal truths of subjectivity, the truths put about through which architecture has legitimated its post-critical and projective turn as progressive and emancipatory. 'Truth games', he said, are implements in the production of subjectivity. They legitimate forms of power that operate on and through the constitution of the self. They are also themselves produced – constituted and constructed by interested parties – before being put into play as techniques of power. The rules of the truth game, though, require that the contrivance of its truths be concealed from the players.[1] This rule maintains the operative capacity of the truths constructed, that they are accepted as the given conditions that determine how things must, of necessity, be managed. Truth games do not rule from outside or above, but by embedding themselves in forms of common knowledge and practice. As Dardot and Laval write in *The New Way of the World*, 'The truth cannot be resisted; it can only be approached. For it does not command, but imposes itself by getting itself acknowledged.'[2]

Neoliberalism is a truth game. Its accounts of human knowledge, social complexity and the economic market legitimate its management of individuals. Among the fundamental truths that neoliberal thought has constructed are those that state that individuals can achieve only a narrow and very limited knowledge of the real complexities of the world; that the planning of society by individuals is, consequently, an untenable proposition; that the economic market is better able to calculate, process and spontaneously order society than the state is able to; that the competition between individuals facilitated by equality of access to the market is a natural state of affairs; that the job of the state is to intervene to ensure the conditions of possibility that sustain the operation of the market and to ensure that individuals are rendered adaptable and responsive to these conditions; that its truths are a guarantee of liberty.

The corollary of these truths is that a specifically neoliberal form of power works to produce the subjects of its competitive market order through the milieu of the market itself, rather than through the direct and disciplinary administration of the state and its institutions. The market exercises control of the subject – its processing, modelling and constitution – through the immanent conditions of an entrepreneurial environment that is itself sustained by these same subjects, and through the forms of strategic state intervention that ensure its survival as the only game in town.

Since their first organized gathering, at the Walter Lippmann Colloquium held in Paris in 1938, attended by figures including Wilhelm Röpke and Alexander Rüstow of the German 'ordoliberal' school, Friedrich Hayek and Ludwig von Mises of the Austrian (later to be Austro-American) school, and the Hungarian polymath Michael Polanyi, the proponents of neoliberalism have concentrated as much effort on the circulation and acknowledgement of their truths as on their construction. What Philip Mirowski describes as the 'Neoliberal Thought Collective',[3] also including figures such as Milton Friedman and Gary Becker, has always been concerned with having its knowledge accepted so as to inform a 'policy of society' and its management, rather than being taken as a purely economic model.[4] 'Neoliberal intellectuals', writes Mirowski, 'identified their immediate targets as elite civil society. Their efforts were primarily aimed at winning over intellectuals and opinion leaders of future generations, and their primary instrument was redefining the place of knowledge in society.'[5] In the 1949 essay 'The Intellectuals and Socialism', Hayek described the precise function of these 'intellectuals and opinion leaders'. He noted the success of socialism in propagating ideas within the working classes that had not, he argued, originated in the minds of that class, and proposed that the methods of socialism be emulated in order to spread the cause of neoliberalism. The intellectual, a figure he described as a 'second-hand dealer in ideas',[6]

> need not possess special knowledge of anything in particular, nor need he even be particularly intelligent, to perform his role as intermediary in the spreading of ideas. What qualifies him for his job is the wide range of subjects on which he can readily talk and write, and a position or habits through which he becomes acquainted with new ideas sooner than those to whom he addresses himself.[7]

In *Law, Legislation and Liberty*, Hayek wrote of the 'need to gain the support of those second-hand dealers of ideas, mainly in what are now called the "media," who largely determine public opinion'. This project – the neoliberalization of common knowledge – pursued through means such as the establishment of the Mont Pelerin society in 1947, and the numerous think tanks and policy units aligned to its trajectory formed since then, has been profoundly successful. As Mirowski writes, 'Neoliberalism as a world view has sunk its roots deep into everyday life, almost to the point of passing as the "ideology of no ideology."'[8]

Architectural culture has, especially since the late 1960s, also been concerned with the propagation of certain truths – about the discipline, its theory and its practice – derived from other fields of knowledge including, but not limited to, those of philosophy, linguistics, media, physics, biology, computation and mathematics. Of late, it has shown signs of readily embracing and propagating the tenets of neoliberalism's truths. Patrik Schumacher, in the essay 'Free Market Urbanism – Urbanism Beyond Planning', argues:

> Perhaps society should allow the market to discover the most productive mix and arrangement of land uses, a distribution that garners synergies and maximizes overall value. The market process is an evolutionary process that operates via mutation (trial and error), selection and reproduction. It is self-correcting, self-regulation [*sic*], leading to a self-organized order. Thus we might presume that the land use allocation and thus the programmatic dimension of the urban and architectural order is to be determined by architecture's private clients.[9]

While architects and architectural theorists have generally been less brazen about their enthusiasms for the subsumption of the urban and architectural orders to those of the market, they have tended, since the mid-1990s in particular, to push those same truths of the way of the world as have served the truth games of neoliberalism. They have adopted models of self-organization, emergence and complexity, endorsed cybernetics, systems theory and ecological thought, denounced the failings of planning in favour of evolutionary paradigms, valorized 'flat ontologies' and enthused over metabolic processes.[10] They have, above all, posited the human subject as kind of post-enlightenment being – environmentally adaptive and driven by affect rather than rationality, flexibly amenable to being channelled along certain pathways, but uninterested in, even incapable of, critical reflection upon its milieu. As with neoliberal thought, much of architecture's intellectual culture posits the construction of the subject and the social order as akin to the operation of natural systems. The function of architecture prescribed by this position is that of producing endlessly flexible environments for infinitely adaptable subjects. As neoliberalism presents itself as a series of propositions in the pursuit of liberty, architecture presents itself as progressive. This is the truth game of architecture.

The confluences between these two truth games, the kinds of theorizing, discourse and practices they legitimate, and the productions of subjectivity that they posit are the concerns of this book. So too are the resources and practices, the turns and manoeuvres, through which architecture has come to serve as an instrument of control and compliance for contemporary processes of neoliberalization.

The book's first chapter, 'The Art of Neoliberal Governmentality', sets out the definition of neoliberalism with which *The Architecture of Neoliberalism* is working. Rather than understanding neoliberalism simply as the unbridled and extreme expression of capitalism, I understand it as an ideology, albeit an 'ideology of no ideology'. As Jeremy Gilbert has recently noted, on the necessity of distinguishing between capitalism and neoliberalism, 'neoliberalism and capitalism are simply different types of thing. Capitalism is not an ideology'.[11] Neoliberalism, he writes, 'is the name for a particular political philosophy and set of beliefs, and the political programmes informed by them, which claim to understand something about human nature and economics, and which claims that their understanding of human nature and economics gives them superior insights into how to use government mechanisms in order to maximise human flourishing'.[12] There is, of course, a relationship between neoliberalism and capitalism. As Gilbert argues, neoliberalism believes 'that the only real way to maximise human flourishing is to maximise the profits of capitalists'. But the distinction between the two needs to be made, not least in order to produce an effectively critical account of architecture's relationship to neoliberalism; one that does more than present the naive and dubious charge that architecture, pejoratively labelled as 'neoliberal', has only lately become enmeshed in systems of power and money.

While I call extensively – though not uncritically – upon a variety of Marxian schools of thought and thinkers throughout this book, I turn outside of these in order to account for and define the ideology of neoliberalism, particularly as it relates to the question of subjectivity. Against Marxian understandings of neoliberalism, particularly those of David Harvey,[13] in which neoliberalism is presented as an outcome of the 'logic of capital', I draw upon the recent work of Philip Mirowski, and Pierre Dardot and Christian Laval, so as to sketch out a historical understanding of what Mirowski has called the 'neoliberal thought collective' in its ideological specificity, and to understand the kind of mentality with which it operates today in what Dardot and Laval tellingly describe as the neoliberal 'way of the world'.[14] It is the work of Foucault on governmentality, on the 'production of subjectivity' and the 'care of the self', however, that is pivotal to the understanding of neoliberalism that I represent here. In the development of neoliberal thought, Foucault remarked, 'the formal principles of a market economy' are projected 'on to a general art of government'.[15] Neoliberalism is understood by Foucault as a form of governmentality with its own particular apparatuses and techniques, its own means of 'taking care' of the self, though not for the self, but in order to render it entrepreneurial, to shape it in accord with neoliberal beliefs about the essential nature of the subject and its relationship to the putatively progressive and evolutionary forces of the market.

This chapter then turns to look directly at the foundational writings of neoliberal thinkers, especially those of Hayek and Polanyi, so as to explore the substance and construction of their arguments, particularly as these pertain to their understandings of knowledge and its circulation. I also address the significance of the notions of 'complexity' and 'spontaneous ordering' as these are developed in the thought of Hayek and Polanyi. These notions, derived chiefly from systems theory and cybernetics, and turned into dogmatic universal principles, become the instruments of neoliberal modes of governmentality; techniques based more on the steering, guidance and control of conduct than on the use of blunt instruments of discipline and the naked exercise of hierarchical power.

An understanding of neoliberal dogma alone, though, cannot be counted on to explain how the framing and control of subjectivity in relation to its environments – through which Foucault claims its power is effected – is actually achieved. This is a process with its own historical development, ranging across the fields of architecture, technology and culture which, while typically informed by cybernetics, systems theory and models of complexity, are not explicitly neoliberal. Chapter 2, 'The Spatial Constitution of the Neoliberal Subject', engages with this history. It begins within an exploration of how figures in the Independent Group in Britain developed and promoted new forms of artistic practice aiming to circumvent existing conventions of distance and judgement in the reception of culture. It also addresses how these ideas and practices correspond with those developed contemporaneously in the United States by figures such as Allan Kaprow, in his writings on Jackson Pollock, and his involvement in the development of the 'happening'. In both cases, immediacy and immersion are affirmed as conditions of spatial and visual experience and in ways that set clear precedents for more recent affirmations of immediacy and affect within contemporary architecture.

Through a comparative analysis of the films *Alphaville* (1965) by Jean Luc Godard, and *THX1138* (1971) by George Lucas, I explore the differing reactions of the New Left and the counterculture to the technocratic fears of the 1960s and early 1970s. Whereas the left, I argue, tended to see technology as an instrument of state power that could itself only be overcome through collective revolutionary social transformation, the counterculture, as represented in *THX 1138*'s individually rebellious protagonist and in the technophilic sensibilities of its conclusion, saw things differently and in ways that were prescient of the development of neoliberal mentalities. The possibilities of a new contract between nature, man and technology explored by the counterculture and its communes, promoted and serviced by Stewart Brand and his *Whole Earth Catalog*, cultivated a cybernetically oriented and entrepreneurial culture that spawned figures such as Steve Jobs, and profoundly influenced architectural culture both in the United States and in Britain and Europe. The turn to cybernetics in architecture was pushed especially by Reyner Banham. His accounts of being transported to some transcendent realm of experience in the fusion of man-machine-nature – riding his bike across the Californian desert, or driving his car along the Los Angeles Freeway – have reappeared in contemporary architectural fantasies of techno-environmental immersion, of the channelling and steering of the subject, of its giving itself over freely to the sensory enjoyments of a cybernetic spatial condition.

Before the 'new architecture' of the 1990s could reconnect with this tendency – I argue in this book's third chapter, 'Architectural Theory: From May 68 to the "Real" of the Market' – it had to deal with the problem of theory. What François Cusset termed the 'madness' of theory had formed, particularly in the fallout from May 68, what was recognized in retrospect as a kind of demonic possession that had to be exorcized from architectural discourse.[16] The intellectual thrills opened up to architecture, especially by what came to be known as 'continental theory', were now castigated by figures like Michael Speaks as obstructions to the proper business of architectural work, that of finding clients and designing for them. I explore the so-called post-critical turn to which this rejection of theory was related, but also argue that this does not so much mark the end of theory as the end of its being allowed to be a disruptive influence. A certain tendency in architectural culture sets itself the managerial task of rejecting the 'negative' theory that obstructs its practice, and sets about locating the type of theory through which it can, in turn, manage its own discourse about itself. On the one hand this newly disciplined theory would be progressive, avant-garde, even emancipatory, on the other it would be practical and fine-tuned to the real needs of the real world 'as found' in post-Fordist capitalism. The prime instruments of this project, in the first instance, are the writings of Deleuze and Guattari and so-called complexity theory. Later these are supplemented with other theories, those of Manuel DeLanda, Bruno Latour and Niklas Luhmann through which Schumacher, Polo, Moussavi and others have constructed arguments in favour of the operation of free markets. Here I analyse the key writings – those by Kipnis, Polo, Lynn, Speaks, Schumacher and others – through which these positions have been articulated, so as to demonstrate and challenge the discursive manoeuvres through which architecture comes to be a managerial practice.

Where the first three chapters of *The Architecture of Neoliberalism* explore how architecture came to operate as an instrument of neoliberal governmentality, and of the conditions, arguments and precedents that opened up this possibility, the following three chapters examine how this has worked out in practice. The fourth chapter, 'Labour Theory: Architecture, Work and Neoliberalism', begins by noting that contemporary architecture is unable to countenance the facts of labour, its hardships, struggles and precarities. It obscures them with the rhetoric of self-organization and autogenic self-creation which its shares with the doxa of neoliberalism. Practically, even the construction of architecture itself is disguised in the phantasmagoria of smooth surfaces and elegant forms wrapped around its structural armatures. Examining the ways in which practices of labour, and its management, have developed according to neoliberal imperatives, I reflect on how these might be critically accounted for, given the existing material on this presented in accounts of immaterial labour, in Boltanski and Chiappelo's *The New Spirit of Capitalism* and in the writings of Moishe Postone. These theoretical reflections are then turned towards an analysis of Zaha Hadid Architects' design for the Central Building of BMW Leipzig. Here, the broader mechanisms of neoliberal governmentality now operative in the former East Germany are shown to be well served by an architecture able to establish a spatial framework for maximizing the productivity of precarious labour while, at the same time, providing an image of socially oriented collectivity. The Office for Metropolitan Architecture's (OMA) China Central Television (CCTV) Headquarters in Beijing is the second case examined in this chapter. I read the form of this building as a refinement of the hyperbuilding prototype earlier developed in Rem Koolhaas' office, one designed to produce more efficient means of corporate staff management. On this basis, I challenge the official account of the CCTV project, circulated by Koolhaas and his partner in the project, Ole Scheeren, that this is some kind of communist project, executed in the service of 'the people'. Rather, I argue, it is a project finely calibrated to the demands placed on the introduction of neoliberal models labour, and for managing the public perception of the state, in the singular conditions of a neoliberalism 'with Chinese characteristics'.

Chapter 5, 'Festivals of Circulation: Neoliberal Architectures of Culture, Commerce and Education', returns, in its analysis of Richard Rogers and Renzo Piano's Pompidou Centre, to an earlier period of cybernetic architecture. As a rare instance of a built project realized from this tendency in architecture, the Pompidou, I argue, stands as a significant precedent for more contemporary projects in which circulation is a central preoccupation. In this project, manifestly informed both by cybernetics and a sympathy for the kind of ludic spatial practices and sensibilities that emerged from the events of May 68, circulation is conceived as a means of breaking down barriers, those between culture and its audiences in particular. Baudrillard's critique of the Pompidou is correct in its claim that the project recuperates the demands of May 68, answering calls for access, participation and informality by turning the museum into a hypermarket for the mass consumption of culture. He is less convincing, I suggest, in arguing that this project fails, that the masses inadvertently sabotage it, destroying culture and meaning in their rush to consume it. Following the analysis presented by Lyotard, in *The Postmodern Condition: A Report on Knowledge*, I explore how, within newly emerging and essentially cybernetic techniques of governmentality, the antagonisms that emerge from May 68 become the fuel for the refinement of its systems.[17] Opposition to the system is answered not by repression but with its sublimation, through its incorporation within a system made more operationally effective by its inclusion. If the Pompidou can be seen, against its initial critical reception, as successful in these terms, it is because it contributes to the forging of a new subject position – the 'cultural consumer' – through its spatial articulation of circulation. Circulation is made productive, but also spectacular, as a visible affirmation of its enjoyments calculated to encourage the subject to step into its currents.

In the analysis of more contemporary projects that follows, I explore the role of an architecture of circulation in fashioning other hybrid and paradigmatically neoliberal subject positions, those of the 'citizen-consumer' and the 'student-entrepreneur'. Through the case of the Foreign Office Architects (FAO) Meydan Retail Complex in Istanbul, I explore the antagonisms between the needs of the disenfranchised poor of Istanbul and the private development of land for shopping malls, and how these are supposed to be resolved by projects such as FOA's in which spaces of consumption are to function, at the same time, as convivial public spaces. In the process I explicate the arguments of Zaera-Polo's essay 'The Politics of the Envelope' in order to contest his claims about the progressive nature of such projects, and so as to indicate the ways in which these effectively serve neoliberal techniques of governmentality.[18] The position of the 'student-entrepreneur' is explored through the antagonisms produced in the marketization of higher education and the consequent subjection of students to conditions of indebtedness. Addressing the case of the New Academic Building designed for the Cooper Union school in New York by Morphosis, of the proliferation of 'hub' spaces in British universities, and focusing on FOA's Ravensbourne College building, I explore how these work to construct new subjects of education, how the university is remade into a space for the practising of new entrepreneurial skills, dispositions and forms of conduct: the so-called 'learning landscape'.

The 'affective turn', and its relationship to both architecture and neoliberalism, is the focus of the book's sixth and final chapter, 'Neoliberalism and Affect: Architecture and the Patterning of Experience'. Against a critical tradition that stretches from Simmel, through Kracauer, Benjamin, Adorno, Baudrillard, and on to Jameson, in which the belief was that one could somehow grasp the larger abstract movements of capital – with architecture frequently the privileged site through which this might be achieved – the discourse of affect suggests that there is nothing to be analysed beyond material immediacy. The turn to affect is premised on the belief that there is nothing to interpret, no moment of cognition, only a feeling for matter. This, I argue, constitutes an essentially a 'pre-critical' turn. Tracing the affirmation of affect in the writings of Zaera-Polo, Moussavi, Lavin and Spuybroek, and the origins of their arguments in the work of Gilles Deleuze, Brian Massumi and others, I contest its insistence upon the immediacy of perception.

The tradition to which the affective turn opposes itself is concerned with critical reflection upon experience, with the possibility of grasping something of the 'totality' – social reality as an interrelated whole – through and from the outward forms that present themselves to the senses. This 'defetishizing critique', founded in the philosophy of Hegel, developed out of a resistance to the idea that the subject might be unconsciously manipulated through a purely sensory stimulation, controlled through a process of aestheticization. It is precisely this danger, I argue, that reappears in the assertions that sensory affect, in a contemporary architecture of immersive environments, liberates the subject from the unnecessary labour of cognition. The discourse of affect in architecture is entirely consonant with neoliberal models of the subject as necessarily ignorant, to the imperative that it give itself over to the trust of processes it cannot, itself, aspire to know or control, to processes rendered efficient and sensually appealing through the new architecture.

Necessary Ignorance: The Art of Neoliberal Governmentality

David Harvey, in his *A Brief History of Neoliberalism*, claims that 'neoliberalization was from the very beginning a project to achieve the restoration of class power'.[1] It is capital, with its logic of unconstrained accumulation and its agenda for the restoration of 'class power', that is decisive.[2] 'The capitalist world', says Harvey, 'stumbled toward neoliberalization' as the answer to its own question: 'How were the conditions for the resumption of active capital accumulation to be restored?'[3] Neoliberalism is granted little agency of its own. The kinds of knowledge it has produced, and its specificity as a particular form of capitalism, are given little consideration. In *Never Let a Serious Crisis Go to Waste: How Neoliberalism Survived the Financial Meltdown*, Philip Mirowski, in response, complains that Marxian approaches have failed to address what is distinctive in neoliberalism. Harvey, he says, 'propounds the Marxist position that it is straightforwardly a class project masked by various versions of "free market" rhetoric. For him, the ideas are far less significant than the brute function of serving the interests of finance capital and globalized elites in the redistribution of wealth upward.'[4]

Pierre Dardot and Christian Laval share these concerns. In their *The New Way of the World: On Neoliberal Society*, they argue that neoliberalism 'employs unprecedented techniques of power over conduct and subjectivities. It cannot be reduced to the spontaneous expansion of the commodity sphere and the field of capital accumulation.'[5] Marxist readings of neoliberalism are 'trapped in a conception that makes the "logic of capital" an autonomous motor of history, they reduce the latter to the sheer repetition of the same scenarios, with the same characters in new costumes and the same plots in new settings'.[6] Against this, Dardot and Laval argue that capitalism does not progress according to an 'implacable "natural law"'. It can encompass and admit of a 'multiplicity of unique forms'. While neoliberalism is certainly a form of capitalism, it must, they say, be understood and analysed 'in its irreducible specificity'.[7]

Foucault and governmentality

Dardot and Laval follow Foucault in formulating their analysis of neoliberalism as a specific form of capitalism possessed and productive of its own apparatus of power. Central to Foucault's analysis, in these terms, is the concept of governmentality foregrounded in later works such as *Security, Territory and Population* and *The Birth of Biopolitics*.[8] In these his concerns turn from a more or less exclusive preoccupation with technologies of domination to a position more attentive to what he terms 'technologies of the self'. As he writes in the essay 'Technologies of the Self', the 'encounter between the technologies of domination of others and those of the self I call "governmentality"'.[9] Here Foucault's agenda shifts from questions of how individuals are subjugated by power to ones of how subjectivity is actively produced. 'Governmentality', as Thomas Lemke elaborates, conceptually unites 'technologies of the self with technologies of domination', and forms a semantic link between 'governing ("gouverner") and modes of thought ("mentalité")'.[10]

In turning from questions of disciplinary power and its centralized, regulatory practices to other forms of governmentality – integrative, continuous, immersive – Foucault sought to understand how non-disciplinary apparatuses of power operated, especially those of neoliberalism. In *The Birth of Biopolitics* he argues that 'American neo-liberalism involves … the generalization of the economic form of the market. It involves generalizing it throughout the social body and including the whole of the social system not usually conducted through or sanctioned by monetary exchanges'.[11] In neoliberalism, the market, its form and logic now coextensive with society as whole, becomes itself a mode of governmentality, an environmental apparatus working to produce the mentalities and dispositions conducive to its continued operation.

Dardot and Laval draw on Foucault's account of governmentality to counter orthodox Marxian perspectives on the emergence of neoliberalism. They argue that the claims made by Harvey, and others, that neoliberalism is adopted by capitalism to solve its crises of accumulation in the 1960s and 1970s are shortsighted, failing to comprehend that neoliberalism serves as a particular mode of power invested in 'controlling the population and directing its conduct'.[12] 'Neoliberalism', they write, 'does not only respond to a crisis of accumulation: it responds to a crisis of governmentality'.[13]

This crisis of governmentality concerns the capacity of the state in this period to direct an effectively functioning capitalist economy while, at the same time, maintaining a democratic social order based on the planning, administration and provision of public services, welfare and employment. The neoliberal answer to this crisis, simply, is that the market economy take on the function of ordering society – the 'market order' – and that the state is reassigned to a role facilitating the operation of the market through the construction of policies and frameworks. A new and beneficent principle of social order will be established through the very same economic principles of free competition that serve as the basis for the accumulation of capital. For neoliberalism the market is not the object of a policy of laissez-faire, but, instead, the very mechanism through which the social order is maintained. As Foucault writes: *— MARKET*

> The problem of neo-liberalism is ... how the overall exercise of political power *—* can be modelled on the principles of a market economy. So it is not a question of *Social* freeing an empty space, but of taking the formal principles of a market economy *order* and referring and relating them to, of projecting them on to a general art of government.[14]

Foucault's assessment of what is distinctive about neoliberalism is confirmed in the writings of its key thinkers. Milton Friedman, for instance, said of the differences between nineteenth-century liberalism and twentieth-century neoliberalism:

> In place of the nineteenth century understanding that *laissez-faire* is the means to achieve [the goal of individual freedom], neoliberalism proposes that it is competition that will lead the way. ... The state will police the system, it will establish the conditions favorable to competition and prevent monopoly, it will provide a stable monetary framework, and relieve acute poverty and distress. Citizens will be protected against the state, since there exists a free private market, and the competition will protect them from one another.[15]

Central to this market-based 'art of government', as implied in Friedman's remarks, is the question of how it will 'take care' of the citizen. Foucault's studies of these matters, of the production of subjectivity and of the 'techniques of the self', are integral to his understanding of the mechanisms of governmentality. His concern with the production of subjectivity, as Sven-Olov Wallenstein notes, was 'meant to displace or circumvent the transcendental claims about subjecthood inherited from the tradition of Descartes, Kant and Husserl'.[16] It was also meant to challenge naïve conceptions of alienation, human nature and liberation. In one of his last interviews Foucault remarked:

> I have always been somewhat suspicious of the notion of liberation, because if it is not treated with precautions and within certain limits, one runs the risk

of falling back on the idea that there exists a human nature or base that, as a consequence of certain historical, economic, and social processes, has been concealed, alienated, or imprisoned in and by mechanisms of repression. According to this hypothesis, all that is required is to break the repressive deadlock and man will be reconciled with himself, rediscover his nature or regain contact with his origin, and reestablish a full and positive relationship with himself.[17]

The subject is never given in advance of or apart from historically specific conditions. As Foucault says in the same interview, 'I had to reject a priori theories of the subject in order to analyze the relationships that may exist between the constitution of the subject and games of truth, practices of power, and so on.'[18]

Foucault pursued his interest in techniques of the self in the contexts of their practice in the worlds of ancient Greece and Rome, published, respectively, as *The Use of Pleasure* and *The Care of the Self*.[19] In these works, and in *The Government of Self and Others* (the title of his lecture series at the Collège de France in 1982–3), Foucault explored how the 'care of the self' served as an ethical imperative within Greco-Roman culture and philosophy.[20] Consisting of practices such as meditation, prayer, writing and collective ritual, Foucault conceived of the 'care of the self' as an art of self-governance and self-mastery. Its techniques served to guard against the enslavement of the self by 'desires, appetites and fears', and against making slaves of others, who must also, ethically, be at liberty to care for themselves.[21] 'The risk of dominating others and exercising a tyrannical power over them', Foucault says, 'arises precisely only when one has not taken care of the self and has become the slave of one's desires.'[22] The care of the self demands 'extensive work by the self on the self', and this work centres on the cultivation of an 'ethos that is good, beautiful, honorable, estimable, memorable, and exemplary'.[23] For Foucault there is nothing innately 'bad' about governmentality. It can, as he shows in his studies of Greco-Roman culture, serve as a 'practice of freedom'. It is impossible to have society without power: 'Power is not evil. Power is games of strategy.'[24] The point is 'to play these games of power with as little domination as possible'.[25]

Neoliberalism, human capital and the entrepreneurial self

Foucault's *Birth of Biopolitics* – chiefly concerned in fact with the birth of neoliberalism – came before his final works on governmentality and does not directly address 'the care of the self'. But he is, in these lectures, evidently concerned with the ways in which neoliberalism is engaged in the production of subjectivity and in the art of government. Focusing on the ideas of German ordoliberals such as Wilhelm Röpke and Alexander Rüstow, he considers how, in the aftermath of Nazism, they were concerned to fully incorporate the subject within capital. Rather than being at the mercy of the economy (as in pre-war Germany), and consequently at risk of being alienated from it, the subject should feel at one with the market, embedded within and nurtured by its multiple enterprises. This proposition was premised on a model of the self as an essentially entrepreneurial being. As Foucault says of the ordoliberal perspective on the subject and its relation to the market:

> The individual's life must be lodged, not within a framework of a big enterprise like the firm or, if it comes to it, the state, but within the framework of a multiplicity of diverse enterprises connected up to and entangled with each other, enterprises which are in some way ready to hand for the individual, sufficiently limited in their scale for the individual's actions, decisions, and choices to have meaningful and perceptible effects, and numerous enough for him not to be dependent on one alone. And finally, the individual's life itself – with his relationships to his private property, for example, with his family, household, insurance, and retirement – must make him into a sort of permanent and multiple enterprise.[26]

Neoliberalism is not a disciplinary power. It does not aim to confine or segregate subjects or attempt to impose normative standards of conduct and behaviour. Foucault's understanding of the neoliberal governmentality of the self corresponds with neoliberalism's own perspectives on how power should, in the interest of liberty, operate: not through the vertical application of external force but horizontally and immanently. The individual is modelled as innately adaptable and responsive to these horizontal relations. Adjusting its conduct and behaviour to the ever-evolving conditions of the market, it will exercise and realize its liberty.

The historical development of neoliberalism represents, in contemporary form, one of those periodic returns to the question of the self and its care that Foucault attends to in his later work. From the aftermath of fascism and the fear of communism, the self and its care, reappear in a discourse about the subject and its relations with others. Neoliberal thought, however, does not afford the individual subject the kind of 'autonomy' that Foucault claims to find within Greco-Roman practices of the self.[27] When neoliberalism rediscovers the care of the self, it is not to reduce domination to 'as little as possible' but to legitimate and extend its reach. The care of the self is not undertaken for the self, as a 'practice of freedom', but in order to maintain the economic order. The 'work on the self by the self' is not an autonomous practice, but one demanded by the conduct of the market to which the subject must accommodate and continually adapt itself. We must, in neoliberalism, give ourselves over to the care of the market.

Neoliberalism 'moves over to the side of the subject' only to the extent that it concerns itself with the cultivation of an economic ethos: 'The subject is considered only as *homo oeconomicus*, which does not mean that the whole subject is considered as *homo oeconomicus* …. It simply means that economic behavior is the grid of intelligibility one will adopt on the behavior of a new individual.'[28] Gary Becker, for instance, employed this 'grid of intelligibility' to conceive of the conduct, habits, education and care of the self as 'investments' in 'human capital': 'Tangible forms of capital are not the only type of capital. Schooling, a computer training course, expenditures on medical care, and lectures on the virtues of punctuality and honesty are also capital. That is because they raise earnings, improve health, or add to a person's good habits over much of his lifetime.'[29]

The self becomes 'governmentalizable' in neoliberalism, says Foucault, as an economic subject. The *homo oeconomicus* who 'responds systematically to modifications in the variables of the environment, appears precisely as someone manageable'.[30] The subject can be managed through the economic processes to which its existence is made immanent, and the very fact of its adaptability renders it amenable to an art of *economic* governmentality. Recursively, the adaptability of the self demanded by neoliberalism is represented as a sign of emancipatory self-transformation. As Mirowski observes:

> Time and again, the supposed success of some teen idol or hedge fund manager or sports star is said to illustrate the tired platitude that 'you can be anything that you want to be, if you want it bad enough'. This presumes a self that can incorporate any attribute, take up any challenge, transcend any limitation and embody any quality.[31]

Foucault understood that Greco-Roman practices of the self had as their object the salvation of the human soul. Neoliberalism has been no less ambitious in its objectives. In an interview for the *Sunday Times* in 1981 Margaret Thatcher stated: 'Economies are the method. The object is to change the soul.'[32] This objective has been served by a carefully constructed apparatus of knowledge founded upon, and legitimized by, a claim about the 'necessary ignorance' of the subject.

Hayek, Polanyi and cybernetics

The proposition that human individuals can have little knowledge of the world in which they live is fundamental to neoliberalism. The world is too complex and the perspective of the individual too limited to grasp its workings, let alone to presume to direct these. Hayek, in *The Constitution of Liberty*, states that the primary requisite for understanding society is that 'we become aware of men's necessary ignorance of much that helps him to achieve his aims'.[33] In *Law, Legislation and Liberty*, he writes of 'the fact of the necessary and irremediable ignorance on everyone's part of most of the particular facts which determine the actions of all the several members of human society'.[34] According to Hayek we cannot and need not be aware of the rules that govern our social order. These rules – the 'natural laws' of traditions, institutions, customs and conduct – have evolved over the course of time without ever having been the products of conscious design by human minds. Hayek considers it an error – 'rationalist' and 'anthropomorphic' – to 'ascribe the origins of all institutions of culture to invention or design'.[35] Far from circumscribing individual freedom, the evolutionary nature of the social order is, argues Hayek, the very basis of that freedom: 'Liberty is essential in order to leave room for the unforeseeable and unpredictable'.[36] The 'unforeseen' and the 'unpredictable' are, within neoliberal thought, the necessary conditions for the experience of freedom and the possibility of progress. 'The advance and even the preservation of civilization', writes Hayek in *The Constitution of Liberty*, 'are dependent upon a maximum of opportunity for accidents to happen.'[37]

Necessary ignorance of the social order disqualifies us from making conscious plans for its progress. It is from the kind of 'conscious planning' practised by a rationalist approach to social progress that, argues Hayek, 'all modern socialism, planning and totalitarianism derives'.[38] Planning can in fact only result in tyranny. The totality of the social order cannot be grasped, and any state that sets out to control and direct this order, even a democratic one, has set itself on the path towards totalitarianism. As Foucault noted in *The Birth of Biopolitics*, German ordoliberals directly equated the Keynesian-inspired policies of the post-war British government with the fascism it had recently fought against. Foucault records the essence of Wilhelm Röpke's attack on the foundation of the welfare state as follows: 'What you are preparing for yourselves with your Beveridge plan is quite simply Nazism. On one side you battle with the Germans militarily, but economically, and so politically, you are in the process of repeating their lessons. English Labour party socialism will lead you to German-style Nazism.'[39] In *The Road to Serfdom* Hayek writes:

> Planning leads to dictatorship because dictatorship is the most effective instrument of coercion and the enforcement of ideals, and as such essential if central planning on a large scale is to be possible. ... A true 'dictatorship of the proletariat', even if democratic in form, if it undertook centrally to direct the economic system, would probably destroy personal freedom as completely as any autocracy has ever done.[40]

The cause of human liberty cannot be served by an anthropocentric rationality. There can be no collective project for changing the world. Common purpose and solidarity, says Hayek, are tribal throwbacks that constitute the greatest threat to a 'free civilization'.[41] Logically and ethically disqualified from presuming to grasp the totality of the social order, humans are supposed to submit to the superior organizational capacities of the market, to individual competition rather than to collective solidarity, as the guarantor of their liberty. As Foucault notes, 'Economic rationality is not only surrounded by, but founded on the unknowability of the totality of the process.'[42]

There is something like an inversion of Immanuel Kant's 'Copernican revolution' at work in the neoliberal truth game. Instead of 'conforming' to *our* knowledge, the world demands that we submit to the innate 'knowledge' of the market, to *its* capacity to spontaneously order our lives and facilitate our freedoms. The true gravitational centre of social agency, supposed to be mistakenly ascribed to the perspective of the subject, is located in the competitive order of the economic market and its unplanned evolution. Kant saw the Enlightenment as the 'age of criticism, to which everything must be subjected', identifying critique as central to its.[43] Neoliberal thought effectively denies the very possibility of the critically reflective subject. Its own critical reasoning rescinded, the subject is itself to be subjected to the reason of the market, a milieu to whose evolutionary development it must continually adapt. As Hayek asserts in *The Constitution of Liberty*, 'Man did not simply impose upon the world a pattern created by his mind. His mind is itself a system that constantly changes as a result of his endeavour to adapt himself to his surroundings.'[44] These surroundings are primarily those of the market and its order, as figured by Hayek, is spontaneous.

Spontaneous orders and complex systems

Hayek drew extensively upon thinkers of the Scottish Enlightenment – Adam Smith, David Hume and Adam Ferguson – in formulating the notion of a 'spontaneous order'. He found Ferguson, in particular, useful in legitimating his arguments against the capacity of the state to consciously direct societal development. In *Law, Legislation and Liberty*, Hayek employs a line from Ferguson's *An Essay on the History of Civil Society* to underscore his point: 'Nations stumble upon establishments, which are indeed the result of human action, but not the execution of any human design.'[45] Michael Polanyi, to whose thought Hayek was deeply indebted, likewise located the origin of the idea of a spontaneous order – often also referring to this as a 'polycentric order' – in the Scottish Enlightenment. Adam Smith presented Polanyi with a model of the market as exemplary of a spontaneous order. 'The most massive example of spontaneous order in society', he wrote in *The Logic of Liberty*, 'the prototype of order established by an "invisible hand" – is that of economic life based on an aggregate of competing individuals.'[46] The logic of the spontaneous order guarantees liberty since, as exemplified in the polycentric medium of the market, it is achieved without the exercise of an external power. In the economic market, he writes, 'Each consumer adjusts his purchases to the ruling price, which he affects in his turn by his purchases.'[47] The mutually coordinating activities of individuals 'exercising their initiative' in their dealings with the market are 'free, for they are not determined by any *specific* command, whether of a superior or of a public authority; the compulsion to which they are subject is impersonal and general'.[48]

Beyond the focus on the market as a prototypically spontaneous order, Polanyi is also occupied, in *The Logic of Liberty*, with extending the reach of this model into other fields, such as those of science and intellectual culture.[49] He finds the logic of the spontaneous order operating in the 'co-ordinative principle of science', since it 'consists in the adjustment of each scientist's activities to the results hitherto achieved by others', and demonstrates the 'co-ordination of individual activities without the intervention of any co-ordinating authority'.[50] He finds the same logic at work in the way fluids and gases spontaneously respond to their environmental conditions, in the formation of crystals, and in 'the growth and form of plants and animals'.[51] In *The Constitution of Liberty*, Hayek follows Polanyi's lead in asserting a scientific basis for the spontaneously occurring organizational properties of the market – the game of 'catallaxy', as Hayek termed it.[52] 'We could never produce a crystal or a complex organisational compound', he writes, 'if we had to place each individual molecule or atom in the appropriate place in relation to the others.'[53] It follows for Hayek that what goes for physics must go for society. 'As in nature', he says, we cannot arrange its elements or design its order, we can 'merely ... create conditions in which an orderly arrangement can establish and ever renew itself'.[54]

Analogical leaps of this kind – from the spontaneous ordering of the physical and natural worlds to that of social and economic ones – were premised on the grounds of their supposed equivalence as complex systems. Precisely because of their complexity, these kinds of systems, maintain Polanyi and Hayek, cannot be arranged from the outside, or ordered from a centre. They can only be ordered, spontaneously and immanently, through the mutual interaction and coordination of their elements. 'The rules that govern the actions of the elements of such spontaneous orders', writes Hayek, 'need not be rules which are "known" to these elements; it is sufficient that the elements actually behave in a manner which can be described by such rules.'[55] Hayek further developed his conception of spontaneous orders and complex systems through his associations with figures such as the mathematicians John von Neumann and Warren Weaver, and the biologist Ludwig von Bertalanffy. Hayek drew, for instance, upon von Neumann's account of the 'logic of automata' – with its analyses of the operations of self-regulation, information processing and the evolution of simple elements into complex systems – to develop his own explanations of evolutionarily and endogenously ordered systems. That von Neumann held that these systemic operations always functioned in the same fashion, whether within thermodynamics, computation or the human brain, also furnished Hayek with the kind of unifying model that could comfortably traverse natural, social and economic orders.

In the essay 'Degrees of Complexity', first published in 1955, Hayek argues for the methodological advantages of theories of 'organized complexity' over those of classical physics.[56] Drawing on the work of Bertalanffy, and especially Weaver (who also advised Hayek on the preparation of the essay), he claims that the traditional methods of physics lack 'universal applicability'.[57] These methods may work for the analysis of 'closed systems', ones composed of a limited number of observable and controllable elements, but they are ill equipped to deal with questions of organized complexity. The progress of fields addressing complex systems, such as the biological, social and economic sciences, suggests to Hayek the advanced path of scientific method.

When dealing with instances of complex systems we cannot expect to comprehend or predict their specific behaviour. The explanatory power of theories of complexity lies in their capacity to identify the kind of outcomes we might expect of certain systems on identifying their type. Hayek writes: 'It seems indeed not improbable that, as the advance of the sciences penetrates further and further into more complex phenomena, theories which merely provide explanations of the principle, or which merely describe a range of phenomena which certain types of structures are able to produce, may become more the rule than the exception.'[58] In place of particular knowledge the sciences can aspire only to 'the ready perception of patterns of configurations' familiar from the observation of complex systems across a number of fields. 'The possession of such a ready-made pattern of significant relationships', argues Hayek, 'gives us a sort of sense for the physiognomy of events which will guide us in our observation of the environment.'[59] Rather than the kind of precise knowledge that would equip us to act directly upon complex orders, and shape them to certain ends, we can perceive them only as phenomena that impinge on our senses in familiar configurations through a process of 'pattern recognition'. According to Hayek we can never hope to know or reflect upon the rules upon which complex orders operate, and this is not least because the human mind attempting to understand them is itself a type of complex order of which we can only have limited knowledge.[60] Writes Hayek in 'Rules, Perception and Intelligibility', 'Conscious thought must be assumed to be directed by rules which in turn cannot be conscious – by a supra-conscious mechanism which operates upon the contents of consciousness but which cannot itself be conscious.'[61] We do not and cannot know our own minds. It also turns out, in a further analogical manoeuvre, that the mind is made to serve as the model of the market which is itself, paradoxically, supposed to be the prototype of a spontaneous order. As Mirowski states, for Hayek 'the "market" is posited to be an information processor more powerful than any human brain, but essentially patterned upon brain/computation metaphors.' It is this account of the market, continues Mirowski, that has become the most culturally dominant, the 'most closely associated with the neoliberal *Weltanschauung*'.[62]

In *Law, Legislation and Liberty*, Hayek writes that 'the only possibility of transcending the capacity of individual minds is to rely on those super-personal "self-organizing" forces which create spontaneous order'.[63] Taking it as read that the type of spontaneous order with which individual minds are going to be most engaged with, from Hayek's perspective, is that of the market; this statement stands as a further iteration of one of his central arguments: human progress is only possible where the subject conforms to the self-organizing and evolutionary logic of the market. Since human minds and economic markets alike are complex orders, they can be integrated. But since the market is possessed of superior self-organizing and evolutionary powers, because it is a 'super-personal' force, it would be to the advantage of human subjects to adapt themselves to the operations of the economic order, to deliver themselves into its care.

In Hayek's concerns with systemic regulation and integration, with information and pattern recognition, his debts to the cybernetics of Heinz von Foerster and Norbert Wiener are made plain. In *Law, Legislation and Liberty*, he enthuses over the emergence of cybernetics as 'a special discipline which is also concerned with what are called self-organizing or self-generating systems'.[64] He employs cybernetics to rationalize the mechanisms of adaptability on which neoliberal truths are premised: 'The process of adaptation operates, as do the adjustments of any self-organizing system, by what cybernetics has taught us to call negative feedback'.[65]

Wiener had derived the term 'cybernetics' from the Greek word *kubernētēs*, meaning 'steersman', noting that this, in turn, is also the source of the word 'governor'.[66] In his *Cybernetics*, Norbert Wiener wrote: 'We have decided to call the entire field of control and communication theory, whether in the machine or in the animal, by the name Cybernetics'.[67] In *The Human use of Human Beings*, Weiner elaborated:

> There is a larger field which includes not only the study of language but the study of messages as a means of controlling machinery and society, the development of computing machines and other such automata, certain reflections upon psychology and the nervous system, and a tentative new theory of scientific method.[68]

Cybernetics promised to unify these different fields by conceiving of them all as information processing systems. The different components of these systems – man, machine and society – could now speak to each other in a common language.

Cybernetics furnishes Hayek with further legitimation for his arguments. Individuals are conceived of according to unifying models that situate them as integral components of larger systems within which they cannot hope to exercise any degree of autonomous control, let alone critical reflection. The subject, possessed only of the capacity for information processing and pattern recognition, functions as a relay within the larger and superior processual order of the market. This is to the advantage of the subject since liberty and progress are dependent upon its integration within a spontaneous order. This order serves, at the same time, as an immanent mode of self-governance in which we are to be 'guided by habit rather than reflection'.[69]

The unifying perspectives to which neoliberal thought has attached itself have equipped it, through the technique of analogy, to transfer its model of the economic market to fields of knowledge and practice spanning the worlds of work, education, health, politics, ecology, welfare, management and design. Its discourse now resides in these and other domains as an almost unquestioned and unquestionable orthodoxy. As Mirowski writes, neoliberalism has 'become a comprehensive worldview'.[70] Adaptability and flexibility appear, through the neoliberal lens, as the qualities of conduct, the ethos that the subject must cultivate in order to thrive in the competitive environment of the market. According to the truth games of neoliberalism there is no choice for the self, politically or ontologically, but to govern itself, and to have itself governed, according to these imperatives.

Neoliberalism as the 'form of our existence'

Far from simply playing out the 'logic of capital', neoliberalism is productive of certain ways of thinking about the very nature of the subject and its relation to the economic market. Its truths have so thoroughly permeated the world as to substantially shape the conception and experience of selfhood as an essentially productive and adaptable enterprise. Foucault's perspective on the concern of neoliberal thought with the production of subjectivity and the legitimating functions of truth games have turned out to be prescient insights into our contemporary condition. As Dardot and Laval write, 'At stake in neo-liberalism is nothing more, nor less, than the *form of our existence* – the way in which we are led to conduct ourselves, to relate to others and to ourselves.'[71]

According to neoliberalism's own account of the order of things, though, this conduct cannot be disciplined into the subject from without, and certainly not under the corrective authority of some external power always readily identifiable as 'neoliberal'. The ethos of neoliberalism is to be shaped in the subject through its encounters with the order of its environment and the apparently immanent and unmediated demands this places upon it to be pliant, productive and competitive. These encounters, in turn, take place through specific practices and techniques, in particular times and places, that typically appear to have nothing to do with neoliberalism. This is the case in a particular 'spacing' of the subject, developed in the second half of the twentieth century, that derived from the post-war artistic avant-garde, the counterculture of the 1960s and 1970s, new models of management and early developments in personal computing. The construction of new relationships between the subject and its environment was supposed to promise the experience of liberation. In effect, and sometimes by design, though, the new environmental spacing of the subject had a good deal in common with the tenets and agendas of neoliberalism. It has also come to constitute a certain doxa through which architectural culture has, of late, staked its claims to being progressive.

The Spatial Constitution of the Neoliberal Subject

Arranged on a domestic shelving unit are animal skulls, bird's eggs and geometric models. There are diagrams of cellular structures, X-rays, microscopic images of organisms and telescopic photographs of galaxies. Richard Hamilton's exhibition *Growth and Form*, held in 1951 at the Institute of Contemporary Art (ICA) in London, comprises a seemingly disparate array of images and objects. Immersed in the atmospherically lit environment of this installation, its visitors are, though, supposed to seize upon the unity underlying the leaps in scale and subject matter. As their attention passes between the items tabulated in its displays, common patterns should appear. Following the thesis of the book that inspired Hamilton's exhibition – D'Arcy Wentworth Thompson's *On Growth and Form* – these are to be understood as expressions of the mathematical laws that universally govern the growth of forms.[1]

Hamilton, Pollock and Kaprow

On Growth and Form, first published in 1917, has been described by Stephen Jay Gould as a 'hybrid theory of Pythagoras and Newton [that] argues that physical forces shape organisms directly'.[2] Thompson himself understood the book as a 'physico-mathematical or dynamical investigation into morphology',[3] a search for the 'community of principles' and the 'essential similitudes' of the 'organic and inorganic', the 'animate and inanimate'.[4] These 'essential similitudes' extended from physics to chemistry, biology and engineering, and were illustrated with a variety of equations, diagrams, drawings and photographs that invited the readers of *On Growth and Form* to recognize, through its visual rhetoric, the universality of the morphological rules to which these fields were all subject.

On Growth and Form had already had some impact within avant-garde circles before the time of Hamilton's exhibition. It had been cited, for instance, by László Moholy-Nagy in his *Vision and Motion* of 1947. Hamilton's take on Thompson's work, though, was original in its focus on the challenge it presented to conventional artistic practices. Planning the exhibition *Growth and Form* in 1950 he wrote:

> The initial stimulus for the proposed exhibition was provided by Thompson's book *On Growth and Form*. The visual interest of this field, where biology, chemistry, physics and mathematics overlap was considered an excellent subject for presentation in purely visual terms. The laws of growth and form pertaining to the processes of nature are quite contrary to the processes of artistic creation. However complex the form … it is the result of very precise physical laws; the complexities of art, on the other hand, are the products of involved psychological processes.[5]

Hamilton contrasts the lawful rules of morphology accessible to science to the wilful drives of artistic creation. The latter appears to him disadvantaged and inadequate. As an expression of 'psychological' factors its meaning will necessarily lack clarity and immediacy. 'Cleansed by science', comments Isabelle Moffat, the kind of forms that feature in Thompson's book and Hamilton's exhibition, 'are free of any connotative meanings and guarantee a kind of directness that [Hamilton] sought also to translate his art'.[6]

In respect of its affirmation of 'natural laws', Thompson's book has been similarly significant in the construction of a certain rhetoric of contemporary architecture, particularly where this touches upon ideas of morphological 'emergence' and 'elegance'. 'We must search for the principles and dynamics of organisation and interaction, for the mathematical laws that natural systems obey and that can be utilised by artificially constructed systems', writes Michael Weinstock in an essay titled 'Morphogenesis and the Mathematics of Emergence'.[7] Patrik Schumacher, appealing to the 'laws of nature', has argued that the morphologies of Zaha Hadid's architecture derive from 'the forms and spaces we perceive in natural systems, where all forms are the result of lawfully interacting forces'.[8]

The ways in which Hamilton chose to make Thompson's ideas sensible to the visitors of his *Growth and Form* installation also foreshadow the 'post-linguistic' and 'affective' turns lately influential in architecture. Hamilton favoured an exclusively visual language in communicating Thompson's theorems and there are, at his insistence, no textual clues of any kind to guide the visitor's interpretation of the work.[9] Interpretation is, in fact, effectively displaced from the scene of *Growth and Form* so as to facilitate more immediate forms of perception, that is, isomorphic pattern recognition and the registration of affect.

Hamilton's concerns with perceptual immediacy, for dispensing with the ambiguities of semantic connotation, were shared by others associated, like him, with the Independent Group (IG) based at the ICA. The interest this group – comprised of Reyner Banham, Eduardo Paolozzi, Nigel Henderson, Lawrence Alloway, John McHale, Hamilton and others – expressed in popular and so-called mass culture hardly needs recounting, but their concern with the new modes of perception made possible through mass media technologies is worth re-emphasizing. Television, cinema and advertising suggested to them more direct and efficient means of communication than those of the art gallery. Rather than contemplative encounters, *Growth and Form*, and other IG shows – *Parallel of Life & Art* (1953), *Man, Machine & Motion* (1955), *This is Tomorrow* (1956) – were geared towards the creation of immersive conditions. The space of the gallery, it was believed, upheld culturally engrained dispositions in the perception and reception of art. It sustained a respectful distance between viewer and artwork and maintained contemplative habits in perception. The space of the installation, though, suggested a condition of environmental immediacy. Lawrence Alloway even claimed that the mass media that served as the model for these shows already constituted a 'natural environment'.[10]

The possibilities of this type of all-encompassing experiential condition had first been explored in the 1920s and 1930s within the European avant-garde. As Fred Turner points out in his *The Democratic Surround*, practices in designing immersive exhibition spaces first developed at the Bauhaus, and elsewhere, were later transported into an America concerned with the making of the 'democratic personality' during and after the Second World War.[11] Exhibitions such as *Road to Victory* (1943) and *The Family of Man* (1955), both held at the Museum of Modern Art in New York, drew upon practices and techniques first developed by Moholy-Nagy in order to envelope the subject's field of vision, such as suspending images from ceilings and placing them below conventional sight lines. Such exhibitions were, however, also concerned with shaping thoughts and beliefs through argumentation and narrative. They were premised on the conveyance of ideas articulated through text and image together. Exhibitions such as *Growth and Form*, *Man Machine and Motion* and *This is Tomorrow*, however, operated according to very different principles of perception.

The American projects described by Turner as 'democratic surrounds' called upon the visitor to arrive at pre-inscribed meanings for which images, objects and texts were only the medium. They required interpretation. They solicited antipathy for dictatorship, racism and inequality, and they cultivated the affirmation of humanist and democratic beliefs. They sought, in effect, to align the subject's moral and political compass with a set of predetermined principles. The exhibitions staged by the IG, in contrast, operated according to a more closed-circuit model of communication. Located in the 'natural environments' of these shows images and objects were supposed to speak directly for and about themselves. Rather than offered up for intellectual judgement or critical interpretation, they could be perceived through a purely immanent logic of information and its patterning. Influenced by the 'non-Aristotelian' principles of categorization exemplified, for them, by the Dadaists, the IG equalized high art, mass culture, science, technology and nature within a continuum accessible to immediate visual experience.[12] Influenced by the mathematics of von Neumann and the information theory of Claude Shannon, they understood communication as a source-to-destination process in which the information itself was value-neutral. As Hamilton said, reflecting on the formative influence of Shannon's theories, 'The idea that you can express everything with something as simple as ones and zeros, and that value judgments don't count – you can't say this is good and this is bad – means you're in another kind of space altogether.'[13] This 'other kind of space', as developed by the IG, served as a kind of milieu in which the human animal would adapt itself to its new informational *umwelt*; a space in which the sensorium could be trained in techniques of associative and analogical perception, and where the old habits of judgement and interpretation could be relinquished.

In the development of these spaces and experiences, and in the formulation of the ideas of information, perception and order on which these were premised, the IG occupied common ground with the neoliberal thought of Polanyi and Hayek. The significance to both parties of figures such as Wiener, Bertalanffy, von Neumann, Shannon and Weaver shows in their mutual concerns with what Hayek termed the 'physiognomy of events which will guide us in our observation of the environment', and with the natural laws supposed to govern their appearance.[14] The natural and spontaneous order that produces Hayek's 'ready-made pattern of significant relationships' is made sensible in the Duchampian 'readymades' Hamilton assembles in *Growth and Form*. Since everything develops according to an evolutionary logic over which the individual has no control, there is no purpose in signalling to the subject of the environment anything beyond immediate impressions, and no point in trying to interpret these. Things are as they are, 'as found', and we need only acclimatize ourselves – as a species of post-political animal – to the latest techno-informational and mass-mediated stage of their evolution.

American avant-garde and countercultural practices of the 1960s and 1970s were similarly invested in an environmental spacing of the subject, but pushed its implications further. Environments – natural, technological, architectural, pharmaceutical, communal – figured as new realms of personal liberation. They suggested escape routes from bureaucracy and promised liberation within a cosmic order of infinite connectivity, the realization of a Zen-like state of oneness.

Allan Kaprow's essay, 'The Legacy of Jackson Pollock', written in 1958, reads as a founding statement of the concerns that would subsequently occupy the American avant-garde, as well as much of the counterculture. Kaprow laments Pollock's passing, two years earlier, since 'it came at the wrong time'.[15] Pollock, he argued, had been on the threshold of destroying painting as it been practised and understood since the time of the ancient Greeks. His large 'drip' paintings, in the manner of their execution and in the experience they presented to the viewer, were poised on the cusp of 'a return to the point where art was more actively involved in ritual, magic, and life than we have known it in our recent past'.[16] The scale of Pollock's works, and the sense of potentially infinite expansion conveyed in their 'skein of lines and splashings', suggested that they 'ceased to become paintings and became environments'.[17] It was this possibility that Kaprow wanted to pursue, through the form of the 'Happening', to the point where 'we must become preoccupied and dazzled by the spaces and objects of our everyday life'.[18]

For Kaprow, one of the originators of this art form, the significance of the Happening hinged on its capacity to dissolve all boundaries between individual and environment. In an essay of 1961, 'Happenings in the New York Scene', he wrote:

> The sheer rawness of the out-of-doors ... in which the radical Happenings flourish is more appropriate, I believe, in temperament and un-artiness, to the materials and directness of these works. The place where anything grows up ... its 'habitat', gives to it not only a space, a set of relationships to the various things around it, and a range of values, but an overall atmosphere as well, which penetrates it and whoever experiences it ... art approaches a fragile but marvelous life, one that maintains itself by a mere thread, melting the surroundings, the artist, the work, and everyone who comes to it in an elusive, changeable configuration.[19]

Kaprow, referring to an exhibition of his own work, wrote that 'we do not come to look *at* things. We simply enter, are surrounded, and become part of what surrounds us.'[20] Affirming the absorption of the subject within the artwork as habitat, Kaprow's position was close to that of the IG. It focused upon the immediate perception of the everyday world and its 'physiognomy of events'. Being absorbed in the immediate experience of one's habitat, 'preoccupied and dazzled' by its 'ready-made patterns' in the form of the art installation or the Happening, however, necessarily precludes intellectual and conceptual reflection on the artwork. Experience is constricted to what Kant described, in his *Critique of Pure Reason*, as 'merely a rhapsody of perceptions', never amounting in itself to a condition of knowledge.[21] While perception is expanded – beyond the picture frame and the space of the gallery – thought is confined in a fashion perfectly consonant with neoliberal epistemologies of 'necessary ignorance'. We do not gain knowledge of the world through experience in order to conceive of acting to change it, but can, at best, only intuit an order of such complexity that it would be sheer hubris to contemplate its rational comprehension or control.

In light of this renunciation of knowledge, the expansion of perception serves a compensatory function; a pay-off for the absence of individual agency glossed as a pseudo-religious experience. This, at least, is how Kaprow understands the promise of Pollock. In Pollock's paintings, he writes, 'The artist, the spectator, and the outer world are … interchangeably involved.'[22] The painter could be said to be 'in' his work at the moment of its creation, steeped in a delirium of 'automatic' gestures from which any trace of conscience crafting or 'artfulness' had disappeared. The form of his paintings, in turn, allowed the viewer 'equal pleasure in participating in a delirium, a deadening of the reasoning faculties, a loss of "self" in the Western sense of the term'.[23] Kaprow presented Pollock's achievement as Zen-like: a 'combination of extreme individuality and selflessness'.[24] Understanding 'selflessness' in this context as the relinquishing of the rational self, the self that maintains a distance – interpretative, critical, reflective – from the objects of its perception, the 'combination of extreme individuality and selflessness' might also stand as a motto for the imperatives of neoliberalism. The subject must fashion its individuality from whatever resources it can grasp from within the systems of circuits, networks and exchanges it inhabits, but this individuality must be outsourced, redistributed and recirculated, within those same systems, in order to be valorized.

THX 1138 and Alphaville

All forms of totalitarianism, fascist and communist, appear antithetical to this process of subjectification since they threaten to subsume the individual to a social order of abstract ideals and bureaucratic plans. Such anxieties about totalitarianism emerged, understandably enough, from the experiences of the Second World War, but they also came to resonate with Cold War-era paranoia of the 'Red Menace' of communism. They were also fuelled, for the counterculture and the left alike, by concerns over the kind of power a totalitarian state might wield if it were to take advantage of advanced technologies, of a 'technocratic' rationality through which the individual would be subject to forms of social programming. These concerns are exemplified in a diary entry made by the young Stewart Brand, later to be the creator and editor of the *Whole Earth Catalog* and a leading figure of the counterculture, in 1957. Listing his fears of Soviet invasion he wrote:

> That my life would necessarily become small, a gear with its place on a certain
>   axle of the Communist machine. Perhaps only a tooth on the gear ...
> That my mind would no longer be my own, but a tool carefully shaped by the
>   descendants of Pavlov.
> That I would lose my identity.
> That I would lose my will.
> These last are the worst.[25]

Such fears found vivid expression in George Lucas's *THX 1138*. Released in 1971, the film is set in a technologically advanced city, located underground and ruled by an inhuman computational logic. The film's mise en scène is populated by utilitarian-clothed figures monitoring closed-circuit television screens in monochromatic interiors. Its narrative concerns technocratic manipulation, surveillance and dehumanization. In the subterranean world of *THX 1138* human identity has been reduced to an alphanumeric code. 'THX 1138' designates the film's protagonist, 'SEN 5421' and 'LUH 341', its other main characters. Communication is condensed into a series of stock phrases, pre-recorded messages and computer-issued commands. Emotions are regulated through mandatory chemical sedation and sexual activity is confined to prescribed norms. State-sanctioned religious conformity is administered through automated confessional booths furnished with over-sized reproductions of Hans Memling's *Christ Giving His Blessing*, Christ's gaze refashioned into an image of panoptical surveillance redolent of *2001: A Space Odyssey*'s HAL. Stationed on the production line or contained within the cubicle-like spaces of their domestic units, the subjects of this world appear as isolated components in a vast machine. Compliance with the city's computational order is maintained by the chrome-faced android police force who arrest, imprison and beat THX – the film's non-compliant hero – before he escapes from his 'electronic labyrinth' in a stolen car.[26]

The concerns addressed in *THX 1138* echo the critiques of technocratic state planning articulated by much of the left at this time. In this respect Jean Luc Godard's *Alphaville* of 1965 might be read as the source material from which Lucas's film is roughly translated.[27] *Alphaville* centres upon the figure of detective Lemmy Caution, assigned to persuade the exiled Professor Von Braun to leave the city of Alphaville and return with him to the 'Outerlands' of the galaxy.[28] Like the underground city of *THX 1138*, Alphaville is a self-contained world with strictly policed borders. It operates according to a rigidly technocratic rationality and is overseen by an omniscient central computer, 'Alpha 60'. The citizens of Alphaville speak in rehearsed and robotic phrases – 'I'm very well, thank you, not at all.' Their sexual needs are catered to by a state-run system of prostitution performed by officially designated 'seductresses'.

Much as Marx put it in his account of the mechanization of industrial labour in the *Grundrisse*, the inhabitants of Alphaville, like those of Lucas's film, have stepped 'to the side of the production process instead of being its chief actor[s]'.[29] But, taking things a stage further, computation has now achieved the mechanization of thought itself. It has subsumed the social to the endless reproduction of a functionally optimized system. In both films, humans are reduced to the role of merely tending to the performance of the huge banks of mainframe computers bearing over them in the control centres of the city. Pharmaceutically numbed and stripped of the language with which to express feeling, they are themselves reduced to the status of automatons, mere relays for the formulaic speech and thought patterns of a computational operating system.

Other similarities obtain between *THX 1138* and *Alphaville*. Alphaville, like the underground city of *THX 1138*, is an *unheimlich* world of constant night, impervious surfaces, institutional corridors, glass-screened laboratory rooms and anonymous apartments. The forward thrust of the narrative is punctuated with extreme close-ups of road signs, switchboards and control panels. The same device features in *THX 1138*, with its close-ups of computer monitors and the pixilated text in which the system's reports and commands are issued. In both films this invokes the all-pervading presence of a purely computational logic. Each warns of an impending technocratic dictatorship.

Alphaville, Colin MacCabe has written, alerts us to the 'future within the present'. The film is concerned with the imminent emergence of a technocratic totalitarianism shared by others in France, and elsewhere, at this time, particularly (but not exclusively) on the left.[30] Henri Lefebvre, and the Situationists, had, like Godard, targeted architectural modernization and urban planning in their critique of capitalism and its presumed trajectory.[31] In *The Urban Revolution* of 1970, Lefebvre noted that 'a kind of overall colonization of space by "decision-making centres" seems to be taking shape'.[32] Arguing that 'urban reality' had been subordinated to a technocratic system of 'general planning' and the 'logistics of restricted rationality', he wrote that this had reduced space to 'a homogeneous and empty medium, in which we house objects, people, machines, industrial facilities, flows, and networks'.[33] In *Society of the Spectacle*, Guy Debord argued that 'urbanism – "city planning" – is capitalism's method for taking over the natural and human environment', its 'technology of separation', and the means by which it refashions 'the totality of space into its own particular decor'.[34] Social scientists of this period, Jean Meynaud and Alain Touraine in particular,[35] also drew attention to the ways in which technocrats 'breached the boundaries between technology and politics'.[36] Technocracy, it was argued, threatened to supplant political democracy with social programmes and economic policies decided upon by unelected 'experts'.

Alphaville, then, speaks of contemporary social and political anxieties.[37] Its characters – Natasha (Von Braun's daughter with whom Lemmy Caution escapes the city), the seductresses, the lab technicians – are confined within the bureaucratic spaces of modern planning and modernist architecture, caught in the circuits of a programme that erases history and memory. Technocratic urbanism appears to produce a subjectivity closed in upon itself, isolated, save for the scripted interactions and formulaic speech patterns through which communication is filtered. It constructs for its operatives a space-time of fixed coordinates and limited perspectives. *Alphaville*'s premonition of all of this is echoed in that of *THX 1138*, in which conditions of confinement and dehumanization are addressed even more emphatically. But *THX 1138* parts company with *Alphaville*, and with the broader critical perspectives of the left that Godard's film had articulated, in the type of escape route it finds for its protagonist. In the final scene of *THX 1138*, its eponymous hero escapes his subterranean confines, climbing out of a ventilation shaft and ascending into the daylight of the world above. The heat-hazed image of the enormous sun setting behind THX frames him as a figure newly (re)born into the natural world. As the credits roll the film's closing images speak of a new beginning, the re-environmentalization of the subject.

The left were unable to so easily envisage any such escape from the spaces and techniques of instrumental reason. Lemmy Caution's flight from Alphaville with Natasha in the detective's Ford Galaxy fails to convince as an escape. The characters remain captured within the film's shadowy scenography, and in their generic roles of hard-boiled detective and vulnerable ingénue. The film's ending is symptomatic of the fact that, for the left, there were no easy exits and no individual escape routes from an increasingly totalizing and technologically facilitated system of control. The left looked to nothing less than revolution, and with it the collective transformation of social, political and historical consciousness, as the means to avert the subsumption of social existence to the programmed logic of technocratic capitalism. In the type of exit it finds for its hero *THX 1138*, though, shows its sympathies to be with American countercultural sensibilities rather than with the politics of the left.[38] Filmed in the West Coast city of Port Hueneme, the film's final scene has THX ascend and escape to the free expanses of the Californian beach.

As captured in the diary of the young Stewart Brand, it was the threat to individual identity and free will posed by technocracy that most exercised countercultural sensibilities, rather than the broader political concerns that occupied the left. In *Alphaville*, Lemmy Caution confronts the central computer, Alpha 60, causing its circuits to break down and the system to collapse. In *THX 1138*, the hero, rather than engaging the system in direct combat, simply evades it. He drops out, leaves it to its own devices. The imaging of a future scenario of technocratic totalitarianism in *Alphaville* is consistent with a left critique of existing structures of power, particularly those concerning urban space and its instrumental rationalization, and with arguments for the necessity of radical social transformation. In *THX 1138*, as in the counterculture in general, the technocratic scenario serves as a foil through which to valorize individualized liberation and self-expression, to achieve immediate freedom from constraints of any kind rather than to collectively confront and transform existing conditions through struggle. Rather than fighting in the streets the counterculture advocated abandoning the technocratically rationalized city altogether. 'Workers of the world, disperse' as the *Whole Earth Catalog* declaimed in 1971.[39]

The counterculture and the technical mentality

The thousands of communes established in America in the late 1960s, many located far from its cities, typified the counterculture's efforts to escape existing power structures rather than to contest them directly. At Drop City in southern Colorado, and in the many others its example inspired, the 'new communalists' were organized into small collaborative and cooperative groups.[40] But these communes were not entirely isolated from one another. Links between them were cultivated, especially through the distribution of Stewart Brand's *Whole Earth Catalog*. Brand's publication, through which the communalists could source the items and equipment required for their enterprises, also served as a networked medium for exchanges of knowledge between the communes, and it linked them to projects and practices possessed of the same 'frontier spirit' in other fields. The *Whole Earth Catalog*, as Turner observes:

> Featured contributions from four somewhat overlapping social groups: the world of university-, government-, and industry-based science and technology; the New York and San Francisco art scenes; the Bay area psychedelic community; and the communes. … When these groups met in its pages, the *Catalog* became the single most visible publication in which the technological and intellectual output of industry and high science met the Eastern religion, acid mysticism, and communal social theory of the back-to-the-land movement. It also became the home and emblem of a new, geographically distributed community.[41]

The Spring 1969 edition of the *Catalog* featured short pieces on Buckminster Fuller's Dymaxion map, adobe construction, D'Arcy Wentworth Thompson's *On Growth and Form*, organic gardening, self-hypnosis, building your own computer and the cybernetics of Norbert Weiner. Described by Steve Jobs as 'sort of like Google in paperback form, 35 years before Google came along', the *Whole Earth Catalog* promoted, and exemplified in its format, the kind of laterally connective, interdisciplinary models of organization enthused over both by the counterculture and within the worlds of contemporary technology and research.[42] The distributed network form, embodied in the *Catalog*, represented an alternative means of organizing the relationship between individuals, communities and information to that of the centralized bureaucratic hierarchies from which the communalists were seeking to escape.

If such diverse themes and interests could be arrayed across the pages of Brand's *Whole Earth Catalog*, this was not, as Jobs's reference to Google might imply, because they were placed together at random. The different worlds onto which the *Catalog* offered its seemingly kaleidoscopic perspectives converged upon a unifying set of models drawn from cybernetics, systems theory and ecological thought. These perspectives held in common the idea that the workings of the human brain, of nature, art and computation could all be understood as information systems – 'patterns' – produced through the interaction of material and energetic forces within given environments. Rather than locating the source of this common principle in any externally directive power, the thought of figures fundamental to the development of the counterculture, like Norbert Weiner or Gregory Bateson, understood it as immanent to the operation of any system. The idea of a universal set of organizational and processual principles not only suggested a commonality to how human beings, art, nature and technology might be understood to operate, it also implied that they could be used to understand each other, and, further, that they could be environmentally integrated with one another to form a cohesive and harmonious whole. It was through this kind of analogical apparatus that the computer, once its miniaturization had become possible by the late 1960s, could become 'personal' and technology could be conceived as a means to facilitate nomadic lifestyles lived beyond the confining spaces of the city and its architecture.

In the thought of figures such as Max Horkheimer, Henri Lefebvre and Herbert Marcuse, in contrast, technology was often figured as an essentially alienating apparatus of power. The latter, in an essay of 1941, wrote:

> Technology, as a mode of production, as the totality of instruments, devices and contrivances which characterize the machine age, is thus at the same time a mode of organizing and perpetuating (or changing) social relationships, a manifestation of prevalent thought and behavior patterns, an instrument for control and domination.[43]

While the left understood that it was within the broader context of capitalist relations of production and instrumental reason that technology acquired such powers of 'control and domination' – Marcuse continued in the same essay: 'Technics by itself can promote authoritarianism as well as liberty' – the counterculture was unburdened by any such perspectives. It didn't have to wait on the revolution. Computational technology, 'personalized' and conceived of as operating according to the same systemic processes as those of nature and mind, could be liberated from technocracy, in the here and now, and put to progressive ends immediately. 'All Watched Over by Machines of Loving Grace', a poem by the written Richard Brautigan in 1967, imagined a 'cybernetic meadow, where mammals and computers, live together in mutually programming harmony ... a cybernetic ecology'.[44] Likewise, as Felicity D. Scott notes, the countercultural architecture/media collective Ant Farm, in 1969, 'imagined tribes of nomads appearing "on the horizon ... to replace traditional lifestyle patterns in a new age of leisure, an age without war, an age with a global consciousness, living in a cybernetic playground"'.[45] Technology was envisaged as enabling nomadic lifestyles, decentralized modes of communication and collaborative working practices within the ex-urban environments of the counterculture and, equally, within the labs and campuses of technological research facilities. Moreover, such seemingly different environments increasingly came to resemble one another. Buckminster Fuller's technologically pioneering designs for geodesic domes served as prototypes for the dwellings constructed at Drop City and other communes, and the collaborative working spaces of Xerox Palo Alto Research Center Incorporated (PARC), a company specializing in the research and development of computational technology founded in 1970, were furnished with bean bags.

The kinds of convergence, exchange and interaction evident in such cybernetic ecologies suggest that relationship between thought and technology is operating differently than in Marcuse's understanding. Rather than serving as 'a *manifestation* of prevalent thought and behavior patterns [emphasis mine]', technology is itself actually productive of ways of thinking and behaving. This is the proposition sketched out by Gilbert Simondon in his essay 'Technical Mentality'; technology, rather than straightforwardly expressive of 'cognitive schemas', is constitutive and productive of these.[46] The 'technical mentality', he wrote, 'offers a mode of knowledge *sui generis* that essentially uses the analogical transfer and the paradigm, and founds itself on the discovery of common modes of functioning – or of a regime of operation – in otherwise different orders of reality that are chosen just as well from the living or the inert as from the human or the non-human.'[47] It is the technical mentality characteristic of any historical period, according to Simondon, that enables these 'different orders of reality' to be conceived of as operating according to the same principles. It might be added, given the specific nature of the technical mentality at work within a cybernetic cognitive schema – one of feedback loops and the interactive regulation of the 'different orders' – that there is a particular concern with the instrumentalization not just of the *analogical*, but of the *practical* relations that might be productively forged between these different orders. The mentality of cybernetics, in other words, may serve to produce a kind of common currency for transactions, conceptual *and* material, between seemingly different fields of knowledge, discourse and practice.

This possibility was exemplified in the organization of the *Whole Earth Catalog*. As an organ of what Simondon termed 'transcategorical knowledge', the *Catalog* organized its contents according to themes – 'Understanding Whole Systems', 'Shelter and Land Use', 'Industry and Craft', 'Communications', 'Community', 'Nomadics' and 'Learning' – that implied a plane of equivalence through which one could move laterally, mentally rehearsing the links that might subsequently be used to create new environments and ecologies. That lateral movement, traversing different fields of knowledge and practice, suggested in itself a new freedom in the breaking of boundaries and the expansion of horizons, an exemplification in practice of the cybernetic technical mentality. A freedom figured in the countercultural imaginary of the beach, the open road and interstellar space. Spaces open to the infinite possibilities of mobility and connection for the technologically equipped nomadic subject. The scenes of the character THX making his getaway from the underground city in *THX 1138* are symbolic of these new cybernetic freedoms. Escaping the city in a stolen car, pursued at speed by the motorcycle police, he enters into a new contract with technology. In the driver's seat he is cybernetically conjoined with a technics of liberation. Technology, earlier figured as the instrument of a totalitarian rationality, now appears connective, intimate, environmental. Sympathetically enabling.

THX 1138 emblematizes the countercultural spacing of the subject, the ascension to the beach in the film's final sequence serving as something like the primal scene of its mythos. In this new spacing stratification between practices, disciplines, discourses and knowledge is suspended. The subject is mobilized as a technologically equipped and cybernetically conceived agent of connectivity, and returned to nature. Unifying and universalizing models provide the traction with which the subject can move with ease between nature, technology and culture in constructing its environment.

The shaping of such environments is an entrepreneurial opportunity for those positioned, like Stewart Brand, to make the connections, exchanges and transactions that will work for their own enterprises. As he wrote in his introduction to the *Whole Earth Catalog*, 'Personal power is developing the power of the individual to conduct his own education, find his own inspiration, shape his own environment, and share his adventure with whoever is interested.'[48] The figure of George Lucas, traversing the worlds of sports car racing, cinematic special effects, avant-garde cinema, narrative mythology and Buddhism, exemplifies the connective ethos of this entrepreneurial spirit. Steve Jobs, who, before founding Apple, had dropped acid, embarked on a journey of spiritual enlightenment in India and been a member of a Californian DIY personal computer group called the 'Homebrew Computer Club', is its archetype.

Figures such as Jobs were central to the valorization of the 'new economy' – supposed to be based on the free exchange of ideas, information and services, rather than on the industrial production of commodities – as a progressive movement towards the realization of individual human potential. In Apple's television advert for the first 'Macintosh' personal computer, aired in 1984, film director Ridley Scott revisited the noirish scenography of Godard's *Alphaville* to depict a world of mass-programmed subjects and autocratic power. The spell of this technocratic tyranny is shattered, at the advert's conclusion, as a lone female athlete hurls her hammer into the huge screen from which the face of 'Big Brother' is orating. 'On January 24th', announces the voice-over, 'Apple Computer will introduce Macintosh. And you'll see why 1984 won't be like "1984".' Released from centralized bureaucratic power and set loose within the connective and mobile spaces of the new environment, we will be free, as an Apple campaign of 1997 claimed, to 'Think different'. This later advert, with its roll call of 'The crazy ones. The misfits. The rebels. The troublemakers. The round pegs in the square holes. The ones who see things differently' – Bob Dylan, Martin Luther King, Buckminster Fuller and John Lennon visualized among them – personified Apple within a countercultural lineage of figures who 'change things', creative individuals who 'push the human race forward'.

Banham, Baudrillard and McLuhan

Architecture's turn to cybernetics, and to the framing of its own practice as one concerned with forging environmental connections between human, technological and natural systems, was contemporaneous with, and related to, that of the counterculture. With an image of an astronaut on its front cover, the February 1967 edition of *Architectural Design*, titled *2000+*, featured contributions from Buckminster Fuller – 'Profile of the Industrial Revolution', 'The Future of the Future' – and John McHale – 'Outer Space', 'Man+', 'The New Symbiosis'. In this latter essay, McHale wrote: 'Recently, as in his natural symbiotic relations with plants and animals, man's relation to cybernetic systems has been subtly changing toward a more closely-woven interdependency resembling his other ecological ties. This trend often is depicted as "intelligent" machines dominating man; but the possibility is more clearly that of organic partnership.'[49]

As Felicity D. Scott records in *Ant Farm: Allegorical Time Warp*, the Ant Farm group had particularly close ties with Stewart Brand and *The Whole Earth Catalog*. Brand had, at one point, commissioned the group to create a mobile environment located in Death Valley from which to produce a supplement to its 1971 edition. An account of this project – 'Production in the Desert' – appeared, in turn, in the publication itself.[50] Ant Farm's Chip Lord and Douglas Michaels styled themselves as 'space cowboys', fashioning mobile architectures and 'enviro-technologies' – such as their inflatable architectures – for the new 'enviroman'. Their 'Cowboy Nomad Manifesto', 'The Cowboy From Ant Farm' provides a flavour of their frontier-spirited take on cybernetics: 'There are cowboy nomads today, living another lifestyle, and waiting for electronic media, that everyone knows is doing it, to blow the minds of the middle class American suburbanite. While they wait the cowboy nomads (outlaws) smoke loco weed around electric campfires.'[51]

Architecture's cybernetic turn also featured in the September 1969 issue of *Architectural Design*. Edited by Roy Landau, this issue explored the architectural implications of cybernetics, information theory and computation in essays by Nicholas Negroponte, Gordon Pask and Cedric Price. In Pask's contribution, 'The Architectural Relevance of Cybernetics', he writes that 'it is easy to argue that cybernetics is relevant to architecture in the same way that it is relevant to a host of other professions; medicine, engineering or law'.[52] 'Architects', he continued, 'are first and foremost system designers who have been forced over the last 100 years or so, to take an increasing interest in the organizational (i.e. non-tangible) system properties of development, communication and control.'[53] Like the communalists of the counterculture, Pask affirms the open and responsive over the fixed and enclosed. He hopes that in urban design the 'inflexible plan' will give way to the 'environmental computing machine'.[54] Following the ideas of Norbert Weiner, Claude Shannon and Warren Weaver, he foregrounds the significance of 'control, communication and system' as the core components of his cybernetic model. Adopting the cybernetic as its own organizational paradigm architecture will, argues Pask, be equipped to engage effectively with other organizational systems. 'Urban development', for example, can be 'modelled as a self-organizing system' so that its outcomes are made predictable. 'There will', he continues, 'be a proper and systematic formulation of the sense in which architecture acts as a social control.'[55]

Also published in 1969, Reyner Banham's *The Architecture of the Well-tempered Environment* proposed rethinking architecture as a practice of environmental management. Banham, as much in thrall to the architecture and teachings of Buckminster Fuller as were countercultural figures like Brand, argued here for 'the close dialogue of technology and architecture',[56] casting architects as the 'creators of actual physical environments'.[57] 'Societies', he wrote, 'through whatever organs they see fit, such as state patronage or the operation of the market prescribe the creation of fit environments for human activities; the architectural profession responds, reflexively, by proposing enclosed spaces framed by massive structures, because that is what architects have been taught to do, and what society has been taught to expect of architects.'[58] 'Civilized' architecture, claimed Banham, encloses spaces and has difficulty in conceiving of "'free" or "unlimited" space'.[59] Space, in the Western architectural tradition, was 'bounded and contained, limited by walls, floors and ceilings'.[60] Other societies – 'nomad peoples' for instance – he argued, made their environments habitable through the manipulation of power and energy, and not through the creation of physical structures. Taking the campfire as exemplary of this 'power-operated solution', Banham argued that such societies enjoy inhabiting spaces 'whose external boundaries are vague, adjustable according to functional need, and rarely regular'.[61] Architecture, acknowledging the significance of contemporary technologies to its theory and practice, might now access similar environmental enjoyments.

Banham's enthusiasm for open environments and technologically equipped architectures is evident in his own proposals for projects comprised of mechanical services – the 'standard of living package' and the 'unhouse' projects of 1965 – and in his sympathies for Cedric Price's Fun Palace (1961-7). In this (unrealized) project for an open-framed 'laboratory of fun', with its moving gantries and multiple points of access, 'many activities' wrote Banham, 'will need no more enclosure than a roof'.[62]

The references to campfires and the arguments against enclosure suffice to suggest Banham's affinities with the environmental visions of the counterculture. His allegiances to its fetishization of the frontier spirit, and to its visions of the unimpeded movement of the cybernetically enabled subject, are epitomized in an infamous photograph of the architectural historian taken by Tim Street-Porter in 1981. In this image Banham, the 'space cowboy', sporting Stetson, bolo tie, full beard and aviator sunglasses, rides his Bickerton bicycle across a Californian salt flat. In a passage from his *Scenes from American, Deserta* Banham describes the rapturous nature of this experience:

> Given a really hard, smooth soda surface like that of Silurian Lake, north of Baker, which is almost glassy and without crackle patterns over much of its area, one can move with a completeness of freedom a cyclist cannot enjoy anywhere else. Swinging in wider and wider circles or going head down for ever-retreating horizon, the salt whispers under one's wheels and nothing else is heard at all but those minute mechanical noises of the bike that are normally drowned out by other traffic. Swooping and sprinting like a skater over the surface of Silurian Lake, I came as near as ever to a whole-body experience equivalent to the visual intoxication of sheer space that one enjoys in America Deserta.[63]

Banham could be similarly transported by the Los Angeles freeway system. In *Los Angeles: The Architecture of the Four Ecologies* (1971), he writes that this is 'a state of mind, a complete way of life, the fourth ecology of the Angeleno'.[64] 'If motorway driving anywhere calls for a high level of attentiveness', he continues, 'the extreme concentration required in Los Angeles seems to bring on a state of heightened awareness that some locals find mystical'.[65] The Angelenos are 'freeway-pilots … their white-wall tyres are singing over the diamond-cut anti-skid grooves in the concrete road surface, the selector levers of their automatic gearboxes are firmly in *Drive*, and the radio is on'.[66]

Banham is clear on the costs of the integration of subject and environment. The freeway demands of its drivers 'the almost total surrender of personal freedom for most of the journey', their 'willing acquiescence' to an 'incredibly demanding man/machine system'.[67] But things could not be otherwise. Echoing the neoliberal trope of our 'necessary ignorance' in the face of an incomprehensibly complex order of things, Banham explains: 'No human eye at windscreen level can unravel the complexities of even a relatively simple intersection … fast enough for a normal human brain moving forward at up to sixty mph to make the right decision in time, and there is no alternative to complete surrender of will to the instructions on the signs'.[68] The 'mystical' experience of the freeway, the opportunity to be 'integrally identified' with the city, effectively serve – much like the participatory delirium of Pollock's paintings – as compensation for the relinquishment of individual agency. Spatial experience can no longer be synthesized into understanding, but we can at least revel in its 'intoxication' of the senses.

Where Banham affirms 'spatial intoxication' as recompense for the evacuation the subject's interiority, Jean Baudrillard's acknowledgement of the new cybernetic grounds of experience – the 'ecstasy of communication' – is registered without celebration.[69] 'Something has changed', he writes in 1983, and the 'period of production and consumption gives way to the "proteinic" era of networks, to the narcissistic and protean era of connections, contact, contiguity, feedback and generalized interface that goes with the universe of communication'.[70] The 'psychological dimension', he continues, 'has in a sense vanished … one feels that it is not really there that things are being played out'.[71] The scene of the 'dramatic interiority of the subject' has been abandoned and the subject has become a mere 'terminal of multiple networks'.[72] For Baudrillard the 'ecstasy' of communication – telematic, neural, even drug induced – is 'cold' and without passion.

Sometime before Baudrillard's 'Ecstasy of Communication', Marshall McLuhan's essay, 'The Invisible Environment: The Future of an Erosion', published in *Perspecta* in 1967, already sounded an unambiguous warning about the ways in which the emerging cybernetic environment might diminish the human subject.[73] McLuhan begins, following a position then recently argued by Jacques Ellul, by suggesting that all environments (the example used here is of language), per se, might constitute modes of propaganda more powerful than any ideology since their 'action … is total and invisible, and invincible'.[74] The 'environment' is not, he says, necessarily 'bad', but its 'operation upon us' is always 'total and ruthless'.[75] It is the threat of erosion placed over the human unconscious within the environmental conditions of the 'Electric Age', in particular, that concerns McLuhan:

> If the unconscious has an important and irreplaceable function in human affairs, we had best look to it – it is being eroded at a furious pace; it is being invaded by dazzling investigations and insights, and we could quickly reach a stage in which we had no unconscious. This would be like dreaming awake. This possibility that we are actively engaged in liquidating the unconscious for the first time in history, behooves us to pay some attention to how it is structured and to what function it serves in human affairs. It may prove to be indispensable to sanity.[76]

McLuhan's writings – *The Gutenberg Galaxy* (1962), and *Understanding Media* (1964) in particular – exerted a significant influence within the IG, the counterculture and the avant-garde architectural groupings of the 1960s and 1970s. But McLuhan was frequently misread in these contexts – as he continues to be – as straightforwardly and uncritically championing cybernetic technologies, the 'global village' and new forms of post-Gutenberg tribalism. As he wrote in response to such misreadings:

> I am resolutely opposed to all innovation, all change, but I am determined to understand what's happening because I don't choose just to sit and let the juggernaut roll over me. Many people seem to think that if you talk about something recent, you're in favour of it. The exact opposite is true in my case. Anything I talk about is almost certainly to be something I'm resolutely against, and it seems to me the best way of opposing it is to understand it, and then you know where to turn off the button.[77]

McLuhan believed that artists were uniquely capable of locating this button. They had, he held, historically assumed the function of rendering emerging environmental conditions available to conscious and critical perception through the creation of 'anti-environments'. The artist, he wrote, 'does not accept the environment with all its brainwashing functions with any passivity whatever; he just turns upon it and reflects his anti-environmental perceptions upon it'.[78] The act of making the environment visible was critical to McLuhan since, while the content of the media are readily apparent, this is their least significant aspect, having 'about as much importance as the stencilling on the casing of an atomic bomb'.[79] The *medium,* famously, is the real 'message'. It is also the 'massage' in that it 'works over and saturates and molds and transforms every sense ratio'[80] while itself remaining invisible. Its 'groundrules, pervasive structure and overall patterns elude easy perception'.[81] The artist, working against this brainwashing, makes the environment apparent as a medium through which subjects are being otherwise unknowingly trained in behavioural, perceptual and communicative habits. What McLuhan termed 'pattern recognition' is the means through which artists and, increasingly, the 'amateur' are able to recognize and counter these environmental controls. His notion of pattern, here, is distinct from, in fact diametrically opposed to, that of Hamilton or Kaprow, for example. Pattern is not the ready-made register of an immanent and universal logic to be 'dazzled' and 'preoccupied' with. It is not an end in itself. It is a vehicle towards interpretation rather than a compensatory alternative to it. Pattern recognition points us towards the possibility of grasping some larger totality and its transformative processes. The anti-environment produced in response is the artist's retort to the ruthless environment. It 'seeks the development of the total awareness of the individual and the critical awareness of the groundrules of society'.[82]

William S. Burroughs and his 'cut-up' literary technique exemplified, for McLuhan, the anti-environmental work of the artist. 'Burroughs is unique', he argued, 'only in that he is attempting to reproduce in prose what we accommodate every day as a commonplace aspect of life in the electric age. If the corporate life is to be rendered on paper, the method of discontinuous nonstory must be employed'.[83] Burroughs' novels *Naked Lunch* and *Nova Express*, wrote McLuhan, were 'a kind of engineer's report of the terrain hazards and mandatory processes, which exist in the new electric environment'.[84] The discontinuities of Burroughs' prose – the ellipses, hyphens, repetitions and reiterations – work to distance the reader from their linguistic environment. Rather than immersed in the medium, carried along by the syntax of each successive sentence, these devices interrupt habitual reading practices. Burroughs' *The Soft Machine,* writes Oliver Harris, is '"unreadable" in the sense of being impossible to read without being forced to wonder what "reading" is at all'.[85] Burroughs aims to interrupt the flows and scramble the codes through which control otherwise functions invisibly, drawing attention, at the same time, to its operations. As he wrote in *The Ticket that Exploded,* 'Communication must become total and conscious before we can stop it'.[86] In Foucault's terms he reveals, and in the process dismantles, the mechanisms of the 'truth game': 'Cut word lines – Cut music lines – Smash the control machine – Burn the books – Kill the priests – Kill! Kill! Kill!'[87]

McLuhan's calls for the creation of anti-environments such as those produced by Burroughs, especially given the context of their being published in the pages of *Perspecta*, gestured towards the possibility that architects might produce some work of critical disclosure, something equivalently disruptive, from within their own medium. Only the Utopie group in France, though, found themselves compelled to speak out in explicit objection to the doxa of 'environments' and 'environmentalism'. In a statement prepared by the group for the Design and Environment Conference at Aspen in 1970 – delivered by Jean Baudrillard and essentially written as an attack on Banham (one of the organizers of the event) and his environmental discourse – they wrote:

> The burning question of Design and Environment has neither suddenly fallen from the heavens nor spontaneously risen from the collective consciousness: It has its own history. Professor Banham has clearly shown the moral and technical limits and the illusions of Design and Environment practice. He didn't approach the social and political definition of this practice. It is not by accident that all the Western governments have now launched (in France in particular for the last six months) this new crusade, and try to mobilize people's conscience by shouting apocalypse.[88]

The Utopie group understood the conference and the emerging 'environmental ideology' as a phantasmagoria – 'Aspen is the Disneyland of environment and design' – a 'Utopia produced by a capitalist system that assumes the appearance of a second nature in order to survive and perpetuate itself under the pretext of nature'.[89] It is instructive, in this context, to note the kind of sponsors the Design and Environment conference could find to invest in its enterprise – Coca-Cola, Ford Motors, IBM, Mobil Oil.

Banham might have been 'bruised' by the experience of Utopie's critical intervention, but, however prescient and incisive, it had as little impact upon architecture as that of the concept of the 'anti-environment' circulated by McLuhan.[90] The dominant tendency within architecture was towards the affirmation of the emerging cybernetic environment, with its transcategorical forms of knowledge, its entrepreneurial orientations, its celebrations of networked mobility and its promises of self-transcending immersion. Even if unwittingly, it came to serve as the vanguard for the spacing of a neoliberal subjectivity.

The push towards destratified, computational and responsive environments in which man, machine and nature might operate as interactive systems, their commutability authorized under the sign of a unifying paradigm, is widespread and familiar in contemporary architectural discourse. The Theodore Spyropoulos, director of the Architectural Association (AA's) Design Research Lab has recently written, in *Adaptive Ecologies: Correlated Systems of Living*, that 'architecture today can serve as an emergent framework that displays a new nature, combining the biological, social and computational in an adaptive and evolving organism'.[91] In the introduction to this book AA director Brett Steele suggests that 'what is called architecture is barely distinguishable from the behaviours making up the natural world all around it – a world, that is, where bodies, organisms, systems and even disciplines share one thing above all else in common: their own malleability'.[92]

Before such perspectives could reach the kind of prominence within architectural discourse that they currently enjoy, and before these could effectively converge with a neoliberal agenda within the discipline, it had first to shake off the dead weight of theory, cut itself free from the unsettling turns this had taken in the wake of May 68. It had to remove the obstacles that had blocked its supplies lines to more straightforward forms of work and productivity. It had to remake its own environment as one of lateral freedoms in order to facilitate new alignments with theories of complexity and affect, with managerial models, with new materialisms and with the philosophy of Deleuze and Guattari. It had, above all, to kill critique.

Architectural Theory: From May 68 to the 'Real' of the Market

Rem Koolhaas, pitching OMA's project for a new office tower in Manhattan in 2012,[1] directs the attention of the competition panel to his authorship of *Delirious New York: A Retroactive Manifesto for Manhattan*.[2] 'What I wanted to do is look at New York as if there had been a plan. Europeans have a lot of manifestos but then don't realize something, but in New York there was a lot of realization but no manifesto' he explains, as the book's cover appears on the screen to his right. 'Anyone thinking about New York has to think about the implications of the grid. It was my conviction that the grid, on the one hand, is very rigorous and authoritarian, but that in that rigor it also enables a lot of imagination,' he continues, visually accompanied now by a map of the city's street plan. A further image of Manhattan's gridiron appears, identifying the location of the tower at 425 Park Lane, so as to illustrate the reasoning behind its torqued form: 'I think it's a site that's pulled in two directions, both to the north and to the south … so we then started to look at shapes that were perhaps expressing, articulating, that double pull.' After elaborating on the ways in which the tower's shape appears to shift in relation to the perspective of the viewer, Koolhaas proceeds to his concluding argument: 'In a city which is almost dying of generic shapes, but which also doesn't need needless extravagance, it is a beautiful in-between of something that has not happened before, but is still very polite towards everything which is there.' Koolhaas credentials are established with *Delirious New York*, but the book's original theses – the 'culture of congestion', the 'technology of the fantastic', the 'archipelago of blocks' – are elided. *Delirious New York*'s paranoid critical method is parlayed into the 'polite' formal novelties of 425 Park Lane.

Architecture has travelled some distance, since the 1970s, to accommodate itself to the present-day pragmatics of doing business. Strategies of disjunction, sorties into philosophy, film and narrative, and raids on the early-twentieth-century avant-garde have been set aside as the discipline has sutured itself more securely to the means and methods of the market. Where some had sought out a radically new conception and practice of architecture, the discipline now constrains its ambitions to market penetration and its purpose to the provision of product innovation for the 'only game in town' – the 'real' of capitalism. Its attentions are turned now to matters of organizational efficiency, research and development, resource optimization. Not only are its design practices and its client relations carried out according to managerial principles, but so too is its discourse *about* these practices and relations.

Alejandro Zaera-Polo, in the essay 'The Hokusai Wave', recounts the moment at which he realized that the conceptual vocabulary in which his practice, Foreign Office Architects (FOA), had typically traded – one of 'material organizations', 'artificial ecologies' and 'circulation diagrams' – was ineffective in communicating with a non-specialist audience.[3] During the presentation of FOA's Yokohama Port Terminal project at a local press conference, he recalls, he realized that their 'message was not coming across'. In a 'burst of inspiration', he writes, 'we terminated the factual process narrative to conclude that what really inspired us was the image of the Hokusai Wave. The room exploded in an exclamation of sincere relief: "Ahh!"'.[4] This moment of realization is itself relayed back to the architectural readership of *Perspecta*. The anecdote is used to identify a 'crucial matter' in the management of architectural discourse – 'the relationship between acquisition protocols and architectural output' – and presented as a lesson in public relations.[5]

The managerialist turn in architecture, now concerned with making things work and pay within the scope of existing arrangements rather than with testing the limits of these, speaks of the discipline's proximity to the post-political that operates, as Slavoj Žižek has argued, through the apparatus of managerialism.[6] 'The ultimate sign of "post-politics" in all Western countries', he argues, is 'the growth of a managerial approach to government: government is reconceived as a managerial function, deprived of its properly political dimension'.[7] The post-political, he writes in *The Ticklish Subject: The Absent Centre of Political Ontology*, is concerned with 'the "administration of social matters" which remains within the framework of existing sociopolitical relations'.[8] The properly political act, in contrast, 'is not simply something that works well within the framework of existing relations, but something that *changes the very framework that determines how things work*'.[9]

Architecture has, of late, undertaken its own post-political turn. It appears similarly unconcerned with, even actively hostile to, changing the 'framework that determines how things work'. It is focused, instead, on making the existing framework – both of the discipline itself and of the larger social processes in which it is implicated – work more effectively within what Žižek terms 'the (global capitalist) constellation that determines what works'.[10]

Post-theory and the post-political

'Sometime in the third quarter of the twentieth century', observes François Cusset, 'in France but not only there, theory joyfully *stopped* making sense, and began cracking all existing frames … theory used to be reasonable, more than strictly *rational*, and for some reason which remains to be fully explained theory turned *crazy*.'[11] Unleashed from its disciplinary demarcations – by figures such as Althusser, Foucault and Derrida – theory began to produce 'a transdisciplinary open field'.[12] Theory turned 'crazy', Cusset suggests, because its critical labour was endlessly multiplied and turned against itself with every encounter it staged between once discrete fields of knowledge. It lost its identity in the multiple displacements, doubts and suspicions arising from these encounters. Troubled and troubling, theory became a 'demon' that 'began to possess the Western intellectual body'.[13]

Something of theory's demonic quality is also apparent in the description of its encounter with architecture given by K. Michael Hays in the introduction to his *Architecture Theory since 1968*: 'From Marxism and semiotics to psychoanalysis and rhizomatics, architecture theory has freely and contentiously set about opening up architecture to what is thinkable and sayable in other codes, and, in turn, rewriting systems of thought assumed to be properly extrinsic or irrelevant into architecture's own idiolect.'[14] Throughout the period from 1968 to 1993 – within which Hays's anthology is framed – theory's presence within architecture is troubling and demonic because it posits all manner of unforeseen connections between architecture, on the one hand, and language, the unconscious, capital, class and gender, on the other. Since these latter concerns are to be found inextricably lodged within the discourse and practice of architecture, the discipline is forced to acknowledge the presence of foreign elements – each bearing its own burden of unresolved contradictions – that have been residing, all along, in the very places where it might have thought itself able to locate its autonomy. Rather than enriched by such encounters, architecture, like theory itself, in its relentless work of translation, correlation and displacement, finds its foundations unsettled and, according to some, its mission compromised. Michael Speaks writes that theory 'attached' itself to architecture, at this time, and then drove it towards a 'resolutely negative' condition.[15] In one sense theory takes possession of architecture, but the exchange could also be two-way, with architects grasping at theory for their own ends.

 Under the self-promotional imperatives of post-Fordism, observe Luc Boltanski and Eve Chiapello in *The New Spirit of Capitalism*, those engaged in artistic and intellectual labour are 'burdened by a strong need to distinguish themselves in the professional universe'. 'Being the one who has done such and such', they write, 'who has had some idea, and having it acknowledged matters.'[16] The production of a distinctive perspective serves as the precondition for acquiring 'projects'. Theory comes to serve as a resource from which architects, among others, access the means to distinguish and identify themselves so as to secure academic positions, to publish, to fashion projects. But if theory works, at this time, in this way, for certain figures within architectural culture, it is the type of theory that they are engaged in that comes to be seen, by some, as troubling for the discipline as a whole. Post-structuralism and deconstruction cannot, beyond a rather limited scope, be readily instrumentalized by architects as the means to service the construction of the built environment according to the managerial and entrepreneurial principles of neoliberalism. As these principles come increasingly, and ever more exclusively, to define the ambitions of its would-be clients, a disconnect between theory and practice becomes increasingly apparent. This, after all, is Speaks' complaint. Theory's 'negativity' gets in the way of the 'real' work of architecture: that of finding common ground with clients and designing buildings for them: 'Theory was interesting … but now we have work.'[17]

The argument that since architecture has now re-established some common ground with its clientele – and this by cutting itself free from any theoretical ties – that the time of theory is now over, superseded by one of practice, is, though, hard to sustain. This is not least apparent in the tendency for arguments for the 'end of theory' to collapse under the weight of their own paradoxical theorization. More problematic still is the fact that the kind of managerial turn in architecture, in which Speaks locates its newly found 'intelligence', is no less invested in theory than are the forms of managerialism with which it identifies. 'Gilles Deleuze' writes Speaks himself, for instance, 'in his little book, *Spinoza: A Practical Philosophy*, gives us a useful way to think about how … post-vanguard practices become more intelligent and therefore better able to adapt to and transform their environments.'[18] The frequency with which figures such as Ulrich Beck, Bruno Latour or Peter Sloterdijk are invoked in the writing of Alejandro Zaera-Polo,[19] or the centrality of Niklas Luhmann's 'autopoiesis'

to Patrik Schumacher's parametricism,[20] attests to the fact that their own work, indeed their own theorizing, does not itself go untheorized.

Maintaining that practice has straightforwardly superseded theory, relegating the latter to an outmoded era of politics and ideology, obscures not only the ways in which theory now works for architecture, but also the politics and ideology at work in the very notion of a post-ideological and post-political architectural practice. Libero Andreotti has perceptively noted how the prefix 'post-' has typically found employment in the promotion of a 'neo-conservative political agenda'.[21] 'The simple logic of the prefix', he observes, 'is almost irresistible to a certain triumphalist state of mind of the sort we often find among proponents of globalization and the "new economy."' In the case of the 'post-political', he argues, the prefix serves to ontologize an inability to grasp contemporary reality in political terms as an unalterable fact. At the same time, its celebration of having superseded the political effectively obscures the fact that the world is becoming not 'post-' but 'hyper-' political. It is 'moving manifestly toward ever more dizzying degrees of economic centralization and control'.[22] The 'post-' marks the intensification of the very thing it signals to have been surpassed. The same might be said of the 'post-ideological'.

Something similar might also be said of the 'post-theoretical' in architecture, though rather than an intensification of theory, the 'post', in this case, conceals the fact that theory has not been not so much surpassed as retooled for architecture's current objectives. Rather than dropped, like some toxic asset, theory has been rendered productive and reasonable, once more. It provides architecture with a rationale for its current identifications with natural laws, flat ontologies and new materialisms, and, through the same logic, with the epistemologies of neoliberalism and the mechanisms of the market. Architecture now manages theory, at the same time as it turns towards theories of management. This marks its reorientation towards a generalized mode of neoliberal managerialism, a movement from the critical to the organizational originating in its turn to Gilles Deleuze and Félix Guattari.

Architecture and Deleuze

Architecture's endeavours to exorcize its theoretical demons were founded, in significant part, on its appropriations of Deleuze's *The Fold: Leibniz and the Baroque*,[23] and Deleuze and Guattari's *A Thousand Plateaus: Capitalism and Schizophrenia*.[24] In *The Fold*, Deleuze, reading the Baroque through the lens of Gottfried Wilhelm Leibniz's *The Monadology*, finds its philosophy, its mathematics and its art sympathetically attuned to a vitalism that finds expression in the form of 'folding'. The Baroque, writes Deleuze, 'twists and turns its folds, pushing them to infinity, fold over fold, one upon the other'.[25] Through his reading of Leibniz, he conceives of matter as continuous, essentially fluid. It cannot be divided into discrete components. As Leibniz states in his *Pacidus to Philalethes* (from which Deleuze quotes): 'The division of the continuous must not be taken as of sand dividing into grains, but as that of a sheet of paper or of a tunic in folds, in such a way that an infinite number of folds can be produced, some smaller than others, but without the body ever dissolving into points or minima'.[26] Matter is not composed of discrete atomistic particles, but folded and unfolded through the vital forces with which it is charged. These continuously elaborate its potential for becoming in a process that complicates distinctions between solid and void. 'Matter … offers an infinitely porous, spongy, or cavernous texture without emptiness, caverns endlessly contained in other caverns: no matter how small, each body contains a world pierced with irregular passages, surrounded and penetrated by an increasingly vaporous fluid, the totality of the universe resembling a "pond of matter in which there exist different flows and waves"'.[27]

But matter, in Deleuze/Leibniz's schema, constitutes only the first level of folding. The 'pleats of matter' resonate with a second level, the 'folds in the soul', and the two levels – material and metaphysical – communicate through a further 'fold between the two folds'.[28] 'Leibniz constructs a great Baroque montage', writes Deleuze, 'that moves between the lower floor, pierced with windows, and the upper floor, blind and closed, but on the other hand resonating as if it were a music salon translating the visible movements below into sounds up above'.[29] Deleuze illustrated this arrangement in *The Fold* with his diagram of 'The Baroque House (an allegory)'.[30] On the lower floor are the 'common rooms, with "several small openings": the five senses', and above this a 'closed private room, decorated with a "drapery diversified by folds"'.[31]

This diagram, taken to represent 'folding' in plainly architectural terms, proved irresistible to some. Its allegorical purpose, in figuring the relationship between the material and the metaphysical, between sensory experience and the workings of the human soul, was, though, largely overlooked within architecture. Instead the diagram, and *The Fold* overall, was treated as a tract in which the philosophy of Leibniz could be straightforwardly read off the formal complexity of the architectural Baroque. Deleuze's treatment of the formal and the material appeared to illuminate for architecture an exit from the semiotic model that had, until then, held it captive. Deleuze appeared, or was made to appear, to offer a philosophical affirmation of 'folding' as an architectural technique. Ontological descriptions were turned to practical prescriptions so that architecture found a rationale for its return to form, a concern supposed to be more proper to the discipline. Freighted with the philosophical ballast of Deleuze, 'folding' was then presented as the new paradigm of a progressive architecture. In 1993 *Architectural Design* published *Folding in Architecture*, featuring essays and projects by Peter Eisenman, Greg Lynn and Jeffrey Kipnis, among others.[32] Here Eisenman, for example, retrospectively claimed to have employed 'the fold' as a generative device in his Rebstockpark project of 1990. John Rajchman's *Constructions* (1998), in turn, offered its own Deleuzian interpretation of the same project.[33]

In *A Thousand Plateaus*, 'smooth space' is conceived by Deleuze and Guattari as a condition of topological complexity and 'continuous variation'. Smooth space is 'nomadic', a realm of invention, difference and becoming through which the subject might drift. Its antithesis, 'striated space', is rigidly partitioned. It isolates functions and contains subjects within conditions of territorialized stasis. Striated space is figured as standardized, disciplinary and imperial. Deleuze and Guattari elucidate the tensions between the smooth and the striated through a number of models – maritime, mathematical, physical and aesthetic. They write of the sea, for instance, that it is the 'archetype of smooth space', but that it is also 'the archetype of all striations of smooth space: the striation of the desert, the air, the stratosphere …. It was at sea that smooth space was first subjugated and a model found for the laying-out and imposition of striated space, a model later put to use elsewhere.'[34] Whatever the positive implications of smooth space emerging from their analysis, Deleuze and Guattari famously cautioned against the straightforward identification of it as essentially or sufficiently radical in and of itself: 'Of course, smooth spaces are not in themselves liberatory. But the struggle is changed or displaced in them, and life reconstitutes its stakes, confronts new obstacles, invents new paces, switches adversaries. Never believe that a smooth space will suffice to save us.'[35]

Despite the qualifications and cautions offered by Deleuze and Guattari, 'the smooth' proved as alluring to architectural Deleuzism as had been 'the fold'. In its apparent appeal to the continuous and the open, the associative operations of 'smoothing', much like those of 'folding', resonated or were made to resonate, with the complex topologies then being explored through new tools in computational design by figures such as Greg Lynn. Both concepts were mobilized in a discourse that implied that their adoption was not so much motivated by formal considerations as it was driven by some kind of progressive social agenda, one that claimed a causal correlation between formal experimentation and the overcoming of existing boundaries, constraints and contradictions.

The case against contradiction in architecture was put most directly by Greg Lynn, in the introductory essay for *Folding in Architecture*, 'Architectural Curvilinearity: The Folded, the Pliant and the Supple'. Architecture, he wrote, had so far only been able to deal with complexity and difference either by amplifying these to the level of contradiction for rhetorical purposes, as in deconstructivism, or else by subsuming them, as in modernism, to universalizing paradigms. An 'alternative smoothness', he argued, served as a manoeuvre through which architecture could escape these 'dialectically opposed strategies'.[36] The smooth would serve as a new way of handling 'difference' in architecture, one that would bypass the logics of both homogenization and exacerbation. The work of architects of the latter tendency, such as Peter Eisenman, Frank Gehry, Bernard Tschumi and Robert Venturi, alleges that Lynn 'represents difference in violent formal terms'.[37] Smoothing and folding, he claims, will liberate architecture, and 'difference' itself, from this violence:

> Both pliancy and smoothness provide an escape from the two camps which would either have architecture break under the stress of difference or stand firm. Pliancy allows architecture to become involved in complexity through flexibility. It may be possible to neither repress the complex relations of differences with fixed points of resolution nor arrest them in contradictions, but sustain them through flexible, unpredicted, local connections.[38]

The rhetoric of escape from the twin evils of the homogenous and the contradictory still serves as common currency in architectural discourse. Writing in 2012, some two decades after Lynn's essay, Jesse Reiser and Nanako Umemoto claim that a 'new plasticity enables the creation of rich and varied places beyond the impoverished tool boxes of modernism and postmodernism'.[39] Likewise Sylvia Lavin's *Kissing Architecture*, published in 2011, inveighs against the failures of modernism and postmodernism/deconstructivism alike to provide architecture with any forward momentum.[40] Architecture must escape its resultant condition of 'paralysis', she argues, through an intimate, immersive and post-critical condition – a 'theory of kissing' – in which opposition and distance are dissolved through affect.[41]

Lynn's position, like those latterly derived from it, is opposed to the strategies of formal contradiction employed within postmodernism and deconstructivism. It is further opposed to opposition as such. Contradiction, however paradoxically, is contradicted. Difference is to be sustained but conflict is contraindicated.

Figure 1 Greg Lynn FORM, Korean Presbyterian Church of New York, 1999, photo: the author, 2006.

Pliancy is projected as the new model through which to achieve this. A 'cunning pliability is often more effective through smooth incorporation than contradiction and conflict', writes Lynn.[42] In formal terms, he continues, 'These kinds of cunning connections discover new possibilities for organization.'[43] But these connections are not merely formal. They organize the relations between architectural form and other 'events' exterior to it: 'A logic of curvilinearity argues for an active involvement with external events in the folding, bending and curving of form.'[44] 'Forms of bending, twisting or folding', he writes, 'are not superfluous but result from an intensive curvilinear logic which seeks to internalise cultural and contextural [*sic*] forces within form.' If pliancy is the logic, smoothing is its tactics: 'Smoothing does not eradicate differences but incorporates free intensities through fluid tactics of mixing and blending.'[45]

Everything is to be processed, blended, in an operation in which difference is valued on condition that it goes with the flow, that it renounces all antagonism. Nothing must be repressed but everything must comply. The very possibility of contradiction is smoothed out of existence. As a result, architectural Deleuzism approaches the neoliberal ideal of the post-political. Renouncing critical opposition, and any possibility of occupying a position of resistance, it can only endorse what 'works well within the framework of existing relations', and only find its validation in making these function more effectively through the managerial 'cunning' of organizational complexity.

How this might impact on the production of subjectivity is made more explicit as Lynn turns to address D'Arcy Wentworth Thompson analysis of the 'flexible type' – a being whose form adapts in response to the forces at play in its environment. Lynn is especially concerned with how this type, treated as purely morphological being, is 'deformed' by its environment, and with how Thompson's model might be extended to encompass cultural and political forces. 'The morphing effects used in the contemporary advertising and film industry', he writes, 'may already have something in common with recent developments in architecture. These mere images have concrete influences on space, form, politics and culture.'[46] Taking the music video for Michael Jackson's *Black or White* to exemplify this proposition, he affirms its 'physical morphing' of Jackson's image in the same terms – the inclusive logic of 'continuous variation' – as those used to valorize his architecture of folding: 'It is significant that Jackson is not black *or* white but black *and* white, not male *or* female but male *and* female. His simultaneous differences are characteristic of a desire for smoothness; to become heterogeneous yet continuous.' 'Form, politics and identity', he adds 'are intricately connected in this process of deformation.'[47] From this Lynn is able to recommend, without balking at the adjectives employed in the process, an architecture 'compliant to, complicated by, and complicit with external forces in manners which are: submissive, suppliant, adaptable, contingent, responsive, fluent, and yielding through involvement and incorporation.'[48]

Figure 2 NOX – Lars Spuybroek, Maison Folie, Lille, France 2001–4, photo: the author, 2004.

The 'smooth' appears translated in the architecture of Zaha Hadid into the spatial trope of the 'artificial landscape', a morphology in which ground planes, walls and envelopes blend into one another as if collectively deformed by some unseen environmental force. Proclaiming the socially progressive qualities of these compositions, Hadid argues:

> Artificial landscapes are coherent spatial systems. They reject platonic exactitude but they are not just any 'freeform'. They have their peculiar lawfulness. They operate via gradients rather than hard edge delineation. They proliferate infinite variations rather than operating via the repetition of discrete types. They are indeterminate and leave room for active interpretation on the part of the inhabitants.[49]

Presenting a similar argument in interview with Hans Ulrich Obrist, she argues that 'we now have the chance to organize things differently …. You can occupy space and make clusters of organization in such a way that people from all levels of society meet each other'.[50]

Folding and smoothing, in this reconfiguration of Deleuze and Guattari's conceptual apparatus, became the means to conceive of new, supposedly progressive, forms of social composition and individual experience. Deleuze and Guattari's philosophy also presented the discipline with a model of the 'new' as 'invention' through which it could further differentiate itself from postmodernism and deconstructivism. Kipnis, in the essay 'Towards a New Architecture', decried postmodernist architecture as politically conservative, even reactionary, due to its supposed inability to produce the 'new'. In its use of collage and historicism, postmodernism's ultimate effect, he argued, was to 'valorize a finite catalogue of elements and/or processes'.[51] Confining itself to a recombinant logic postmodern architecture, he wrote, 'enabled a reactionary discourse' of 'the nothing new'.[52]

The 'new architecture', in contrast, departed from any semiotic or linguistic paradigm, even the most radically conceived (as in deconstruction), in favour of the supposedly Deleuzian orientation adopted by figures such as Greg Lynn and Sanford Kwinter. These, wrote Kipnis, had turned from 'post-structural semiotics to a consideration of recent developments in geometry, science and the transformation of political space, a shift that is often marked as a move from a Derridean to a Deleuzean discourse'.[53]

Though inaccurate – Derrida had by then made plain that 'deconstruction is inventive or it is nothing at all' – this polarization of Derrida and Deleuze nevertheless effectively served architecture's instrumentalization of philosophy

Figure 3 Zaha Hadid Architects, London Aquatics Centre, London, 2005–11, photo: the author, 2014.

according to its own discursive ends.[54] However untenable the proposition that Deleuze could think the new in terms of 'political space', while Derrida was mired in a realm of 'post-structural semiotics', this was nonetheless the notion circulated by figures like Kipnis and Zaera-Polo in order to provide the new architecture with its distinguishing features. Deleuze, modelled as a philosopher of the 'new', was made amenable to an architecture seeking to establish an image of novelty for itself. For the 'new architecture', the 'new' was doubly significant. It distanced the discipline from recent trends and it underscored its allegiance to a philosophy of becoming. In Reiser + Umemoto's *Atlas of Novel Tectonics*, for instance, Deleuze and Guattari are read as philosophers of matter, emergence and becoming. In subscribing to this philosophy the architects claim to be in pursuit of an agenda of 'difference' and 'the unforeseen': 'Beneficial novelty is the preferred condition to stability and the driving agenda behind architectural practice.'[55]

The new architecture undertook, in the emphatic affirmation of its newness, to establish its autonomy from linguistic and semiotic concerns. It also sought to distance itself from critique. Through its alliance with the 'post-critical' position emerging contemporaneously in American architectural discourse – marked by the publication of Robert Somol and Sarah Whiting's 'Notes Around the Doppler Effect and Other Moods of Modernism' in the journal *Perspecta* in 2002 – it opposed critique as extrinsic to the 'proper' concerns of architecture and castigated its practice as counterproductively negative.[56] Kipnis described criticality as a 'disease' that he wanted to 'kill', 'once and for all'.[57] For Zaera-Polo criticality was anachronistic and, in its 'negativity', ill equipped to address contemporary conditions of complexity:

> I must say that the paradigm of the 'critical' is in my opinion part of the intellectual models that became operative in the early 20th century and presumed that in order to succeed we should take a kind of 'negative' view towards reality, in order to be creative, in order to produce new possibilities. In my opinion, today the critical individual practice that has characterized intellectual correctness for most of the 20th Century is no longer particularly adequate to deal with a culture determined by processes of transformation on a scale and complexity difficult to understand. … If we talk in terms of the construction of subjectivity, the critical belongs to Freud a Lacan [*sic*], what I called 'productive', to Deleuze.[58]

Zaera-Polo's reconstruction of Deleuze is contrived, however unconvincingly, to obscure such aspects of his philosophy as its debts to Lacan.[59] However fabricated, arguments such as these aimed at recruiting Deleuze to the affirmative

Figure 4 Foreign Office Architects, South-East Coastal Park, Barcelona, 2004, photo: the author, 2005.

'productivity' of the new architecture, and to legitimating the proposition that architecture position itself within the complexities of contemporary society so as to 'manipulate' them from the inside. Where Deleuzism in architecture was to be autonomous from any engagement with linguistic paradigms or critical perspectives, it would become progressive through its engagement with the inventive capacities of its own formal and material practices. It would make its cause immanent to that of a new order of complexity.

The new agenda for architecture

In her Pritzker Prize acceptance speech of 2004, Hadid remarked: 'I believe that the complexities and the dynamism of contemporary life cannot be cast into the simple platonic forms provided by the classical canon, nor does the modern style afford enough means of articulation. We have to deal with social diagrams that are more complex and layered when compared with the social programs of the early modern period.' Her work was, she continued, 'concerned with the expansion of the compositional repertoire available to urbanists and designers to cope with this increase in complexity'.[60]

Hadid and Schumacher, claiming that the formal complexity of their architecture coincides with the social complexity of the conditions it is designed to service, have represented their work as a contribution to a progressive project. This claim is also premised on the turn to complexity undertaken within contemporary models of managerialism. Schumacher, in 2005, remarked upon a 'recent trend towards an "architecture of folding" … congenial to the new ideas in organisational and management theory'. 'Architectural notions such as "superposition," "multiple affiliation" and "smoothness"' he continued, 'correspond to organisational tropes such as "matrix," "network" and "blur"'.[61]

These remarks served to introduce a research project – 'Corporate Fields' – conducted by Schumacher and others within the Design Research Laboratory (DRL) at the Architectural Association between 1997 and 2001.[62] In the essay, 'Research Agenda: Spatialising the Complexities of Contemporary Business', Schumacher introduces the programme as follows:

> Each of our teams [of architectural students] collaborated with one of the following corporate quasi-clients: BDP, DEGW, M&C Saatchi, Arup, Microsoft UK or Razorfish … creative leaders in their own fields. These companies and their organisational strategies served as a point of departure for the development of

experimental design scenarios. On a more general level these scenarios respond to the innovative work patterns of a 'post-industrial' economy.[63]

The rationale for this project derived from the argument that while the contemporary business organization – particularly within those advanced sectors of the 'knowledge economy' represented by Schumacher's choice of 'quasi-clients' – was undergoing rapid change, reorienting itself towards paradigms of complexity and 'liquefaction', architecture had, so far, failed to embrace such changes: 'New ways of organising labour are emerging, as witnessed in countless new organisational and management theories. … The business of management consultancy is now thriving while the discipline of architecture – with few exceptions – has yet to recognise that it could play a part in this process.'[64]

For Schumacher, the organizational models employed within these most advanced sections of business represented a departure from the rigidly segmented and hierarchical work patterns of the 'Fordist' era. They signalled a positive movement towards those that were 'de-hierarchised' and based upon flexible networks. Architecture, in its adoption of formal tropes such as 'smoothness' and 'folding', he argued, might make itself 'relevant' by entering into a relationship with the 'new social tropes' with which business organizations and management theories were already engaged. This would enable architecture to 'translate organisational concepts into new effective spatial tropes while in turn launching new organisational concepts by manipulating space.'[65]

Not only might architecture achieve some greater degree of relevance through this pact with post-Fordist managerialism, it might also, suggested Schumacher, identify the basis for an emancipatory project. While acknowledging that organizational tendencies towards de-hierarchization and flexibility were currently 'tied' to the ideology of neoliberalism, and might, for the labour force, result in an experience of 'existential insecurity', he argued, nonetheless, that there was 'today no better site for a progressive and forward-looking project than the most competitive contemporary business domains.'[66] Schumacher's argument was sustained by his insistence that left-wing activism had all but 'disintegrated', that the traditional models of radicalism were now stagnant and regressive.[67] Contemporary forms of activism, the anti-corporate 'movement of movements', for instance, were similarly disparaged: 'The recent anti-globalisation movement is a protest movement, i.e. defensive in orientation and without a coherent constructive outlook that could fill the ideological vacuum left behind since the disappearance of the project of international socialism.'[68]

The 'progressive realities' capable of filling this 'vacuum' – 'de-hierarchisation, matrix and network organisation, flexible specialization, loose and multiple coupling, etc.' – could, claimed Schumacher, only be found within the contemporary business organization.[69] These 'progressive realities' were, in any case, not produced by business itself but had been 'forced upon the capitalist enterprise by the new degree of complexity and flexibility of the total production process'.[70] They could, then, be bracketed from their existing neoliberal and corporate contexts and pursued, in themselves, as a new agenda for architecture.

Schumacher located complexity, and its progressive potentials, within post-Fordist organizational practices. Alejandro Zaera-Polo and Farshid Moussavi found it in matter itself. Drawing on the work of Ilya Prigogine and Isabelle Stengers, the self-organizing and 'emergent' capacities imputed to matter were held up as evidence of an essential, all-pervading, order of complexity.[71] This order was then valorized such that anything appearing to follow its 'materialist' organizational principles might be accorded progressive status.

In 'Order out of Chaos: The material organization of advanced capitalism',[72] Zaera-Polo writes that a contemporary 'restructuring of the capitalist space unfolds a "liquefaction" of rigid spatial structures'.[73] The 'spatial boundaries' of the city, he continues, lose their importance within the new composition of capital. From this, Zaera-Polo infers a progressive tendency within the process of contemporary urbanism since, 'through this growing disorganisation of the composition of capital, the contemporary city tends to constitute itself as a non-organic and complex structure without a hierarchical structure nor a linear organisation'.[74] The post-Fordist city now operates as a complex system whose organization is composed exclusively of local interactions so that it escapes any externally directive power:

> At the end of the 60s, due to the rise of the late-capitalist mode of production, emerging patterns of urban organisation began to consolidate as new forms of urbanity and material organisation. These changes in the urban topographies coincided in time with the emergence of a new scientific paradigm which has come to replace the long-lasting validity of conservative systems – those based in models where systems are considered isolated and maintaining matter and energy constant – by an emerging epistemology that understand systems as vaguely delimited locations crossed by flows of matter and energy.[75]

From this perspective the role played by corporate capital within the contemporary city can be claimed as subversive. 'The complex formed by the AT&T, Trump and IBM headquarters in Manhattan not only integrates a multiple programmatic structure, but also incorporates systematically the public space within the buildings: a subversion of the established urban boundaries between public and private.'[76] The 'dynamics of contemporary urban phenomena' represent 'the manifestation of emerging complex orders'.[77] The political becomes the morphological. A progressive project is one that dissolves boundaries, achieves flexibility and embraces complexity. Spatial closure is conflated with the apparatus of a disciplinary society and boundaries between academic disciplines similarly construed as brakes on an underlying, and essentially emancipatory, order of complexity. 'To operate within the contemporary city', Zaera-Polo declares, 'we have to evolve the disciplines related to material practices: it may be by looking at the sciences of complexity that we understand a reality that our disciplines are no longer able to operate.'[78]

In a later essay, 'The Politics of the Envelope', Zaera-Polo extends the designation 'complex order' to economics, politics, culture and the social.[79] These are now to be understood as *material* organizations so that notions such as ideology and practices of critique – based as these are in the supposedly *de-materialized* world of concepts and ideas – are now rendered anachronistic. In the case of the political, writes Zaera-Polo, we now inhabit the post-ideological condition of a new materialism where 'contemporary power structures operate as physical aggregates where behavior is created through the localized complex association of molecular components'.[80]

The turn towards matter, and the investment in its productive complexity, is similarly articulated by Kipnis in the essay 'On the Wild Side'. Here matter is affirmed against the 'dematerialized-idealist' world of semiotics, criticality and other products of the 'cult of ideas'.[81] Criticality is singled out as an especially pernicious practice likened, in its 'violent' and 'sadistic' character, to that of vivisection. A 'stalled' enterprise, now 'less thoughtful than mean', its time is over.[82] Now, claims Kipnis, is the 'time of matter'. It has in fact been so since the birth of the universe when 'there were no signs, no ideas, no concepts, no meanings, no disembodied spirits, no dematerialized abstractions whatsoever around during the first couple of seconds after the Big Bang, nor during the first million or billion years, or, for that matter, even these days'.[83] 'Nothing escapes materiality', writes Kipnis, and this fact guarantees our liberty since 'matter is freedom itself'.[84]

The 'sciences of complexity' are the new grounds upon which architecture's discourse and practice are to be fixed. They will equip it with the means to become progressive and the truths with which to silence critique, once and for all. Complexity heralds a new and progressive order in which productivity, invention and the new issue from matter itself, escaping external disciplinary powers. This renders critique, predicated on the interrogation of the ideology of power, redundant. There is no ideology, there is only matter. Architecture can exorcize its theoretical demons and dispense with the cult of ideas. It has had, though, to observe a strict and conspicuous silence regarding the possibility that complexity, as it has been appropriated by the discipline, might itself be amenable to critique. Not least where this possibility stems from the very sources on which its foundations have been consecrated.

Complexity, says Isabelle Stengers, is not itself a science but rather 'a discourse *about* science'.[85] Complexity does not provide science with a new foundation, but disturbs the very grounds on which it is based. Architecture, conversely, has understood complexity as a property discovered to be immanent to matter and its organization. Yet Stengers, in 'Complexity: A Fad', had already, in 1987, issued advanced notice to the contrary: 'It is not possible to speak of a "discovery of complexity"'.[86] Complexity does not expand scientific knowledge, it complicates it. The discourse, practice and authority of scientific method are undermined by the observation of phenomena described as 'complex'. Stengers and Prigogine describe, for instance, how the 'thermodynamics of irreversible processes' are liable to 'drive certain systems far from equilibrium'. These processes, they write, 'can nourish phenomena of spontaneous self-organization, ruptures of symmetry, evolutions toward a growing complexity and diversity'.[87] For Stengers these behaviours and potentials are significant not because they give us 'another scientific vision of the world', but because they suggest that 'it is the notion of a vision of the world, from the point of view of which a general and unifying discourse can be held, that in one way or another must be called into question'.[88]

Stengers is concerned, however, that what began as a critique of scientific knowledge has effectively renewed and re-legitimized that knowledge. Complexity appears now as a progressive scientific instrument: 'It allows one both to defend science against the charge of "reductionism" and at the same time to envisage science's conquest of what until now had escaped it,' she laments.[89] Where complexity, as 'a discourse *about* science' might have challenged practices of mastery and control, it appears now that it may be serving to further extend the reach and scope of such processes of 'capture' for instrumental means.[90]

Stengers' concerns are well founded. Not only architecture, but military strategy, marketing, urban planning, organizational theory, policing and management techniques have all in recent years been transformed through their engagement with models of complexity, emergence and self-organization. Adopted as a self-legitimating scientific rationality, the discourse of complexity has become hegemonic within a number of disciplines. Outwardly presented as an ecologically redemptive alignment with newly discovered laws of nature, complexity functions as a practice of knowledge employed to achieve more effective means of capture and control. Networked patterns of communication, mobility, industrial and 'immaterial' production, research, marketing and warfare, and the vast scales on which these are globally integrated require sophisticated means of modelling, analysis and systemic steering. Far from driving such systems 'far from equilibrium' complexity harvests more effective means of control, efficiency and productivity from them. Complexity is both the pretext and the means for neoliberal managerialism. What Adorno and Horkheimer said of the Enlightenment's instrumentalization of nature holds true for its more contemporary incarnations: 'Knowledge, which is power, knows no obstacles: neither in the enslavement of men nor in compliance with the world's rulers. … What men want to learn from nature is how to use it in order to dominate it and other men.'[91] What architects want from complexity are rules of governance. Organizational truths located in an irrefutable materialism. The 'laws' of natural systems and the 'orders' of complexity.

Architecture remains unperturbed by Stengers' proposition that unifying theories and visions of the world should themselves be put into question. Instead its own vision of the world is upgraded to one better able to reinforce laws and legitimate order. The discipline can displace its agency to the 'real' of matter. Nothing is called into question, other than critique, only in order that it be disenfranchised from calling things into question. The order-words of this architecture – 'self-organization', 'emergence', 'continuous variation', 'material organization' – are circulated until they metabolize into a new doxa. Or until they mesh seamlessly with the existing doxa of neoliberalism so that architecture is relieved of its critical labours and unburdened of its ideas. Neoliberalism, in turn, is itself increasingly figured within architectural discourse as a largely beneficent manifestation of the new order of complexity.

Architecture and the market

'No longer exclusively an homogenizing force', writes Farshid Moussavi in *The Function of Form* (2009), 'capitalism now contributes to the production of difference and novelty'.[92] Taking Ragú Spaghetti Sauce, Starbucks and Volkswagen as exemplary sources of mass customization, product differentiation and novel hybridity, while also suggesting that phenomena such as these might indicate a challenge to platonic idealism, she argues that architecture should pursue the same means in its own development of novel forms. Architecture, she argues, can use this market-based model of development for ends other than those of the market itself. 'The fundamental challenge for architects and other producers of culture,' she writes, 'is to imbue the production of forms with a diversity of goals and causes which are not solely market-driven, thereby contributing to an environment that connects individuals to multitude [*sic*] of choices.'[93]

Alejandro Zaera-Polo's 2010 essay 'Cheapness: No Frills and Bare Life' addresses contemporary conditions of accessibility brought to us by figures like Alan Greenspan – 'cheap money' – and Bill Gates – 'cheap automation' – and by brands such as EasyJet, Ikea and Primark. The social transformations wrought by these are considered representative of a non-ideological and post-ideological politics of 'cheapness' with which architecture should now connect. In the case of clothing and air travel, for instance, Zaera-Polo argues:

> If Chanel or Issey Miyake are supposed to be adding a wholesome aura or lifestyle to the body and are duly priced upward, some of the low-cost operators have resorted to a radical minimization of production costs. In this mode of operation, the relationship between style, price, and value is inverted and the political agency of production is reframed, emptying out the product of any explicit ideological ambition, jettisoning the spectral surplus value of the commodity.[94]

With the qualification that 'it is not clear that equality of means necessarily implies the equality of rights that characterizes democratic life', he writes that accessibility constitutes a 'de facto democraticizing spirit in the neo-liberal markets. In a market-driven culture, *affordability* is the byword for democracy.'[95]

Patrik Schumacher argues that 'society should allow the market to discover the most productive mix and arrangement of land uses, a distribution that garners synergies and maximizes overall value. The market process is an evolutionary process that operates via mutation (trial and error), selection and reproduction. It is self-correcting, self-regulation [*sic*], leading to a self-organized order.'[96] Interviewed by Peter Eisenman, in 2013, he reports 'I am trying to imagine a radical free-market urbanism. ... I am trying to theorize an architectural discourse that does not rely on or create its order through state planning and heavy central, prescriptive regulation but could be possible through open-ended interventions by many participants.'[97]

In these arguments the market is valorized for its accommodation of difference and choice, hailed as a post-ideological force for democratization, and naturalized as an evolutionary agent of self-regulating order. The putative benefits of the market might be further intensified while its seemingly incidental tendencies – towards the exacerbation of economic inequalities and the production of existential precarity – somehow passed over as its unfortunate side effects. As if they were not the very essence of its mechanisms.

Thinking it is engaged in the subversion of neoliberalism architecture only joins it in its ongoing truth game. The discipline effectively aligns itself with the promulgation of truths first scripted in Mont Pelerin in 1947: the market has not been planned; the market is a spontaneously arising spontaneous order; the market is a manifestation of the irresistible ontological truths of the 'way of the world'; these truths guarantee freedom and liberty. The machinations of what Mirowski terms the 'Neoliberal Thought Collective' in the strategic promotion of these truths, including Hayek's recruitment of intellectuals as 'second-hand dealers in ideas' for this work, remain invisible within architecture's encomiums to the market.

This invisibility is actively produced by the subsumption of thought to the model of spontaneous order. History is presented as if driven by an entirely unplanned and spontaneous matter of emergence. Rather than acknowledging the conscious mobilizations of knowledge towards trans-categorical and entrepreneurial practices in the 1960s, Zaera-Polo writes of the '*emergence* of a new scientific paradigm [my emphasis]' at this time.[98] The 'emergent' appears as if it were some self-scripting manifestation of the laws of nature. The political is similarly subsumed to the 'localized complex association of molecular components'.[99]

In the absence of an understanding of the concrete social practices and production of mentalities through which complexity has been fashioned into a hegemonic apparatus, and of the interests this might serve, turns to materialism and complexity appear as if they had themselves simply materialized from the same 'self-organizing' processes they claim to account for. This results directly from such dogma as 'now is the time of matter'. But, since its legitimation in the thought of figures like Deleuze and Guattari or Stengers remains susceptible to contradiction, the new architecture has scaffolded its dogma with more readily amenable sources.

DeLanda, Latour and Luhmann

The work of philosopher Manuel DeLanda, for instance, has long served as a de-Marxifying filter for the reception of Deleuze and Guattari within architecture.[100] He posits the philosophers' attachments to Marx, such as their concerns with the 'economic infrastructure', as their own Oedipus complex.[101] DeLanda's 'assemblage theory', cured of this disorder, models organization as a matter of 'isomorphic' processes operating at different scales across the biological, the geological and the social. This model allows for causal agency between different 'singularities', but admits of no force of capture directing them towards any preconceived end: 'In this ontology all that exists in the actual world is singular individual entities (individual atoms, cells, organisms, persons, organizations, cities and so on) whose main difference from each other is spatio-temporal scale. There are no totalities, such as "society as a whole …".'[102]

De Landa's ontology is resolutely 'flat'. It admits of singularities emerging at different scales in the relations between parts and wholes, but discounts the possibility of any larger totality, such as capital, or the 'social machine' (as it is also called by Deleuze and Guattari), which might capture these singularities for its own productions. He is then – usefully for any supposedly Deleuzian architecture – at odds with what he conceives of as the pathologically Marxian residue within Deleuze and Guattari. In *Anti-Oedipus*, they figure the 'capitalist system' as an 'axiomatic': 'The true axiomatic is that of the social machine itself, which takes the place of the old codings and organises all the decoded flows of scientific and technical code, for the benefit of the capitalist system and in the service of its ends.'[103] In DeLanda's flat ontology, the very possibility of any such axiomatic is ruled out. His position is echoed in Zaera-Polo's refusal to countenance the operation of any instrumental totality. In 'The Politics of the Envelope', he argues that 'it may be good to stop speaking of power in general, or of the State, Capital, Globalization in general'.[104]

This putatively materialist position has also been sustained with recourse to the thought of Bruno Latour, the philosopher of science whose work is also referred to at length in 'The Politics of the Envelope'. In Latour's ontology there are only 'actors' and 'networks'. His 'actor-network theory' recognizes no hierarchies at work, only agents – human and non-human – interacting amid a network within which there are no privileged centres. Latour has also proved valuable to the new architecture in his denouncements of the 'negativity' of critique. This has, he argues, 'run out of steam' – 'critical theory died away long ago.'[105] Politics, such as it is within this ontology, is transformed into a '*dingpolitik*', a matter of *things* and their organizational relations.[106]

Patrik Schumacher, in his two-volume treatise *The Autopoiesis of Architecture*, has derived the ontological basis for architecture's 'new agenda' from the sociologist Niklas Luhmann.[107] Luhmann's not uncontroversial extension into sociological terms of Humberto Maturana and Francisco Varela's account of biological autopoiesis – in which living systems are understood as 'bounded' structures self-reproducing through their interaction with the environments to which they are 'structurally coupled' – has, in turn, been extended by Schumacher to conceptualize architecture. Here, again, accounts of biological and material processes are extended to assertions about social, economic and cultural ones, the authority of which appears underwritten by indisputable 'laws of nature'. And, again, these assertions are mobilized to undermine any basis from which architecture might reflect critically and politically on its disciplinary practice. The bounds by which architecture is circumscribed as an autopoietic system, according to Schumacher, foreclose the very possibility of its exercising any critical faculties or political agency. Schumacher insists that architecture's accommodation of the existing social order must now be absolute since 'it is *not* architecture's societal function to actively promote or initiate political agendas that are not already thriving in the political arena'.[108] Following the arguments of Luhmann, the political is understood strictly and exclusively as that which is exercised by elected political parties. This is the 'specific medium' of the political to which all are entitled to participate 'via voting in political elections' as the legitimate extent of their contribution to the social order which architecture is henceforth to serve unquestioningly.[109] 'Those who want to debate architecture should keep their political convictions to themselves,' stipulates Schumacher, adding that 'political agendas must be pursued in the political system', and that 'those who want to argue politics should enter politics proper'.[110]

The real subsumption of theory

With this latest turn Schumacher proposes the absolute exclusion of the political from the architectural. While Zaera-Polo's 'The Politics of the Envelope' proposed to locate the political, refashioned as a purely 'materialist' phenomenon, within the agency of architecture, Schumacher deems it off limits. That this can be proclaimed signals the 'real subsumption' of theory to architecture. If theory were once subject to a 'formal subsumption' – its existing forms selectively recruited for architectural ends – then now theory is to be designed and produced by architecture itself as an instrument of post-political managerialism. It bears repeating, at this point, that the 'post' typically marks the intensification of the thing it claims to have surpassed. The real subsumption of theory to an architecture in thrall to the virtues of the market marks the turn at which the discipline, in its renunciation of all antagonism towards existing arrangements, becomes most intensively political.

This movement towards the real subsumption of theory is advocated by Schumacher in *The Autopoiesis of Architecture, Volume I.* Here the design of theory comes to replace theories of design. Schumacher writes of the 'the "designed" nature of all theory',[111] and asserts that theory 'is a designed apparatus to give order to the phenomena we experience'.[112] Further underlining this instrumentalization of theory for an end itself unquestioned and already given in advance – in this case the ontological model of autopoiesis – he writes that the 'theoretician's theory succeeds when its guiding premises, conclusions and turns of argument diffuse into the ongoing autopoiesis of architecture'.[113]

If theory can be understood as now disciplined by an architectural culture itself taking its cues from currently valorized forms of neoliberal production, a similarly significant reconception and repurposing of the avant-garde can also be observed. Rem Koolhaas and Hans Ulrich Obrist's *Project Japan*, for instance, identifies an heroic quality in the Japanese Metabolist movement as an avant-garde whose mission was inextricably bound to national economic and bureaucratic agendas, as well as in the prescience of its ecologically derived models.[114] Whereas Manfredo Tafuri argued, in his *Architecture and Utopia: Design and Capitalist Development*, that the work of the early-twentieth-century avant-garde, despite its anti-capitalism, had effectively, and largely against its own visions, served the process of restructuring everyday life for late capitalism, this critique is now rendered redundant by a new conception of the avant-garde as, by definition, something like a research and development department for capital. 'It is the task of the avant-garde segment of architecture,' writes Schumacher, 'supported by architectural theory, to continuously innovate the disciplinary resources in line with the demands of society.'[115] These demands themselves are not to be reflected upon by architects or theorists, but taken as given within 'parliamentary democracy'.[116]

Architecture has sought to sanitize the 'madness of theory', to dispossess itself of its theoretical demons. Theory has been worked over until it can be put to work for and within neoliberalism. The 'smooth' and the 'folded' have been instrumentalized in the affirmation of flexibility and compliance, 'complexity' employed to dissimulate neoliberal imperatives as the laws of nature. The way of the market comes to appear as the way of the world, and vice versa. Through theory, architecture has fashioned itself as a service provider for the 'real' of the market, a resource for the spatial articulation of neoliberal modes of managerialism.

Labour Theory: Architecture,
Work and Neoliberalism

Zaha Hadid has found herself at the centre of recent controversies concerning the conditions of labour under which her projects are constructed.[1] She has been criticized for distancing herself from these concerns, and for arguing that conditions of building construction are beyond the control and responsibility of the architect. Rather than evidence of the moral failings of the architect, however, Hadid's perspective is perfectly consistent with the 'new agenda' of architecture already theorized by her partner in practice, Patrik Schumacher. Social, political and governmental matters are not to be reflected upon or criticized by architects. The discipline is to operate strictly within the confines through which it is autopoietically circumscribed, adhering only to its own 'societal function'. This, argues Schumacher, consists solely in 'the ordering and framing of communicative interaction'.[2]

The reluctance to dwell on the conditions of labour through which projects such as Hadid's stadium are built and the efforts to distance the architect from this work are also logically consistent with the conformity of this architecture to the commodity form. The 'mysterious character' of this form, as Marx noted, lies 'simply in the fact that the commodity reflects the social characteristics of men's own labour as objective characteristics of the products of labour themselves, as the socio-natural properties of these things'.[3] If labour is to appear as the 'socio-natural' property of the commodity itself, then it cannot appear, at the same time, as the property of the labourer. The mystifying, 'phantasmagorical', form in which the commodity appears is predicated on maintaining the invisibility of the concrete labour through which the commodity is produced.[4]

Architecture and the image of labour

In his *In Search of* Wagner, Adorno, extending Marx's critique into the sphere of cultural production, described the compositional and scenographic practices of Wagnerian opera as premised on the 'occultation of production by means of the outward appearance of the product'.[5] The stagehands working the machines that make the Rhine Maidens appear to float above the stage in *Der Ring des Nibelungen* are obscured from the audience. The musicians – the productive forces – are hidden from view in the orchestra pit. Following Marx's criteria, Adorno identifies Wagner's operatic works as essentially phantasmagorical. Conditions of labour are concealed so that the products of these can appear in the commodity form, as fetishized objects of consumption.

As stages for the mass consumption of cultural production, the contemporary architecture of stadiums, concert halls and museums is obedient to the same formal laws. Today's architectural phantasmagoria is similarly invested in the 'occultation of production'. The work of building is of no concern to architects because the real work of architecture, as a commodity, is to positively express the abstract structures and concepts of neoliberal capitalism while mystifying its actual conditions of production. This work acquires a special sense in those forms of architecture most closely aligned with the ontology of neoliberalism. The formal tropes of an architecture of flexibility and adaptability advertise accommodation to the spontaneous order that stands as the truth of the neoliberal way of the world. Free of any suggestion of internal contradiction or struggle, their pliant envelopes and organic contours read as affirmations of the immanent and self-realizing powers of life and matter. Productivity appears as the innate property of natural forces to materialize themselves in architectonic form. The real material conditions of architectural construction are most forcibly occulted where architectural form most emphatically affirms its autogenic powers.

Not only is what Marx called 'concrete labour' occulted in the phantasmagoric appearance of the commodity, it is also disavowed as the means through which our social relations might be grasped. In capitalism, argued Marx, these relations cannot be experienced directly through labour, but only through the exchange of commodities produced from it. As Moishe Postone elaborates, 'A new form of interdependence comes into being where no-one consumes what they produce, but where, nevertheless, one's own labor or labor-products function as the necessary means of obtaining the products of others'.[6] In neoliberalism the disavowal of labour also extends to the types of labour the subject must

Figure 5 Zaha Hadid Architects, Galaxy Soho, Beijing, 2009–12, photo: Shengze Chen, 2012.

undertake upon itself. There must now be a continuous, and ever more intensive, undertaking to work upon the self so as to qualify for and sustain employment. The self is to be an ongoing project fashioned through programmes of physical, intellectual and psychological training and qualification. Its performance is to be tracked, measured and rated. It is to present itself as flexible, adaptable, communicative and enterprising, to be amenable to working long or unsociable hours, to shifting swiftly between tasks and assignments, to undertaking unpaid work in order to gain experience that potential employers might look upon favourably. But the labourious experience of this work – its hardships, stresses and burdens – cannot be acknowledged as such. The imperatives of neoliberalism are spun into the positive-speak of choices and freedoms. Life as competition is affirmatively ontologized as the natural way of things. There is no struggle, there is only opportunity. The belief in universal laws that state that all things possess the capacity to spontaneously develop, evolve and order themselves, without need of external compulsion, obscures all signs of struggle, tension or contradiction. In neoliberalism, everything is productive but nothing is laboured.

Labour is also disavowed in neoliberalism in another sense. The narrative of the post-political has no role for labour as the antagonist or antithesis of capital. The class struggle is overcome in the discovery of the evolutionary nature of the social order, the proletariat relieved of its historic mission in the process. In this natural order everyone is at liberty to find their opportunities and take their chances. The real burden of having to work at one's employability, as well as at one's employment – the labour of qualifying for the opportunity to labour – cannot be acknowledged, as such, within the political and managerial discourse of neoliberalism. Instead the old question of whether one lives to work, or works to live, is rendered seemingly redundant in the merging of the one into the other. This is accomplished through the practice of skills, habits and techniques required of both work and non-work within an overall schema of productivity. These practices are accommodated in spaces designed to productively blur the boundaries between work and its other.

Ubiquitous workspace

The desire to eliminate the boundaries erected between work and life is not in itself necessarily neoliberal. This same desire had, for instance, an earlier iteration in the thought of Henri Lefebvre. In the new spaces of leisure of the 1970s – the hotels, chalets and tourist resorts developed for the new industries of mass tourism – Lefebvre identified the traces of a utopian impulse. These spaces spoke of a wish to abolish the existing fragmentation of everyday life into separate practices, times and spaces. 'Leisure', wrote Lefebvre in *The Production of Space*, 'is as alienated and alienating as labour; as much an agent of co-optation as it is itself co-opted; and both an assimilative and an assimilated part of the "system" … leisure has been transformed into an industry, into a victory of neocapitalism and an extension of bourgeois hegemony to the whole of space'.[7] And yet, paradoxically, as Lefebvre argued, 'The space of leisure *tends* … to surmount divisions: the division between social and mental, the division between sensory and intellectual, and also the division between the everyday and the out-of-the-ordinary (festival)'.[8] Spaces of leisure are at the same time the 'best' and the 'worst' of capitalism. They are 'parasitic outgrowths on the one hand and exuberant new branches on the other – as prodigal of monstrosities as of promises (that it cannot keep)'.[9]

These promises have been fulfilled in neoliberalism – the divisions in question have indeed been surmounted – but in monstrous form. The separation between work and non-work is progressively dissolved so that a general condition of constant productivity prevails at all times, in all spaces. Rather than the hoped for dissolution of the alienating condition of labour, or the (at the time) seemingly reasonable expectation that living standards would continue to rise and working time be lessened, the reach of work, as productivity, now extends far beyond the nine-to-five of the workplace. At the same time, the image of labour, as such, tends to be obscured behind an appearance of convivial and casual informality. As Moishe Postone has argued, the extension and expansion of labour is an inevitable feature of capitalism:

> Higher socially general levels of productivity do not diminish the socially general necessity for labor time expenditure … instead that necessity is constantly reconstituted. In a system based on value, there is a drive for ever-increasing levels of productivity, yet direct human labor time expenditure remains necessary to the system as a whole. This pattern promotes still further increases in productivity.[10]

The imperative towards ever greater levels of productivity is served, in part, by new managerial strategies arguing for the gains in productivity to be achieved through informality, interaction, cooperation and networking within the workforce, particularly that of the office. The implementation of this strategy has been dependent, to a significant degree, on the design of spaces supposed to facilitate the cultivation and performance of the requisite workplace dispositions. In a report titled 'The Future of the Workplace is Now', the British office design group DEGW stated: 'The office has to be designed as a centre of high intensity collaboration, formal and informal, scheduled and ad hoc, large and small scale, virtual and real. The paradigm of the office as a centre of collaboration replaces the paradigm of the office as a place where the staff is physically gathered to work individually.'[11] Likewise, the 'Future of Work' report produced by Capital One in 2005, in consultation with DEGW, focuses on 'enabling mobility and workplace settings that support knowledge work when and where it is most effective', and 'enabling work, anyplace, anytime'.[12] Capital One subsequently introduced collaborative and mobile working practices within a workspace now reorganized into team-based 'neighbourhoods'. The returns on these investments were reported as greater 'portfolio flexibility', 'business agility', 'productivity' and 'employee satisfaction'.[13]

Managerial strategies premised on informality, collaboration and mobility as the means to render workers, and space itself, more productive, are widespread. The workspace of the office is re-shaped to accommodate work 'anyplace, anytime', to inculcate in employees flexible, adaptive and communicative dispositions. The spatial typologies of non-work – the cafe or the lounge – are transplanted into those of work. Spaces outside that of the office are progressively transformed to accommodate the new modalities of labour. Office team-based working lunches are catered for in bars and restaurants furnished with elongated refectory tables. Domestic spaces are reappropriated for the home office. The availability of wireless and mobile computing technologies, coupled to a ubiquitous telecommunications infrastructure, enable the extension of work, and working hours, into the spaces of leisure and travel, its extensive dispersal into domestic and public space.

The popular literature of management presents the new practices of labour, and the reconfigurations of space designed to serve them, as progressive. Don Tapscott and Anthony D. Williams, in their *Wikinomics: How Mass Collaboration Changes Everything*, write that in the past corporations were run as rigid hierarchies: 'Everyone was subordinate to someone else,' 'there was always someone or some company in charge, controlling things at the "top" of the food chain.'[14] Now, though, 'profound changes in the nature of technology, demographics, and the global economy are giving rise to powerful new models of production based on community, collaboration and self-organization rather than on hierarchy and control'.[15] Breakout spaces, open offices, informal dress codes, the casualized deportment of bodies and the flexibility of working patterns afford escape from the confinements and constrictions of less enlightened (and less productive) regimes. These new freedoms are valorized as affording workers the liberty to engage in what are presented as the essentially human practices of being communicative, cooperative and sociable. Naturalized, the instrumental contrivance of the new managerial strategies and any struggle of workers to accommodate themselves to the demands of these are obscured.[16]

Boltanski and Chiapello, Postone, and the thesis of 'immaterial labour'

Schumacher's argument, that the new post-industrial and post-Fordist models of managerial and workplace organization constituted 'progressive realities', 'forced upon the capitalist enterprise' is contradicted by that put forward by Luc Boltanski and Eve Chiapello in their *The New Spirit of Capitalism*.[17] The strategies of the new managerialism, rather than forced upon the 'capitalist enterprise', were, they argue, recuperated from an earlier critique of alienated labour. Autonomy, spontaneity, availability, informality, conviviality – the central features of this managerialism – were appropriated from the 'repertoire of May 1968'.[18] This repertoire, originally directed against capitalism, was seized upon within management literature and detached from the broader context of its attack on all forms of exploitation. Its themes were then 'represented as objectives … valid in their own right, and placed in the service of forces whose destruction they were intended to hasten'.[19]

Rather than motivated by any concession to the validity of worker's demands, the subsequent dismantling by managers of workplace hierarchies and bureaucratic structures was adopted so as to increase productivity. Recognizing the organizational advantages latent in workers' demands for 'self-management' employers now required workers to manage themselves. Self-motivation, flexibility and interpersonal skills become the requisite attributes of a new organizational paradigm in which mechanisms of control were to be effectively internalized by the worker. As Boltanski and Chiapello suggest, '"Controlling the uncontrollable" is not something with an infinite number of solutions: in fact, the only solution is for people to control themselves, which involves transferring constraints from external organizational mechanisms to people's internal dispositions, and for the powers of control they exercise to be consistent with the firm's general project'.[20] The critique of alienated labour is reappropriated by management, who, in their tactical concessions to demands for autonomy, use these to render labour more efficient and productive.

Boltanski and Chiapello's thesis, though, can only account in part for the new strategies of labour management. These are derived not only, and not most substantially, from the recuperation of critique, as they are from the truths propagated within neoliberal thought. More than the critiques and practices for which May 68 was the epicentre, contemporary managerialism draws on a specifically neoliberal conception of liberty, on the ontologies supposed to legitimate it, and on the organizational forms supposed to be consonant with its realization. People are most free when they are able to act in concert with the universal laws of self-organization, when they are not subjected to external commands and interference. Neither the evolution of the corporation nor its workforce can be effectively directed by individuals isolated at the summit of a rigidly hierarchical structure. As Hayek wrote in *Law, Legislation and Liberty*, 'The only possibility of transcending the capacity of individual minds is to rely on those super-personal "self-organizing" forces which create spontaneous order.'[21]

These are the truths that inform contemporary forms of managerialism, and through which its practices are rationalized. The universal laws of spontaneous order, essentialized as innately human properties and predispositions, legitimate the pursuit of de-hierarchization, self-organization, connectivity and mobility as simultaneously natural, liberating and productive. In *The Digital Economy*, Don Tapscott claims that 'industrial hierarchy and economy are giving way to molecular organizations and economic structures.'[22] The new enterprise, he continues, 'has a molecular structure. It is based on the individual. The knowledge worker (human molecule) functions as a business unit of one. Motivated, self-learning, entrepreneurial workers empowered by and collaborating through new tools apply their knowledge and creativity to create value.'[23]

Theories of complexity and emergence feature frequently in such manuals of business innovation. Rather than as an antagonistic force to be disciplined by management, workers are figured through these theories as molecular agents. In a book whose title makes plain the vitalist tenor of its contents – *It's Alive: The Coming Convergence of Information, Biology, and Business* – business gurus Christopher Meyer and Stan Davis claim, 'We will again have scientific management – but this time the underlying science will be "general evolution." The theories that drive biology will be adopted in the way we use information, and the way we manage our enterprises. Biology, information, and business will converge on general evolution.'[24] Reinscribed within a scientistic discourse, the naturally adaptive potential of worker-molecules resides in their capacity to spontaneously 'self-organise' into larger aggregates of 'distributed intelligence' or 'swarms': 'A type of collaboration in which large numbers of geographically dispersed people quickly self-organize in a peer-to-peer network to deal with a problem or opportunity … a fluid, shifting network with no central control or hub.'[25]

The so-called 'immaterial labour' thesis, derived from the Italian Marxist current of post-autonomia, has come to serve as something of a default position from which to critique these new forms of managerialism. Maurizio Lazzarato, one of the originators of the term, defines it as 'the labor that produces the informational and cultural content of the commodity'.[26] The informational content concerns 'the changes taking place in workers' labor processes in big companies in the industrial and tertiary sectors, where the skills involved in direct labor are increasingly skills involving cybernetics and computer control'.[27] The cultural content of the commodity, on the other hand, 'involves a series of activities that are not normally recognized as "work" – in other words, the kinds of activities involved in defining and fixing cultural and artistic standards, fashions, tastes, consumer norms, and, more strategically, public opinion'.[28] The immaterial labour thesis has also been taken up in Michael Hardt and Antonio Negri's works *Empire* and *Multitude*.[29] As does Lazzarato, though in slightly different form, Hardt and Negri recognize two distinctive features to immaterial labour. The first is 'primarily intellectual or linguistic' and produces 'ideas, symbols, codes, texts, linguistic features, images'.[30] The second is subcategorized as 'affective labour'.[31] This is labour that 'produces or manipulates affects such as a feeling of ease, well-being, satisfaction, excitement, or passion', the kind of labour put to work in the service and hospitality industries.[32]

However inflected, the thesis invariably proposes that immaterial labour appropriates various competences either innate to, or created by, the worker as a social being. Affective skills, linguistic and communicational capacities, creative dispositions and inclinations to collective cooperation all exist prior to their instrumentalization within new modes of capital accumulation. As Lazzarato argues, 'The cycle of immaterial labor takes as its starting point a social labor power that is independent and able to organize both its own work and its relations with business entities. Industry does not form or create this new labor power, but simply takes it on board and adapts it.'[33] If industrial capitalism exploits the muscle power of manual labour, then post-industrial capitalism goes further, deeper into the core of the human, to mine its very essence. Capitalism is not content with our bodies; it now demands our minds, even our souls. Lazzarato writes, 'Today it is "the soul of the worker which must come down into the factory." It's his personality, his subjectivity which must be organised and commanded.'[34] Similarly, Franco 'Bifo' Beradi writes in his *The Soul at Work* that 'industrial exploitation deals with bodies, muscles and arms …. The rise of post-Fordist modes of production … takes the mind, language and creativity as its primary tools for the production of value.'[35] 'Our desiring energy', he argues, 'is trapped in the trick of self-enterprise, our libidinal investments are regulated according to economic rules, our attention is captured in the precariousness of virtual networks: every fragment of mental activity must be transformed into capital.'[36] Capitalism captures and exploits what is properly the property of the worker – 'our' sociability, language, ideas, emotions and desires.

The thesis of immaterial labour and the discourse of neoliberal managerialism, then, share a common proposition, though seen from opposing perspectives. Both assert the self-organizing and productive potential of the communicative subject, and that its faculties, qualities and dispositions exist prior to any use made of them by capital. One talks negatively – in the language of exploitation – of the capture of this potential in 'production for production's sake', the other talks positively – in the language of emancipation – of the release of this potential within humanized conditions of productivity.[37] Neither can conceive, openly at least, of the ways in which the subject may be transformed by capitalism. Were neoliberal managerialism to credit itself with producing the facilities it claims to find, already formed in the subject, it would have to forego its claims that it is liberating anything in its new modes of labour and workplace organization. Post-autonomist thought argues that what is captured of the subject, as immaterial labour, might escape and overcome capital. The potentials of cooperation, communication and self-organization, as the properties of the social subject, might be realized in the form of the 'multitude', capable of collectively refusing 'the rule of capital'.[38] Creativity and productivity cannot be conceded, within this schema, to capitalism itself.

Neither perspective has any investment in considering production – the production of subjectivity, the production of mentalities, the production of apparatuses of power – as a property of capitalism. By default, post-autonomist accounts of labour reinforce the 'truth games' of neoliberalism. The productive – as distinct from simply exploitative – mechanisms and apparatuses through which power operates on and through the constitution of the subject remain obscure. Contrary to this, Foucault's anti-essentialist critique of 'human nature' circumvents the transhistorical tendencies of the immaterial labour thesis, as does Simondon's account of the production of technological mentalities. Moishe Postone's critique of traditional Marxism, especially in its theorization of the relations between labour and capital, also runs counter to both post-autonomist theory and neoliberal discourse so as to address how contemporary forms of power are invested in the constitution of subjectivity.

In *Time, Labour and Social Domination: A Reinterpretation of Marx's Critical Theory*, Postone argues, against traditional Marxism, for a 'critique of labour in capitalism', as opposed to a 'critique of capitalism through labour'.[39] In traditional Marxism, the proletariat is charged with the historic mission of overcoming capitalism. Postone counters – following the mature Marx of *Capital* – that the proletariat has itself been constituted, through and for capital's production process, as a historically specific class.[40] 'Marx's critical theory', he writes, 'tries to show that labor in capitalism plays a historically unique role in mediating social relations, and to elucidate the consequences of that form of mediation.'[41] The consequences, argues Postone, are that in capitalism labour 'mediates a new form of social interdependence'.[42] From this perspective, the self-organizing, sociable and productive qualities attributed to the subject in neoliberal doxa, and within post-autonomist theory, cannot be conceived as either immanent or transhistorical properties. These are in fact mediated by the practices of labour constituted by capital, becoming 'the necessary means of obtaining the products of others'.[43]

In specifically neoliberal conditions of labour management and organization, then, it is not the 'soul' of the worker, or some transhistorical being whose essence is dragged into the factory or the office to be exploited. The already mediated skills and dispositions of a subjectivity practised in the fields of consumption, exchange and self-management are productively recirculated within the new conditions of labour. If, as Postone asserts, following Marx, the 'fundamental form' of social relations is that of the commodity, then it is in this form that the social relations mediated by labour in neoliberalism must be addressed. The outer appearance with which neoliberalism and its managerial strategies imbue the appearance of work – a humanized practice now giving free reign to naturally sociable and cooperative forms of productivity – has to be understood as phantasmagoric, as the 'occultation of production by means of the outward appearance of the product'. The labour that is disowned and disavowed through this appearance, the struggles, contestations, strategies and designs at work in the production of new forms of labour and its requisite subjectivities are the productions that demand explication. A critique of the architecture of the workplace in neoliberalism, in turn, would need to explicate its role in the production of spaces designed both to produce the productivity of the worker, and to advertise this productivity, in phantasmagoric form, as a 'progressive reality'.

Zaha Hadid Architects and BMW Leipzig

In 2001 BMW launched a competition for the design of a Central Building for its new production plant in Leipzig. This was to serve as the plant's 'central nervous system'. It would connect the three production facilities clustered around it – car body manufacture, car assembly and paint shop – and join these to the office and administrative areas contained in the Central Building itself.[44] The brief also specified that the production line be routed through the Central Building so that the BMW 3 Series produced at the plant would be visible to all employees, the 'quality of the product transparent in the centre of work activities'.[45] The Central Building was to be 'a "marketplace" for information', its architecture serving to 'improve communication'.[46] Located at its centre there would be an 'audit area' where the workforce would spontaneously gather, inspect and discuss the resolution of any problems on the production line.[47] The production process is placed centre stage, presented as a new commons in an environment of collective participation and mutual endeavour. It is not enough that employees turn up to work simply to do their jobs. They must feel themselves to be part of a community. They must share, with management and each other, a common set of values, beliefs and goals. They must act as one, exchanging ideas and knowledge, so as to maintain and improve the process of production and the quality of the product. Peter Claussen, responsible for the planning of BMW Leipzig, noted that at other plants shop-floor workers 'didn't feel they could speak up'.[48] This issue would be addressed at the new plant.

BMW Leipzig was not the company's first venture into new modes of workplace management and organization. Since the 1970s, when it first introduced performance-related pay, BMW had been moving from Fordist models of production towards the Toyota system of 'lean' and 'just in time' production.[49] It turned to strategies of 'continuous improvement', developing the new forms of workplace organization through which these were to be realized. It adopted practices already prevalent within the 'knowledge economy' – the levelling of workplace hierarchies and the move towards collaborative team work. Through these it would generate environments from which ideas and innovation could be cultivated from the workforce as a form of 'knowledge work'.[50]

BMW developed new models in plant circulation and layout towards this end. The company's Spartanburg site in South Carolina, on whose plan the Leipzig plant is based, located executive management alongside manual workers so as to facilitate communication between both parties.[51] BMW Leipzig's Central Building would further integrate the circuits of production with those

Figure 6 Zaha Hadid Architects, exterior, Central Building, BMW Leipzig, 2001–5, photo: the author, 2009.

of communication. The company's movement from a classically Fordist model of mass production towards one of mass customization also demanded the reprogramming of these circuits. Introducing the provision of online custom-ordering for its vehicles, it had plugged consumer-generated specifications directly into the production process.[52] As a consequence it would need to address complexities in the organization, planning and execution of production not typically encountered within the Fordist factory. Workers, at all levels, would be required to cooperate in order to respond effectively to these. The circuits of the contemporary factory would be radically reconfigured from those formulated in the first half of the twentieth century.

Albert Kahn, the architect of the Ford River Rouge Complex (1917–28), had standardized the design of industrial manufacturing facilities by the 1920s: a 'one-story structure of incombustible materials, with enormous uninterrupted floor spaces under one roof, with a minimum number of columns'.[53] This formula derived from the functional requirements of the production line. 'The form of the building', notes Federico Bucci, 'was determined by its floor plan; and in turn, the floor plan was determined by the manufacturing flow'.[54] The industrial factory was designed 'according to a single idea of simplification of the flow of materials'.[55] The contemporary factory, however, no longer serves so straightforwardly as a site for the repetition of simple and identical tasks performed on identical products. The production line need not necessarily consist of a procession of identical commodities. The flows that constitute the kind of production process exemplified at BMW Leipzig are structured around more complex, networked and recursive patterns, ones composed not simply of material processes, but that also comprise information, communication and ideas. The architecture of the contemporary factory has to provide for the spatial and environmental conditions of this new mode of productivity. It has to articulate the material flows of industrial production in relation to the circulatory patterns of the workforce, to equip the corporation with a spatial environment through which the perceptual, affective, and communicational capacities of its employees are to be collectively engaged in the technical supervision of the production process.

In Zaha Hadid Architects, who won the competition to design the Central Building, BMW engaged the services of an architectural practice already concerned with the productive articulation of complexity for a client similarly engaged with the application of new organizational models in the workplace. The abstract formal manoeuvres developed earlier in Hadid's practice, combined with the strategies for mobilizing collaborative and knowledge-based work practices gleaned from Patrik Schumacher's Corporate Fields project at the Architectural Association, were recruited to the agenda of contemporary industrial manufacture. The full significance of the type of work being performed here by the architect for the client, though, can only be fully grasped through an understanding of the kind of post-communist territory into which BMW were venturing at Leipzig.

Figure 7 Zaha Hadid Architects, interior open structure, Central Building, BMW Leipzig, 2001–5, photo: the author, 2009.

Locating its new plant 9 kilometres north of Leipzig, within the former East Germany, BMW qualified for an EU subsidy of $454 million towards a total construction cost of $1.6 billion.[56] It placed itself in proximity to a regional tradition of car manufacturing and its 'skills pool'; to favourable transport and infrastructural conditions and, critically, to the availability of a 'flexible' workforce.[57] The unemployment rate for the region, stood at the time, at 21 per cent – double that of Western Germany.[58] This put the company in an advantageous position from which to negotiate with works councils and the metal workers' union IG Metall, as the precondition for its investment in Leipzig, an agreement to set wages at 20 per cent below those of its other plants in Germany.[59] It would also be able to implement a labour regime based upon variable shift patterns, productivity bonuses and the extensive use of a temporary workforce.[60] This 'formula for work' was designed by BMW's management to enable the plant's production routines to be readily responsive and adaptable to economic and market fluctuations.[61]

What was described as a 'community of fate' was founded for BMW with the cooperation of local government, employment agencies and the nearby University of Halle in establishing a training and recruitment programme, 'Poleposition', for the new factory overseen by PUUL GmbH (an enterprise set up for this purpose by BMW itself).[62] Conditions favourable to new modes of workplace management are found in the territory newly exposed by the withdrawal of state socialism – a potential labour force incentivized by economic hardship to accept work under almost any terms and conditions, and an apparatus of governmental agencies and trade unions willing to fashion and offer up, to the corporation, those it is charged with representing. In this respect BMW Leipzig is as much a social project invested in the production of subjectivity as it is a manufacturing enterprise.

In itself, this is not entirely novel. The history of the corporation is also one of social engineering. Nineteenth-century industrial communities such as Saltaire, Bournville and Port Sunlight in England, and Pullman in the United States, were strategically located, by their paternalist patriarchs, beyond the supposedly corruptive realms of the city. Henry Ford pursued similar pastoral ambitions, his desire to model the moral substance of his employees exemplified, especially, in his Village Industries and Greenfield Village museum enterprises.[63] Tomáš Baťa, with his company towns such as those established in Tilbury, England, in 1933, catered to the health and recreational needs of his employees. In the aftermath of the Second World War, the Italian Adriano Olivetti, at his Olivetti plant in Ivrea, pioneered the use of psychoanalytic and sociological perspectives in industrial management.[64]

What is distinctive of the kind of neoliberal managerial practices exemplified at BMW Leipzig is that the company no longer even feigns concern with the ongoing welfare of its individual employees, but only – if and when these resources might be called upon – with their efficient functioning as 'molecular' components, as inputs and relays within an always adaptable system. It offers no commitment, and concedes no responsibility, to the worker. It deals only in opportunities – to be offered, withheld or withdrawn as it determines economically efficient – to join its putative community on an always provisional basis.[65]

Under these conditions – variable shift patterns, temporary contracts, low wages – the post-political ideal of the workplace as a site of mutual cooperation and endeavour will be especially hard won by management. Antagonisms, inequalities and insecurities will need to be smoothed over if the circuits of communication and cooperation are to function effectively, if the factory is to operate as an 'open' and apparently self-organizing system. The production of this apparition, as absent of tension, conflict or hierarchy, and the productive channelling of the system's components through its open circuits, will be the phantasmagorical and organizational work of architecture. BMW's awareness of the nature and significance of this task, and of the importance of architecture's contribution to its achievement, is made plain in its report on the progress of the Central Building:

> On the one hand, this building is to serve as the main entrance for employees and visitors. On the other, it is to be the site of all the plant's planning and administrative employees' workplaces. ... There are no hierarchies or managers' offices in this open space, just 740 identical workplaces for everyone from the trainee to the plant director. Here everyone is immediately accessible to everyone else. 'Structure creates behaviour' is the motto, and the open structure of the central building creates greater motivation, more intensive communication and thus higher productivity.[66]

The urban diagram of the new factory

In the planning and design of BMW Leipzig Hadid and Schumacher invoked the dynamics of the city and the collective order of the urban. Hadid proposed, in response to the complexity of the programme, to 'urbanize' the site.[67] Schumacher's stated ambition was to reproduce within it the 'complexity and the unpredictability of city life'.[68] Seeking to articulate and organize the multiple circuits passing through the Central Building in accord with these ambitions, Hadid first calibrated their dynamics through a series of vector diagrams from which both the building's plan and its internal circulatory pattern were derived. Hadid has described this technique as a process in which she is attempting to 'turn space into linear lines', a generic design tool employed in a number of her projects, such as the MAXXI Museum in Rome.[69] For the Central Building, this technique is brought to bear on the particular task of channelling the movements of the plant's workforce according to the cooperative and communicative programme advanced by its managers.

Production line workers, office workers, administrative staff and management alike are gathered together, as they enter the plant, through the Central Building's single point of collective access. The various currents converging on this gateway are then released into the open arena of the building's 'market place' – a reception and social area designed to promote the interaction of employees as they cross paths or congregate in its cafeteria. This serves to channel the workforce towards the forms of socialization from which collective knowledge can be harvested. According to the plant's tour guides, this is where employees gather to freely exchange knowledge of the production process. The collectivized

Figure 8 Zaha Hadid Architects, radial cornering patterns, Central Building, BMW Leipzig, 2001–5, photo: the author, 2009.

knowledge accumulated at this point is then fed back into the system to further its 'continual improvement'. Likewise the attention of workers is directed towards the audit area, in Hadid's vectorized diagram of the plant, by locating this at the intersection of the main routes through the building.

Figure 9 Zaha Hadid Architects, main entrance, Central Building, BMW Leipzig, 2001–5, photo: the author, 2009.

Other means are also employed to articulate what Hadid has referred to as the 'transformation of a production field into an urban field'.[70] Rather than vertically stacking the programmes of the Central Building within discrete floors assigned to specific functions, the floor plates are modulated by inclines, openings and cantilevers. These are designed to articulate an interactive spatial condition. 'Although the structure is open', said Hadid, 'it's the layering that makes it complex. Our idea was to achieve openness, layering and complexity simultaneously'.[71] All workers will encounter and communicate with one another on equal terms in a deterritorialized environment: 'The idea is that you have a wide range of activities happening together in one space. There's a mix of blue- and white-collar areas, which prevents an exclusive domain from being established'.[72]

As well as mobilizing the putatively open and interactive conditions attributable to the 'urban field' to this end, Hadid also invokes the topographical qualities of the design of the Central Building. 'The interior structure', she says 'has a landscape quality to it'.[73] These qualities are apparent in the terraced 'cascades' that accommodate the plant's planning and administrative offices. In their open-plan layout these adhere to a by now generic model of the 'office landscape' or *Bürolandschaft* developed in West Germany in the 1950s. But these offices are landscaped in section too, through a stepped and 'cascading' floor plate that forms a continuous terrain between offices and other elements of the Central Building. The effect of continuity is reinforced through the open trusses designed so as not to obscure the vista of the workplace as 'artificial landscape'.

The architecture's scenographic performance and the smooth trajectories of its circuits are underscored in the visual orchestration of its components and the use of materials. As Schumacher states:

> We employed only homogenous, continuous materials such as concrete and welded steel; we strove to eliminate as many columns as possible; and we minimized the number of corners. … The eye is drawn along continuous concrete walls; seamless, welded steel handrails; even the conveyor belts overhead. These lines flow in parallel, they bifurcate, they travel up and down through the section, but always tangentially. … Here, the eye never comes to rest. As one moves around a corner, new vistas open up in all directions. In the best instances, it almost gives one a sense of flying.[74]

The aesthetics of controlled convergence and continuous mobility also appear in the Central Building's exterior cladding. Here the vector diagrams used to plan the building's circulation patterns are presented in ornamental form. Translated from plan to elevation, their parallel trajectories promote the qualities of the factory's managerial paradigms. Fluidity, responsiveness, circulation and mobility are reassuringly aestheticized in forms advertising the ease, efficiency and elegance with which these qualities can be achieved. The organizational imperatives of neoliberalism are rendered appealingly in their dynamism.

In the sense that the appearance of architectural form gives positive expression to these imperatives, it constitutes a practice of what Manfredo Tafuri, in his analysis of the German architecture of Erich Mendelsohn, termed (borrowing form Adolf Behne) *reklamearchitektur* – advertising architecture. In adapting avant-garde modes of formal expression to serve commercial interests, Mendelsohn occupied a singular place within the architectural culture of Weimar Germany, argued Tafuri. In his department stores, cinemas and factories the formal 'exasperation' of Expressionism was sublimated to the dynamics of the capitalist metropolis: 'Mendelsohn chose to work for monied capitalist clients who could sponsor projects that permitted him to enter into the quick of the urban substance.'[75] Mendelsohn's architecture 'took its place in that chaos of stimuli which is the commercial center and which, with him, could lose that anguished aspect attributed to it by Expressionism and propose itself anew as a dynamic force to the public of Weimar Germany'.[76]

The cornering of Mendelsohn's buildings, confluent with the circulation of the city's traffic, and the articulation of their stacked horizontal elements, underscored by artificial illumination, advertised speed and mobility as the essence of the metropolis and its new architecture. This architecture – the

Mossehaus press offices in Berlin (1921–3), the Shocken department store in Stuttgart (1926–8) or the Woga-Komplex and Universum-Kino, also in Berlin – acted as shock absorbers for the experience of the metropolis. The frenetic effects of the city were harmonized so that the public might be actively immersed within, rather than alienated by, what Simmel had termed its *nervenleben* (nervous life). The stylistic evolution of Hadid's architecture recapitulates this movement from the avant-garde to the commercial. The constructivist- and suprematist-inspired aesthetics of earlier projects – The Peak, Hong Kong (1982–3), the Vitra Fire Station (1994) – have been largely abandoned since around the time of the design of the Central Building for BMW. The juxtapositional and explosive dynamics of the 1980s and 1990s have given way to ones that speak of composure and elegance. In projects such as the Central Building, the MAXXI Museum and the Innovation Tower in Hong Kong (2014) massed linear elements, recalling those employed by Mendelsohn, describe parallel circuits around facades and form smoothly contoured patterns of circulation within.

What is advertised in these architectures is a *Weltanschauung*. The world view of neoliberalism in phantasmagorial form. An appeal to alignment with continuous variation rendered as a 'progressive reality'. Emancipation from stasis and constraint. Schumacher has claimed that the kind of formal elegance that now typifies Hadid's projects is the means through which their architecture articulates

Figure 10 Zaha Hadid Architects, exterior panelling, Central Building, BMW Leipzig, 2001–5, photo: the author, 2009.

complexity so that its work appears as 'an effortless display of sophistication'.[77] Elegance works to conceal and to doubly disavow labour – both that involved in the subjection of the worker to the new conditions of labour in neoliberalism, and that of architecture in accommodating itself to the new managerialism.[78]

Koolhaas, OMA and CCTV

Designed by Rem Koolhaas/OMA as a new headquarters for CCTV (China Central Television) within Beijing's Central Business District, CCTV HQ is located on an 180,000 square metre site that also accommodates a cultural centre – 'TVCC' – a service building and a media park within its complex. Completed in 2012, CCTV HQ is 234 metres in height, with a total floor area of 465,000 square metres. It is designed to be in continuous occupation by 10,000 workers, and accessible to the public through its internal 'visitor's loop'. Combining production, administration and management facilities within its structure, it also serves as the centre from which 250 television and radio channels are broadcast.

Ole Scheeren, Koolhaas's chief partner in the project, described CCTV as 'some kind of new utopia, partly social, partly constructive, [that] reclaims

Figure 11 OMA/Rem Koolhaas, construction, CCTV Headquarters, Beijing, 2002–12, photo: Ana Abram, 2008.

the ground from the seemingly rational territories of the global market economy .... It is a scale beyond the simple addition of its individual components: Bigness.'[79] Such statements exemplify the ways in which OMA has sought to manage the perception of this project. In its conception and design, however, CCTV reclaims ground for, and not from, the 'global market economy'. It manages subjectivity for the new conditions of labour now being realized in China. CCTV is a governmental, not a utopian project. Rather than realizing the promise of 'Bigness', or the related theorems of *Delirious New York*, the project makes apparent the distance travelled by Koolhaas in his journey from the avant-garde to managerialism, from theory to work.

Challenging the modernist conception of metropolitan 'efficiency', Koolhaas turns, in *Delirious New York*, to the surrealism of Salvador Dali and his 'Paranoid Critical Method', or 'PCM'. 'Dali', he writes 'proposes a second-phase Surrealism: the conscious exploitation of the unconscious through the PCM.'[80] The PCM, he continues, 'is defined by Dali mostly in tantalizing formulas: "the spontaneous method of irrational knowledge based on the critical and systematic objectifications of delirious associations and interpretations".'[81] Dali's PCM, Koolhaas suggests, promises that 'the world can be reshuffled like a pack of cards whose original sequence is a disappointment'.[82] It is through this method that Koolhaas identifies, within the singular history of Manhattan's urban and architectural development, within the proto-surrealist spatial juxtapositions of its skyscrapers, the project of 'Manhattanism': a delirious mode of urban production – a 'culture of congestion' and a 'technology of the fantastic' – that will inform his own 'metropolitan architecture'.

These ideas are carried forward into Koolhaas's essay 'Bigness: The Problem of Large'.[83] Concerned with the emergence of large-scale architectural and infrastructural projects in Europe in the late 1980s, Koolhaas channelled lessons learnt from the New World back to the Old: 'Against the background of Europe, the shock of Bigness forced us to make what was implicit in *Delirious New York* explicit in our work.'[84] Bigness is conceived of as a 'radical break' 'with scale, with architectural composition, with tradition, with transparency, with ethics'.[85] Like Manhattanism, Bigness is opposed to architectural rationalization and normative perceptions of the city: 'Where architecture reveals, Bigness perplexes; Bigness transforms the city from a summation of certainties into an accumulation of mysteries. What you see is no longer what you get.'[86] The juxtapositions of spaces and programme potentiated at the scale of Bigness enable 'the assembly of maximum difference'. 'Only Bigness', writes Koolhaas, 'can sustain a promiscuous proliferation of events in a single container.'[87] As a kind of refuge from the organizational protocols of contemporary urbanism, Bigness stands against and in contradistinction to its urban context: 'Bigness is no longer part of any urban tissue. It exists; at most, it coexists. Its subtext is fuck context.'[88]

The tenets of Bigness are reversed in the CCTV project. Coherence and transparency are substituted for perplexity and mystery so that what you see is, after all, what you get. Programmes are productively integrated rather than deliriously juxtaposed. The building is conceived as a complement to its urban context – Beijing's Central Business District – rather than as offering refuge from it. In place of the intensification of difference promised by the Paranoid Critical Method, CCTV is designed to produce identity and erase paranoia. Where the shock effects, schisms, and juxtapositions of earlier projects by OMA – the Kunsthal in Rotterdam, or the Deux Bibliothèques Jussieu, in Paris, for instance – originate in the discoveries of *Delirious New York*, the architecture of the CCTV building emerges from the model of the 'hyperbuilding'.

The hyperbuilding makes its first appearance, as a new object of research and possibility for OMA/Koolhaas, in their project for the headquarters of Universal Studios in Los Angeles in 1996. In place of the deep volumetric massing characteristic of Bigness, the architecture of the Universal Studios headquarters is composed of four vertical towers connected by a horizontal slab of office floors. Each tower is designed to serve a specific component of the corporation. Suspended between them is the 'Corporate Beam': 'A glass volume that consolidates corporate activity with special needs and shared support departments.'[89] The composite structure of the hyperbuilding is likened to urbanism in its organizational capacities: 'At this scale of organization, architecture approaches urbanism. Universal is not so much an office plan as an urban plan, a map: the building as an organizer of different elements. The organizational diagram resonates more with a subway map than with a building plan.'[90]

Much as in Hadid and Schumacher's trope of the 'urban field', the organizational powers of architecture are likened to those of urbanism. This conception is foregrounded in the form of the hyperbuilding. Its bundled towers and intersecting beams – Universal Studios headquarters, the Hyperbuilding in Bangkok and the Togok Towers in Seoul – imply a compositional logic of infrastructural integration; its task to facilitate systems of circulation and communication, rather than to contest or critically reconfigure these from within its own territory. Subsuming architecture to urbanism's organizational imperatives, OMA's hyperbuilding architecture aligns itself with an essentially governmental and managerial practice that first emerged in the latter half of the nineteenth century.

With Ildefonso Cerdá's plan for the extension of Barcelona (1859), and his *Teoría general de la urbanización* (The General Theory of Urbanization), published in 1867, as its founding instruments, urbanism was, and is still, premised on the planning and optimization of circulation. Urbanism *engineers* the movement of goods, services and citizens throughout its territory. Its infrastructural components choreograph these movements, systematically, and integrate them according to principles of efficiency and productivity. The development of urbanism coincides, historically, with that of large-scale factory production, and with the managerial practices designed to produce forms of subjectivity compliant with the imperatives of urban industrialization. Ross Exo Adams has described Cerdá's *urbe* as 'the simultaneous enclosing of all of society in a new "urban" order which systematizes (and thus *politicizes*) life's natural cycles of production and reproduction.'[91] Urbanism, Adams continues, produces a 'new order of life' founded 'on the *normalization and management of human behavior*'.[92] These conditions of reproduction now extend to the organization and distribution of knowledge and information – laterally dispersed as well as hierarchically orchestrated – upon whose exchange the modern corporation depends. Mentalities of cooperation, social exchange and interaction are, through the order of the urban, to be elicited and maintained as the new conditions of labour.

These are the managerial demands on the production of subjectivity that the hyperbuilding is designed to serve. It offers the 'virtue' of 'an enormous controllable critical mass' with the capacity to 'forge a new entity from disparate parts.'[93] In an interview conducted in 2008, Koolhaas remarks: 'When we were planning the Universal Studios headquarters in Hollywood, a problem we had was that the company's individual components are spread across a large area – so we designed the building to bring the components together again. It includes a common space where people who work in distant offices could pass and run into each other.'[94]

This 'common space' – the 'beam' that integrates the company's various departmental components – becomes a 'corporate theatre', rather than the 'collective' one affirmed within the theorems of Bigness. The now corporate articulation of common space is framed in the language of managerialism: the 'calculated integration of Universal City's current fragments … improves its flaws and corrects its flows'; 'No matter how turbulent the composition of the company becomes, the office floors provide the necessary flexibility.'[95] Business, according to the Koolhaas of *Delirious New York* is only an 'alibi' for Manhattanism, only one of its possible worlds.[96] The skyscraper is a 'laboratory'; 'the ultimate vehicle of emotional and intellectual adventure'.[97] The hyperbuilding, though, posits an architecture in which business, and its management, is the world. The CCTV headquarters project, designed, with its composite form of inclined towers and horizontal bridging structures, to produce interdepartmental integration and to manage flows of workers and visitors, further develops the hyperbuilding typology.

Given the fact that CCTV functions, still, as the mouthpiece of the Chinese Communist Party (CCP), OMA have had to carefully stage-manage the perception of their involvement in this project. Koolhaas has presented OMA's decision to compete, in 2002, for the CCTV project over that of the Manhattan World Trade Center competition as being driven by a principled choice to pursue 'integrity', and an architecture of 'the people', over that of business and monumentality.[98] His rationalizations ought also to be understood within the context of the controversy surrounding his decision to work in China. Ian Buruma, for example, wrote that China's 'record on human rights is still appalling. ... It's as though Tiananmen never happened.'[99] He described OMA's decision to build for the 'centre of state propaganda, the organ which tells a billion people what to think' as nothing short of 'reprehensible'.[100]

In their counteroffensive against this kind of criticism, Koolhaas and Scheeren justified the CCTV project as representative of their commitment to the public over the private, to communism over the capitalist free market. Koolhaas argued against capitalism's negative effect upon architecture in producing a situation in which 'there's no more public'.[101] CCTV should be understood, he continued, as an 'attempt by us to see whether the more traditional work of the architect – somebody working for the public good – would still be possible in a communist context'.[102] He has also described the project in relation to his early interest in the 'communist architecture' of Russian Constructivism: 'It's a kind of re-visiting the communist history, and moving beyond a classical position of "capitalism good, communism bad."'[103] In the introduction to the issue of *Architecture and Urbanism* in which these comments were published, Scheeren similarly glossed the 'public' and 'democratic' qualities of the CCTV headquarters: 'The declared aim is to become the BBC of China, and the many publicly accessible functions of the new building program point towards a democratization of the institution ... becoming the icon for a new contemporary China.'[104]

Koolhaas and Scheeren refuted the kind of argument raised by Buruma against building in China. While Scheeren conceded the role of CCTV in editing and censoring the 'voice of China', he argued that it was 'also driving forward the transformation process and opening up of this country. On its path, it is carefully manoeuvring between (radical) change and (apparent) retention of existing principles'.[105] 'Risks are inherent – central control paired with untamed financial dynamics', he continued, 'yet the emerging hybrid also creates new dimensions of visionary scope and quality'.[106]

The argument that China has not embarked on a straightforward path towards capitalism, particularly in its current and globally hegemonic neoliberal form, has some element of truth to it. Giovanni Arrighi, in his *Adam Smith in Beijing: Lineages of the Twenty-First Century*, for example, challenges the notion that the recent global ascent of the People's Republic can be understood simply on the basis of its 'alleged adherence to the neo-liberal creed'.[107] 'The success of Chinese

Figure 12 OMA/Rem Koolhaas, construction detail, CCTV Headquarters, Beijing, 2002–12, photo: Ana Abram, 2008.

reforms', he argues, 'can be traced to *not* having given up gradualism in favor of the shock therapies advocated by the Washington Consensus.'[108] Equally, this doesn't legitimate Koolhaas and Scheeren's narrative of China as a still communist state in pursuit of the kind of reforms that would offer architects the opportunity to work, free from the demands of the market, for the 'public good'. Rather than operating beyond the logic of the market, China's reforms have been understood by some as directed towards a very particular form of market-based economy. Rather than Deng Xiaoping's 'socialism with Chinese characteristics', Wang Hui has written of 'a special character to Chinese neoliberalism'.[109] 'China', he writes, 'has promoted radical marketization; in addition, under the guidance of state policy, China has become one of the most enthusiastic participants in the global economy.'[110]

The 'special character' of neoliberalism in China lies in its structurally unique combination of market and state – a market-oriented political economy under the strict management of a centralized state authority. That the state should have a role within neoliberalism – principally that of legislating for and legitimating the conditions of the 'free market' – is, of course, by no means unique to China. It is the state form – that of the single party – and the powers of governance it has inherited from the era of Mao, that defines its 'special character'. The apparatus of the party has been retained but redirected towards managerial rather than political objectives. As Hui observes of the party's depoliticization: 'In contemporary China the space for political debate has largely been eliminated. The party is no longer an organization with specific political values but a mechanism of power.'[111] This 'depoliticization process', he continues, 'has had two key characteristics: firstly, the "de-theorization" of the ideological sphere; secondly, making economic reform the sole focus of party work.'[112]

China's movement towards a market economy, whatever the supposed gradualism of its transition, has involved the country in massive upheaval. While there is huge investment in urbanization and infrastructural development, arable land has become scarce. This has led to environmental crises and concerns over food security. The *danwei* (labour units), which once functioned as the essential instrument of social and political cohesion, have been progressively dismantled, cutting the citizen loose from their point of access to party ideology, as well as adrift from the basic mechanisms of social welfare. These radically changed conditions have not been received passively. Protests and 'mass incidents' of social unrest (scrupulously monitored and recorded by the CCP), around environmental and social problems, are frequent and numerous. Stabilizing these volatile conditions has become central to the work of the party, a task for which the mechanisms of neoliberal governmentality have been recognized as key.[113] Lisa Rofel identifies neoliberal governmentality as a 'project … to remake national public culture'.[114] Aihwa Ong, theorizing neoliberalism as 'a new relationship between government and knowledge through which governing activities are recast as nonpolitical and nonideological problems that need technical solutions',[115] notes the emergence of the concept of 'reengineering the Chinese soul' within organizational discourse in China: 'Reengineering has become a metaphor for converting Chinese employees from particularistic cultural beings into self-disciplining professionals who can remanage themselves according to corporate rules and practice'.[116]

In the post-political, post-ideological conditions of post-reform China, image management has also become a central concern of the CCP. As Yuezhi Zhao writes, 'As part of Deng's "no debate" decree and perhaps the party leadership's own increasing cynicism over its "truth," the party has more or less given up its mission of political indoctrination to simply concentrate on the management of its own publicity'.[117] These, then, are the practices of governmentality in which OMA's CCTV headquarters are implicated – reengineering labour, remaking the public, stabilizing the social and managing the image.

Architecture as infrastructure

As with OMA's earlier hyperbuilding projects, the form and structure of the CCTV headquarters is designed to integrate multiple departments within a coherent whole. Each section of CCTV – administration, broadcasting, news, production, new media, service – is assigned a particular location within an architectural loop that links them in a productive circuit. This looped structure, and the now seamless continuity of its towers and bridges, suggests a further refinement of the hyperbuilding. The management of organizational efficiency is signified, and in such a way as to authorize a certain discourse about its operation.

Describing the significance of the building's looped form, Ole Scheeren states that 'CCTV is a loop folded in space, it creates a circuit of interconnected activities and joins all aspects of television making in one single organism. The loop acts as a non-hierarchical principle, with no beginning and end, no top and bottom, in which all elements form part of a single whole'.[118] The 'non-hierarchical principle' of the loop is supposed also to integrate CCTV's employees within an organic whole:

The coexistence of all functions involved in the process of television-making in one single building allows administration and management, production studios and news departments, research and training divisions, technical areas and broadcasting centres to enter into a continuous dialogue – not only reminding all parts of each other's existence, but clearly illustrating their mutual dependence: a system, in which the 'heads know what the hands are doing' – and vice versa. There are hierarchies – of managers and workers – but the building is not simply broken down into different sections, but a loop of communal circulation with associated social areas, canteens and meeting rooms exploits the shape of the building and promotes direct exchange and contact between the departments. The organisation is more continual than vertical; the top floors of the skyscraper – normally reserved for the board and leadership – are accessible to all employees in the 'Staff Forum'.[119]

Despite the fact that such strategies of integration can be found within the West, and that these have been developed precisely to facilitate a form of neoliberal managerialism, Koolhaas claims them as possibilities only to be found in the exceptional conditions of China. 'In the free market', he writes, 'architecture = real estate'.[120] 'But in China', he argues, 'money does not yet have the last word. CCTV is envisioned as a shared conceptual space in which all parts are housed permanently, aware of one another's presence – a collective. Communication increases; paranoia decreases'.[121] With such claims Koolhaas manages the publicity of his practice no less than the leadership of the CCP now manage theirs. If the creation of the shared space of a 'collective' were only possible outside of a market economy, then how could OMA have argued for the design of 'common spaces' of interaction for their Universal Studios headquarters in Los Angeles? If this type of space were only realizable for architects working in China, then how is it that precisely the same means – the articulation of circulation, proximity and transparency – have been employed for precisely the same ends – the integration of the production process, and the workforce, into a seemingly non-hierarchical and self-aware whole – in projects such as Hadid's BMW Central Building in Leipzig? Rather than a possibility unique to a putatively communist China, the 'collective' Koolhaas speaks of is a function of a now globalized model of labour management – such as is employed in Toyotaism – designed to optimize productivity and to minimize antagonism. It is within the context of this instrumentalization of the 'collective', as well as its specific resonance within post-reform China, that the motivations for increasing communication and reducing paranoia appear.

The elimination of paranoia emerges as a governmental concern in post-reform China, in general, and in the specific case of CCTV, as a consequence of its social instability. Chinese society, writes Zhao, is 'one of the most inequitable

Figure 13 OMA/Rem Koolhaas, exterior, CCTV Headquarters, Beijing, 2002–12, photo: the author, 2011.

in the world ... characterized by a fractured structure, acute divisions along class, rural/urban, ethnic, and regional cleavages, and heightened conflicts.[122] Rather than led by concerns to produce a 'collective' which emanate, as Koolhaas implies, from an essentially communist political programme, the elimination of paranoia is a post-political strategy designed to manage the deterritorializing forces set in motion by China's turn – however qualified by its special circumstances – to neoliberal marketization. Efforts to stabilize the workforce of CCTV, in particular, respond to changed employment practices resulting from the withdrawal of state funding for the broadcasting institution and its increasing commercialization. Zhao, describing conditions of employment at CCTV, around the time at which OMA were awarded the project for its redevelopment, writes: 'CCTV, with its five classes of permanent employees and flexible casual workers with staggeringly different job security and welfare entitlements well into the early 2000s, epitomized the hierarchical, highly exploitative, and almost feudal labor structure in the Chinese media industry.'[123]

The flexibilization and casualization of employment at CCTV, the turn to outsourcing and temporary contracts – under the liberalizing reforms of its presidents Yang Weiguang (1991–9), and then Zhao Huayong (1999–2009) – are documented in Ying Zhu's *Two Billion Eyes: The Story of China Central Television*.[124] These practices are also recorded in a report, by Shu Taifeng, on CCTV's system of 'remuneration by invoices' through which it sought, beginning in the early 1990s, to bypass China's labour regulations.[125] These methods, writes Taifeng, have 'lead to a series of negative consequences ... caused the existing wage system to collapse, brought about huge income gaps and sowed the seeds for corruption.'[126] It seems not unreasonable to suggest that it is the paranoia induced by these conditions of labour that OMA's CCTV is designed to remediate.

Communication – the remedy prescribed here for paranoia – is to be increased through the arrangement of departments and facilities within the building, through their orchestration within the 'non-hierarchical' structure of the loop. In the skyscrapers of Manhattan there are no loops to circuit, just the vertical movement articulated by the elevator and punctuated by the miscellaneous programmes to be found on each floor: the stacking of an 'exquisite corpse' of incommensurable experiences. CCTV, though, is zoned for organizational efficiency. Each facility is consigned to a designated stack of floor plates and located within the loop according to a logistical syntax of productivity. These floor plates also serve to structure the relations within the workforce according to

Figure 14 OMA/Rem Koolhaas, exterior with advertisement, CCTV Headquarters, Beijing, 2002–12, photo: the author, 2011.

the model of the 'typical plan' first referred to by Koolhaas in an essay appearing in *S,M,L,XL*.

Written in 1993 'Typical Plan' has been described, by Roberto Gargiani, as 'another chapter of *Delirious New York*' since its subject matter – the floor plan of the American office – appears to coincide with that of the earlier publication.[127] This assessment neglects a crucial distinction: 'Typical Plan' affirms an architecture of business rather than one of delirium. 'From the late 19th century to the early 1970s', writes Koolhaas,

> there is an 'American century' in which Typical Plan is developed from the primitive loft type (ruthless creation of floor space through the sheer multiplication of a given site) via early masterpieces of *smooth space* like the RCA Building (1933) – its escalators, its elevators, the Zen-like serenity of its office suites-to provisional culminations such as the Exxon Building (1971) and the World Trade Center (1972–73). Together they represent evidence of the discovery and subsequent mastery of a *new architecture*.[128]

'The ambition of Typical Plan' argues Koolhaas, 'is to create new territories for the smooth unfolding of new processes, in this case, ideal accommodation for business.'[129] The typical plan is a neutral ground, a 'degree-zero' of architecture, whose open spaces give free rein to the essentially 'formless'[130] existence of business: 'Typical Plan is to the office population what graph paper is to a mathematical curve. Its neutrality records performance, event, flow, change, accumulation, deduction, disappearance, mutation, fluctuation, failure, oscillation, deformation.'[131]

Manhattanism figures the metropolitan subject as the agent of his or her own experience of the city, the architect of a critical paranoia, but the 'typical plan' is an exercise in efficiency. It posits the subject as a component of an 'office population' whose performance it orders, modulates and records. The mode of subjectivation valorized in 'Typical Plan' is thoroughly managerial. The appearance of the 'generic floor plate', in the hyperbuilding architecture of Koolhaas/OMA, and, specifically, in the 'Universal Floor' of the Universal Headquarters building, has been traced to the ideas expressed in the 'Typical Plan' essay.[132] The generic floor plate, as a managerial instrument, appears too in the CCTV headquarters. The vast 'smooth spaces' of the administration sections, located in the overhang joining the building's two towers, for instance, enable 'staff circulation' and 'communal facilities'.[133] The 'formless' practice of business is accommodated within the 8,000 square metres floor plates 'allow[ing] for ultimate flexibility in office layout'.[134] Many of the 'staff facilities' –

meeting rooms, canteens, gyms, lobbies – occupy similarly large-scale floor areas. These are designed to 'allow workers to gather, socialize, and exchange information', a kind of forced collectivization falling into line with contemporary managerial strategies in the West – knowledge management and the extension of work into the spaces and times of recreation.[135] It appears designed also to minimize, through communication, the paranoia born of workplace divisions and inequalities. Workers will understand their place and significance within a coherent and cooperative whole.

Through the device of the visitor's loop, relations between CCTV and its public, like those within its workforce, are similarly subject to 'collective' refashioning. These relations have been strained both by the continued perception of CCTV as the mouthpiece of state propaganda, and by the implications of its turn to seemingly Westernized commercial values. OMA's CCTV complex has itself become the focus of animosity towards the institution. Ying Zhu, writing of the impact of the fire that severely damaged TVCC (adjacent to CCTV headquarters) notes: 'Since its groundbreaking in 2004, the building had been the subject of popular jests – though one could argue that citizens resented less the building itself than what it stood for: CCTV and the Chinese Communist Party – and once the fire broke out, schadenfreude spread throughout the city and online.'[136]

The visitor's loop is designed to admit the public to CCTV headquarters, channelling them through the building along its prescribed circuit. Koolhaas and Scheeren describe it as 'a dedicated path circulating through the building and connecting to all program elements while offering spectacular views across the CBD and the city'.[137] 'Multiple event spaces', they continue,

> allow for divers programming and direct views into some of the technical areas of the building give the visitors insight in the functioning of a television station. The visitors enter the main lobby in Tower 1 and descend to the first basement level. After passing security control, wardrobe and a cafe, the path moves along a media wall around the central production are while providing views into television studios and actors lounges.[138]

Opening up a previously closed organ of the state to public inspection, the visitor's loop is to serve as an instrument through which the image of CCTV, and by extension that of the party itself, may be remade. Exposing its inner workings to the public CCTV shows it has nothing to hide, that a new rapport, based on openness and transparency, can be established between itself and its public. As crucial as this image management is to both CCTV and the party, the visitor's loop is also implicated in a reciprocal transformation of the very idea of the 'public'. Indeed the 'public', and the 'public sphere', are currently subject to processes of refashioning in accord with the radical marketization of China's economy and the de/post-politicization of the party. The central role of state media in these processes has been to maintain the image of the People's Republic of China as a still communist society, while, at the same time, reconstructing and managing its subjects as an 'audience' according to commercialized models of media production and reception. As Zhao argues in *Communication in China*: 'To stay in power, the party must continue to articulate and rearticulate its communistic pretensions, otherwise ... communism threatens to once again become a powerful subversive ideology against party-led capitalistic developments in China.'[139]

Without entirely disposing of Leninist and Maoist strategies of propaganda, the party has also turned to the public relations and image-making techniques of the West. 'Leadership image design', notes Zhao, 'has become a new topic for applied communication research and everyday media management practices' (ibid).[140] Included among its techniques are methods previously castigated by the party as 'bourgeois', such as opinion polls and audience surveys, and the broadcasting of images of the party's leadership interacting with, and coming to the aid of its citizens that are 'designed to project a "pro-people" popular leadership'.[141]

The perspectives offered from the visitor's loop out onto the activities of workers in the studios, suites and production facilities of CCTV, and those of the organizational integrity of the entire operation, are to perform an image of communicative efficiency. They are to impress upon the visitor a picture of interactive coherence, the productive cooperation of a whole that stands both for the work of CCTV and, analogously, for that of the party for which it is still the official voice. The visitor's loop articulates communism's core values via the very operations through which these are being refashioned into a neoliberal governmentality – the mobilization of cooperative productivity in the service of accumulation. At the same time, the loop inducts the public into the role of a participatory audience, a 'critical mass' whose opinions are to be solicited so as to secure their contribution to a 'pro-people' China.

Circulation as labour and image

Both at BMW Leipzig and at CCTV architecture is implicated in the introduction of new and distinctively neoliberal modes of labour and its organization. It is engaged in the retraining of subjectivities, in rendering them cooperative and flexible. It smoothes over precarities, struggles and contradictions. Architecture finds its turn from theory to work rewarded. It is enlisted in the inscription of neoliberal governmental and managerial practices in the workplace. It finds it concerns with post-political ontologies of complexity and emergence, with the self-organized massing of swarms, mirrored in the discourse and agenda of managerialism. Architectures centred on the design of open, landscaped and connective spaces, on the production of spaces designed to facilitate communicative, networked, cooperative behaviours and dispositions, proclaim themselves – as does the managerial agenda they work to realize – to be aligned with a progressive reality. In order to sustain this deception, the image of labour as strife, struggle or hardship has to be absolutely negated, eradicated through elegant design and phantasmagoric appearance.

The image of the worker is refashioned into that of a molecular component of a naturalized order, occupied – naturally – in the business of circulation, cooperation and communication. In the architecture of BMW Leipzig and CCTV, and numerous other instances of contemporary workplace design, this image itself is subject to circulation. The circulatory performance of labour is made visible, throughout the new landscapes and collective commons of corporate space, so that it will serve as a motivational example, as a catalyst for participation in the forms of conduct it advertises. This spatial technique originates within cybernetically inspired architectural practices of the late 1960s and has, latterly, found employment not only in the production of spaces of labour, but in other realms – education, culture, retail – where circulation operates as a primary instrument in processes of neoliberal valorization and subjectification.

Festivals of Circulation:
Neoliberal Architectures of Culture, Commerce and Education

The Centre Beaubourg was conceived from within the cultural establishment of France and authorized, in 1969, by its President, Georges Pompidou (after whose death in 1974 it was subsequently renamed). Proposed as a 'multidisciplinary cultural centre of an entirely new type', and located in the Plateau Beaubourg, Paris, it would accommodate a major public reading library, the collection of the National Museum of Modern Art, the Centre for Contemporary Art and Pierre Boulez's IRCAM music project.[1] In Richard Rogers and Renzo Piano's winning submission for the building competition the architects stated, 'We recommend that the Plateau Beaubourg is developed as a "Live Centre of Information" covering Paris and beyond.'[2] The statement might all too easily be read as revealing of some suspiciously technocratic ambition on the part of the architects. Indeed this is precisely how the building was received by John Partridge of the *Architectural Review* in 1977. The exoskeletal structure of the architecture, together with the way in which its services – air ducts, ventilation pipes, power supplies, escalators – are, famously, exposed on its exterior, lend it the appearance of 'a menacing building which stands like a man in full armour in a room full of civilians'.[3] For Partridge, the project represents a 'supreme moment of technological euphoria', a negative utopia already recognizable as one that if widely pursued 'would be so offensive that it would remove true freedom from the face of the earth'.[4]

The Pompidou as Fun Palace

Rather than summoning up a technocratic nightmare of the kind envisaged in Godard's *Alphaville*, however, the design of the Centre Pompidou was indebted to the specifically cybernetic sensibilities of recent British architecture, as well as to its countercultural affinities. In its overt display of technology, the building followed precedents already established, in projects by Banham, Price and Archigram, for an architecture comprised chiefly of mechanical services. In Banham's 'standard of living package' or 'unhouse' proposals, in Price's Fun Palace, or in Peter Cook's Plug-In City, technology figures as a ludic, emancipatory instrument of mobility, access and connectivity, rather than as one of repression and containment.[5] Concomitant with this, such projects tended to privilege unplanned and spontaneous patterns of use within spaces unburdened of dividing walls or restrictive programmes. This tendency also informed Piano and Rogers' design for the competition, with its exoskeletal supporting structure accommodating a stack of five vast, uninterrupted floor plates within, each measuring 48 × 170 metres, to be flexibly programmed and spontaneously occupied.

The news and mass media of communication that had been a central preoccupation of the Independent Group, and whose significance had been explored in the architecture of figures such as Banham, Price and Cook, also found expression in the 'media wall' originally proposed for the building's main facade. 'The building was conceived as a tool', said Rogers and Piano in 1977, 'whose exterior should have been the contact surface … a surface of screens – TV screens, movie screens, written messages, newsreels.'[6] The architects were eventually forced to abandon this feature of their design for political reasons. As they put it, 'A center for free information that the students could have occupied and put to highly effective use was something very threatening.'[7] Nevertheless, their ambition attests to the architects' affinities with a critique first articulated from within the Independent Group. Where the gallery – the sanctified space of the art object – engendered an essentially passive mode of reception, the mass and popular media of film, television and advertising could activate a participatory public.

Even without its media wall the facade of the Pompidou would still serve as an information screen. The movement of visitors made visible through the transparent escalator tubes on the building's exterior, and, within, through its glass curtain walls, would present an image of popular activity for which the building itself was a mere support, a service provider. As Rogers said, the centre would be 'a large building that would not be a monument, but a festival, a large urban toy'.[8] Its image of animated and spontaneous activity would be displayed to the occupants of the large sunken plaza onto which the building faced. Advertising a newly informal disposition towards culture, it would act as a deterrent against overly reverential attitudes towards the world of art.

Figure 15 Richard Rogers and Renzo Piano, Pompidou Centre, Paris, 1972–6, photo: Savia Palate, 2011.

'The architects', stated the official publicity, 'believe in a framework which allows people freedom to do their own thing.'[9]

As much as this cybernetically progressive conception of the Pompidou Centre owed its origins to tendencies in British art and architectural culture, it was also called for by, and precisely suited to the purposes of, those responsible for directing the project. The Secretary General of the centre, Claude Mollard, had stated: 'The President of the Republic himself wished for the center to be established in a working-class neighbourhood and open to a very broad public: the cultural events should not remain in spirit the privilege of a small, elite [group].'[10] As Rebecca J. DeRoo notes in her analysis of the Pompidou:

> Many of the center's visitors came for the kind of sites and activities that [Pierre]Bourdieu had approved of as a means to draw in visitors, such as the cafe, store and view of the city from the top floor. While high art was shown, the curators downplayed the scholarly background that was necessary to understand to make it seem accessible to all. The museum's collection prominently featured works of Pop Art that were embedded in the vocabulary of the mass media and advertising, evoking a resonance with contemporary, urban culture with which the curators contended all could identify. The consumption of culture was thus promoted as a form of entertainment.[11]

In aiming to make art accessible, and in focusing on accessible art, the Pompidou Centre conformed to what Adorno, in *Aesthetic Theory*, had called a contemporary 'push for the deastheticization of art'.[12] 'Its unmistakable symptom', he wrote, 'is the passion to touch everything, to allow no work to be what it is, to dress it up, to narrow its distance from its viewer.'[13] Art's autonomy is desacralized in that the public's relations to it are modelled on those of the consumer to the commodity. The artwork becomes a 'thing among things'.[14] Baudrillard, in his critique of the centre, 'The Beaubourg Effect: Implosion and Deterrence', reached a similar conclusion: 'For the first time, Beaubourg is at the level of culture what the hypermarket is at the level of the commodity.'[15] Those who planned the Beaubourg might not, however, have viewed this accusation negatively. As Ewan Branda has argued, large stores such as FNAC and Leclerc had built a popular reputation as progressive institutions in post-war France. In their 'democratic access, openness, and plenitude', they represented a 'revolution' of 'lower prices and open information' which had been influential in the conception of the Pompidou.[16] Seeming to share these perspectives, Richard Rogers noted that 'certain critics, disoriented by the multiplicity of its activities and the resulting perception of disorder, have complained about its resemblance to a "supermarket"; this comparison has never bothered me: a supermarket is always more lively than a museum'.[17]

The impetus towards the supposedly progressive desacralization of art might also be understood as originating from within the avant-garde itself. As Adorno wrote in his analysis of the commodification of the art object, 'Art responds to the loss of its self-evidence ... by trying to pull itself free from its own concept as from a shackle: the fact that it is art.'[18] Addressing art's efforts to escape its condition of isolation, Claire Bishop, in *Artificial Hells: Participatory Art and the Politics of Spectatorship*, has observed that a number of tendencies in France's artistic and political culture of the 1960s converged upon a rhetoric of participation and access that aimed, in different ways, to challenge art's socially unengaged and autonomous character.[19] She notes, in particular, the Situationist International, with their critique of the separation between art and everyday life: the Groupe Recherche d'Art Visuel, with their inclusion of the public as participants in their staged and street-based events, and the 'eroticized and transgressive Happenings' of Jean-Jacques Lebel.[20] As Bishop also notes, 'All three claimed a central role in the events of May 1968.'[21] Whatever the truth of these claims, it was clear that in the events of May 1968 popular feeling against bureaucratic forms of control, demands for access and information and an artistic critique of contemporary culture had momentarily coalesced to form a problematic to which the Pompidou Centre would respond. May 1968 was, among other things, a catalyst for the spatial articulation of new modes of governmentality of which Rogers and Piano's design was prototypical, although few at the time recognized the centre's significance in these terms.

Crowd modelling

At its opening, in 1977, Renzo Piano and Richard Rogers' Centre Pompidou in Paris was critically received by Reyner Banham as already anachronistic. Counter to Rogers' description of the Pompidou as 'a large building that would not be a monument', Banham wrote, in *Architectural Review*, that it was, after all, a 'terminal monument' erected to the megastructural projects of the 1960s that had inspired it:

> Even that colour scheme seems to say "Archigram" (if not "Yellow Submarine"!), the concept of a stack of clear floors that can be adapted to a variety of cultural and recreational functions seems to recall the "Neo-Babylon" of Constant Niewenhuis [*sic*], or the Fun Palace of Cedric Price and Joan Littlewood, even if the project was never as radical as the floorless Fun Palace or as casually innovatory as Price's Interaction Centre.[22]

Not only did the centre's form lack originality, but its aesthetic was similarly out of date. Its 'transparency and colour' were 'true' only to the 'departed aspirations of "the swinging '60s".'[23] 'Seen against low raking winter sunlight in the fresh snow of the last day of 1976', wrote Banham, 'the west facade flashed with those "explosions of fire, ice and light" that we were bidden to observe with our "third eyes of the soul" a psychedelic decade earlier.'[24]

Alan Colquhoun, writing in Architectural Design in 1977, considered the centre to be a 'problematic' attempt to 'combine "modernity" and traditional institutionalism, populism and gigantism'.[25] In the Pompidou Centre 'we are presented with a conception of functionalist and expressionist art which is a rehash of the catchphrases of the 1920s, as if nothing at all had happened during the intervening forty years.'[26] While Colquhoun joins Banham in charging Rogers and Piano's building with architectural anachronism, he does at least recognize what is novel, and, for him, troubling in its architectural and cultural implications. 'What evidently appealed to the jury', he argues, 'was the uncompromising way in which the building interpreted the center as a supermarket of culture and gave no spatial plastic form to the various departments exhaustively specified in the brief.'

Banham's erstwhile adversary, Jean Baudrillard, also reckoned the Pompidou to be a monument, but one commemorating something more profound and epochal than the mere passing of architectural fashions. For Baudrillard, the building signalled the end of power, the end of representation, the end of meaning. In some respects, if not these, his analysis is astute. The openness and accessibility of the building, he notes in the 'The Beaubourg Effect', indicate that distinctions between interior and exterior no longer hold. This reveals the truth of a contemporary predicament where inside and outside, in terms that are simultaneously cultural, social and spatial, are now collapsing into one another. This is the 'truth of Möbius'.[27] The centre captures and reconfigures the lessons of May 68 in its affirmations of the social and its new forms of organization – 'participation, management, generalized self-management'.[28] Attempting to both produce and signify these forms of the social, the architecture, observes Baudrillard, is one of 'flux and signs, of networks and circuits'.[29] It 'proclaims' that 'our only temporality is that of the accelerated cycle and of recycling, that of the circuit and of the transit of fluids'.[30] But Baudrillard also claims that the centre actually fails in these terms. It appears to him to implode under the pressure of the masses attracted by its magnetic pull. 'The circulation of fluids is unequal', he writes, 'the "traditional" fluids circulate there very well. Already the circulation of the human flux is less assured.'[31] The masses, too numerous to be efficiently channelled through the centre's circuits, assume unwieldy and destructive patterns of occupation.[32] The proximity of the masses to culture liquidates the space in which reflection, representation and meaning once existed. The 'supreme irony', in which Baudrillard delights, is that the masses 'throw themselves' at the centre 'not because they salivate for that culture which they have been denied for centuries, but because they have for the first time the opportunity to massively participate in this great mourning of a culture that, in the end, they have always detested'.[33] Culture is annihilated in the very process of being made accessible to its newly enfranchized consumers. Not only this, but power collapses in the process. Its circuits can no longer manage the volume and behaviour of the masses.[34] For Baudrillard, the new forms of power developed in the aftermath of May 68, those invested in the management of circulation and participation, are stillborn.

Against Baudrillard's proclamations, some indication that the Pompidou Centre might constitute power's reformulation, rather than its disappearance, can be found in Jean-François Lyotard's *The Postmodern Condition: A Report on Knowledge*. Here he writes that the 'breaking up of the grand Narratives ... leads to what some authors analyze in terms of the dissolution of the social bond and the disintegration of social aggregates into a mass of individual atoms thrown into the absurdity of Brownian motion. Nothing of the kind is happening'.[35] This is in reply to Baudrillard. The reference to Brownian motion – the random movement of particles – alludes to the latter's *In the Shadow of the Silent Majorities*, published in 1978. Here the failure of power to manage the masses, of which the Pompidou Centre's putatively overloaded circuits are deemed symptomatic in 'The Beaubourg Effect', is diagnosed as the absolute 'end of the social'.[36] The masses – and this is why Baudrillard insists on referring to them as such – never resolve into discrete individuals, never coalesce into a unified whole. They can be neither object nor subject of power or knowledge. They cannot be managed: 'All manipulation plunges, gets sucked into the mass, absorbed, distorted, reversibilised'.[37] They cannot be analysed: 'No analysis would know how to contain this diffuse, decentered, Brownian, molecular reality. ... No more object of knowledge, no more subject of knowledge'.[38]

Lyotard's purpose, in *The Postmodern Condition*, is to 'report' on the new formulations of knowledge, and with it those of power, rather than to proclaim the exercise of either now impossible. His findings are, in some respects, not dissimilar to the arguments to be found in Foucault's lectures on neoliberalism. From the perspective of a mode of power ever more focused upon economic performance, the state, seeking to govern society through centralized planning, comes to be seen as a problem of 'interference', as 'noise' in the system. The market, taken to be the remedy for this situation, is valorized as the exemplary paradigm to whose logic all social practices and institutions should now conform. In the field of education, for instance, 'the relationship of the suppliers and users of knowledge to the knowledge they supply and use is now tending, and will increasingly tend, to assume the form already taken by the relationship of commodity producers and consumers to the commodities they produce and consume'.[39] The welfare state is no longer seen from an 'optimistic' perspective, but is subject to the accusation of being 'technocratic' in its totalizing powers. Cybernetic systems will now assume power in order to mobilize productivity, and devolve responsibility for this to the performance of the subjects of its open circuits. 'The true goal of the system, the reason it programs itself like a computer', writes Lyotard, 'is the optimization of the global relationship between input and output – in other words, performativity'.[40] The subject, at once systemic input and output, will be incentivized to act and think in accord with the optimal functioning of the system: 'Administrative procedures should make individuals "want" what the system needs in order to perform well'.[41] The subject will be both a 'nodal point' within circuits of information, and itself be circulated, mobilized, so as to stave off the system's entropic exhaustion.[42]

Where Baudrillard holds that the systemic turn to circulation overburdens and overwhelms power, Lyotard understands it as already positively effective. Power draws upon knowledge and practices gleaned from its enemies so as to optimize its own performance. The focal point of Lyotard's critique is the systems theory of Niklas Luhmann, whose essentially cybernetic model, influenced by sources also fundamental to the development of neoliberalism – Norbert Weiner and Claude Shannon, for instance – is centred on systemic performance rather than on the welfare of its subjects. These now merely comprise its operative components. Just as neoliberalism demands individuals submit to the superior organizational capacities of the market they must, for Luhmann, submit to the efficiencies of the autopoietic system, and to their role in contributing positively to this. This, writes Lyotard, 'entails a certain level of terror'.[43] The demands of the system are 'be operational (that is, commensurable) or disappear'.[44] Individual needs are delegitimized in being figured as subservient to those of the system. 'The needs of the most underprivileged', writes Lyotard, 'should not be used as a system regulator as a matter of principle: since the means of satisfying them is already known, their actual satisfaction will not improve the system's performance, but only increase its expenditures. … It is against the nature of force to be ruled by weakness'.[45] The human only regains legitimacy in being refashioned as instrumental to the system. Where, to this end, the subject is refigured in neoliberalism as 'human capital', in systems theory it is refigured, in similar fashion, as a systemic component to be shaped and deployed for systemic ends. As Lyotard writes of this process, 'The system seems to be a vanguard machine dragging humanity after it, dehumanizing it in order to rehumanize it a different level of normative capacity.'[46]

Luhmann's agenda has been both sustained and intensified within architecture, most notably within Patrik Schumacher's parametricism. The system theorist's autopoietic imperatives – condemned by Lyotard as a new 'terror' – are emphatically asserted by his architectural acolyte:

> Contemporary network society demands that we continuously browse and scan as much of the social world as possible to remain continuously connected and informed. We cannot afford to withdraw and beaver away in isolation when innovation accelerates all around. We must continuously recalibrate what we are doing in line with what everybody else is doing. We must remain networked all the time to continuously ascertain the relevancy of our own efforts.[47]

Our relevance is contingent upon and calculated by our performance as informatic operators. 'We', subjects of a system whose order must be facilitated, unquestioningly, are to be moulded to its demands. These demands are derived from the 'evolutionary' order of the 'market process' which, through its systemic autonomy from interference, leads us towards a 'self-organized order'.[48] Within the now compulsory conditions of networked circulation, architecture is to 'conceive of the functions of spaces in terms of dynamic patterns of social communications; i.e., as parametrically variable, dynamic event scenarios'.[49] Schumacher assigns to architecture the task of modelling the behavioural performance of occupants – their patterns of circulation and interaction – according to these scenarios. 'The agent's behaviors might be scripted', he suggests, 'so as to be correlated with the configurational and morphological features of the designed environment; i.e., programmed agents respond to environmental clues.' Accessing computational tools in crowd modelling – Miarmy, AI.implant, Massive – the architect can rehearse the performance of simulated agents until the script is perfected, the architecture tweaked until its environmental cues elicit the appropriate behaviour. The computational agents come to serve not only as simulations, but as models of responsive behaviour, paradigms of compliance for their real-world counterparts.

Luhmann's autopoietic systems are not, however, composed of closed or unchanging circuits. Their evolution must be constant. They must harvest difference and antagonism so as to fuel the continued improvement of their own performance, so as to ward off entropic decline. Lyotard's provocation, in this regard, is to suggest in *The Postmodern Condition* that events such as May 1968 serve to sustain and enhance the functioning of the system by these means:

> Even when its rules are in the process of changing and innovations are occurring, even when its dysfunctions (such as strikes, crises, unemployment, or political revolutions) inspire hope and lead to belief in an alternative, even then what is actually taking place is only an internal readjustment, and its result can be no more than an increase in the system's 'viability'. The only alternative to this kind of performance improvement is entropy, or decline.[50]

Baudrillard announces the end of the social, of its disaggregation into randomized particles that escape power and elude analysis. Lyotard posits that power improves its performance through a 'systemic rehumanization' of subjectivity. For Lyotard, Baudrillard's masses are not a silent majority casting their shadow over power, but the active instruments of its cybernetic optimization. Given that the masses have not, after all, eclipsed the manipulative capacities of power, let alone caused its collapse, and that power had already, by the 1970s, begun to assume new and interrelatedly cybernetic and neoliberal forms, it seems that Lyotard is closer to the mark. The significance of the Pompidou Centre might be better captured as being prototypical of the kind of performative purposes to which architecture has, since then, come to be focused.

If the centre is a project whose impetus derives from the aftermath of the events of 1968, then, following Lyotard, its task must be to refashion the negativity of those events into positive terms. These events, driven, in part, by critiques of bureaucracy and of the passivity of life in spectacular society – as infamously articulated in Guy Debord's *The Society of the Spectacle* – demand a response that promotes participation, informality and access to information.[51] Rather than a concession to such critiques, however, this project aims for their sublimation. Increased participation, circulation, informality and mobility are developed into newly refined instruments of power. In this the cybernetic enthusiasms of Rogers and Piano serve the project's planners with the requisite architectural equipment. Their 'centre of information', with its stack of uninterrupted floor plates, provides the conditions for open access, informal circulation and flexible programming. The new organizational logic, in turn, becomes informational output, a signal – the circulation of the visitors through the escalators – projected from the facade to the plaza, which itself serves as an image of informal circulation for those looking down on it from the escalators and interior. Envelope and ground, together, form a feedback loop in which the relays between vision, mobility and participation are captured and amplified.

Visitors exercise their freedom to participate, to interact, to break down barriers to culture and information. At the same time, and through the same process, they constitute an exemplary image of these actions, a performance. The image of the people formed out of the events of May 68 – barricades, street battles, strikes, occupations – is refashioned into one of collective participation to be experienced and affirmed as an end in itself. The patterns of circulation at the Pompidou Centre are staged to 'rehumanize' the subject, to optimize it around prototypically neoliberal figures of subjectivity – the cultural consumer, the informationally enfranchized citizen. More contemporary forms of neoliberal subjectivity, shaped, in significant part, by similar spatial practices, include the 'citizen-consumer' and the 'student-entrepreneur'.

Citizen-consumers: FOA's Meydan Retail Complex

The Meydan Retail Complex in Istanbul, designed by Foreign Office Architects, was conceived within the context of the commercially driven processes of urban transformation that have taken place in Istanbul since Turkey's economic conversion to a free-market model in the 1980s. As a major instrument in this transformation, shopping malls – of which around forty have been built since the city's first in 1988 – are largely financed through international investment and have served to steer the basis of the economy towards leisure, travel and tourism. In this same period, the population of Istanbul has more than doubled to reach 13 million,[52] much of which has been absorbed into informal squatter settlements, the *gecekondular*, in which the city's dispossessed are crammed.[53] The settlers have then been subjected to further displacement so as to make way for the mall-based developments, often militantly opposed, being driven through these areas. Istanbul is a city riven by social polarities threatening to unsettle the economic stability on which further international financial investment depends.[54]

The developers for the Meydan complex, the international retail company Metro Group, frame the project in terms of a commitment to public access presented as being in distinct contrast to the privatized character of other malls in the region. 'The architecture of the shopping square', reads the company's website, 'acts as a public space in the center of the rampant sea of houses in this district of the city. The urban planning concept picks up on the existing and predictable paths the residents will take to reach the site, and brings them to converge on the square.'[55] Such commitments to public space and open access, or at least the expression of these, should be understood in the context of the stark contrasts in wealth and access to urban infrastructures threatening to undermine the further financial development of Istanbul as a 'global city'. The strategy of the Metro Group in Istanbul, and in similar contexts globally, has been to position itself as an investor in socially inclusive urban development rather than in consumerist enclaves for the middle classes.[56]

These are the practices of a neoliberal urban governmentality. Private enterprise assumes responsibility for social regulation through the territorial expansion of the market form. Subjects and populations regarded as problematic to its project are, wherever possible, not to be excluded but incorporated. They are better managed and valorized as productive participants in the game of the market. In Istanbul, specifically, retail-led urban transformation includes in its objectives the making of what Tuğal terms the 'urban citizen-consumer', a form of subjectivity critical to the amelioration of the city's social and economic polarization.[57] Retail complexes such as Meydan, in its production of an urban spatial condition that is simultaneously commercial and, apparently, public, serves to put such forms of subjectivity into circulation.

Alejandro Zaera-Polo's essay 'The Politics of the Envelope', published in 2008, is similarly concerned with the ameliorative and socially inclusive performance of urban development projects.[58] He notes that significant portions of the urban environment are being captured within large-scale architectural envelopes sealed off from their surroundings. The most extreme manifestation of this phenomenon, he observes, is to be found in Norman Foster's 'Crystal Island', 'a project in Moscow that would contain 2.5 million square meters under a single envelope, the world's biggest building, approximately five times the size of the Pentagon building'.[59] While such urban enclosures may find some justification in environmental terms, their political performance, as Zaera-Polo understands it, is questionable. 'The political dangers of the scale of the flat-horizontal envelopes', he argues, 'lie in the scale of space they regulate.'[60] More permeable envelopes would, however, stand as safeguard against social exclusion:

> The only way to ensure that the skin of flat-horizontal envelopes does not create a radical split between those who are included – let's say shoppers with a certain acquisitive power – and those who are excluded is to devise equally sophisticated mechanisms of permeability across the skin. And the larger the envelope becomes, the more sophisticated the interface has to be to guarantee an appropriate level of mix in the population of the envelope.[61]

FOA's retail-based projects, claim Zaera-Polo and Moussavi, challenge the tendencies towards urban fragmentation and social exclusion of the standard mall typology through a new prototype. Based on the traditional urban square, and exemplified in their Watermark WestQuay development in Southampton, as well as the Meydan complex, this, they argue, enables retail-led development to act as a catalyst for forms of urban growth that can accommodate the 'appropriate' mix of urban populations. This is to be achieved through multiple programmed developments and articulated through permeable architectural envelopes. Zaera-Polo and Moussavi have stated that their interest, in developing their winning proposal for the Meydan complex, was with its 'urban potential', that they were 'perhaps less concerned with producing an architecture which can simply be described in formal terms, and more with defining architecture in terms of the links and forms of public space'.[62]

The chief claim for the urban potential of their design is that it will function as an integrative centre upon which the various, and otherwise divided, populations of the city will converge. In this ambition the architects identify themselves with the ideas of Victor Gruen who, in the 1950s, envisioned the suburban shopping mall as a new form of communal urban space. Gruen, they state, 'was interested in the way that space and the interplay of programmes

Figure 16 Foreign Office Architects, Meydan Retail Complex, Istanbul, Turkey, 2005–7, photo: Murray Fraser, 2012.

function. In this respect he is closer to FOA than most other architects of his time.' Zaera-Polo and Moussavi's clients appear to share these interests and inspirations. In *Meydan Shopping Square: A New Prototype by FOA*, they argue against urban developments such as the 'gated communities' and 'fashionable housing enclaves' that fragment and divide the city.[63] 'The METRO Group Asset management', they declare, 'is now attempting a solution to this problem. And what they are planning here in the middle of Ümraniye, between a motorway junction and proliferating residential buildings, is reminiscent of the visions of Victor Gruen.'[64]

Zaera-Polo and Moussavi suggest that the circulation of the Meydan complex is inspired, in part, by early-twentieth-century functionalist approaches, Margarete Schütte-Lihotzky's celebrated 'Frankfurt Kitchen'[65] scaled-up as an arrangement of the complex's components – 'casual world', 'sports world', cinema, department store – around a central plaza. In line with the proposal to have this plaza function as the centre of a wider urban network, it is also made permeable to multiple access routes. Rather than connecting the complex to its urban context only by road, the mall is designed to accommodate pedestrian access. This, the architects propose, will ensure that it does not become privatized and will, instead, fulfil a range of properly civic functions. 'While other malls often define their roles as a private site with signs and security fences', they write, 'these elements will not exist at Meydan.'[66]

These are the politics of the envelope, a 'politics of things' inspired by Bruno Latour's *dingpolitik* in which the 'thing' is conceived of as 'an assemblage between humans and nonhumans, politics and nature as well as concerns and facts'.[67] FOA understand the architectural envelope as the thing that undertakes this combinatorial, and supposedly political, work. 'We have focused', writes Zaera-Polo, 'on the envelope as an optimal domain to explore the politicization of architecture and, possibly, the development of a *Dingpolitik*.'[68] Suggesting, for instance, the assemblage of the natural and the constructed, the structures of the Meydan complex appear to emerge from and return to the ground through a series of oblique planes, as if geologically formed as much as architecturally designed. The swathes of terracotta-coloured paving and brickwork further the earthly connotations, and the green-turfed roofs – supposed to function as a further layer of public space and circulation – intimate the scenic modulations of a landscape. With its permeable envelope the complex modulates the relations between inside and outside as ones between public infrastructures and the private sector.[69] Tapping into the reserves of geothermal energy beneath the site, for light, heating and ventilation, the envelope assembles an environmental hybrid of the natural, the technical and the human. The political agency of such assemblages is held to consist in their capacity for what Latour describes as 'making things public'.[70] They bring to light the hybrid processes from which 'things' are constituted within what he refers to as an 'object-oriented democracy'.[71] This, argues Latour, is how the truly material basis of what were misconceived in critical theory as ideological issues is revealed. The agency of objects is duly recognized. Objects, says Latour 'bind all of us in ways that map out a public space profoundly different from what is usually recognized under the label of "the political" '.[72]

Latour's argument is useful to Zaera-Polo in supporting his contention that the conception of the political in architecture needs to be shifted from its ideological, critical or representative definition towards one based upon things and their material organization. Support for this position is also drawn from the work of the philosopher Peter Sloterdijk, a figure who, in his conception of space as a politics of 'atmospheres', and in his concern with making explicit the connections through which these are produced, is close to Latour (as he is too in his aversion to critique). Explaining the relevance of Sloterdijk's thought to his pursuit of a 'politics of the envelope' Zaera-Polo writes that 'as an alternative to ideology as a tool for a politically engaged architecture and utopia as its form of representation we have been testing an architecture of explicitation – to use

Figure 17 Foreign Office Architects, Meydan Retail Complex, Istanbul, Turkey, 2005–7, photo: Murray Fraser, 2012.

the term coined by Peter Sloterdijk – through the analysis of the architectural envelope'.[73] As the instrument of this politics, the envelope performs an 'architecture of *explicitation*'. It has the capacity to 'capture new political affects and processes of diversification, to communicate that certain manipulations of the ground and the roof index the politicization of nature, or to explain that the breakdown of the correlation between interior and exterior and private and public signals more advanced social structures'.[74] Zaera-Polo asserts that the politics of the envelope – the specifically architectural manifestation of a wider politics of things – is socially 'advanced', that it enables a 'progressive politics'.[75] However, the progressive cannot be thought, consistently, in terms of the disavowed politics of abstractions and totalizations such as 'society', or indeed of the supposedly anachronistic politics of left and right repudiated by Sloterdijk, with whom Zaera-Polo is in agreement. And, logically, if architecture consists in making the progressive or advanced explicit, then these qualities must already exist, elsewhere and prior to architecture, in order to be revealed as such by the discipline.

What Zaera-Polo understands by the terms 'progressive' or 'advanced' is never itself made explicit in 'The Politics of the Envelope'. Yet his contention that the market is today 'the most important medium of power distribution within the global economy'[76] goes some way towards suggesting an answer to this concern. The market is, for Zaera-Polo, the mechanism through which 'progressive' values in architecture must be pursued. Furthermore, the market inherently tends, within its own logic, to break down hierarchical power into heterarchical forms. 'We are witnessing', he writes, 'the emergence of a heterarchical order which increasingly constructs its power by both producing and using diversity'.[77] Compared to older, rigidly bureaucratic and hierarchical forms of power, Zaera-Polo argues, the market 'is probably a better milieu to articulate the current proliferation of political interests and the rise of *micro-politics*'.[78] Evidently, it is the market that is advanced and progressive because it advances and progresses beyond bureaucratic hierarchies, because it flattens everything within its heterarchical order. It accommodates diversity, hybridity and the equality in status of 'humans and nonhumans, politics and nature'. It allows for their continual configuration and reconfiguration in the multiple assemblages of its 'object-oriented democracy'. This, it seems, is what is explicitated in the politics of the envelope. We are, in some sense, still in the presence of arguments concerning the 'essential similitudes' of the 'organic and inorganic', the 'animate and inanimate', first put forward in D'Arcy Wentworth Thompson's *On Growth and Form*.[79] Everything exists equally, on the same plane, and is subject to the same laws. The assembling of any particular configuration of objects, as with Richard Hamilton's 'Growth and Form' exhibition of 1951 (based around Thompson's work), is enough to affirm the general principle of their equivalence. The laws in question now, though, are those of the market, rather than those of mathematics. The innately progressive powers of the former are affirmed, in general, whatever the particular configuration of its objects, as in the explicitations of the politics of the envelope.

Figured as always already implicated within these assemblages, the subject, lacking any privileged place or external vantage point, is conceived to be in no position to engage in interpretation or critique. This is how the politics of things works for the neoliberal truth game. Noting, in this regard, the resonance between neoliberalism's antipathy towards planning and Latour's disavowal of critique in favour of assemblage and composition, Ben Noys, in 'The Discreet Charm of Bruno Latour, or the critique of "anti-critique"', writes:

> Against what Latour regards as the reductionism of critique and its tendency to take a position transcendent to the world, he poses compositionism as an addition to reality that is always immanent to that reality. It is not surprising that such a position is attractive in all its consonance with the 'democratic ideology' that places itself within and amongst a thoroughly equalized set of thin of critique and its tendency to take a position t 'imposition' of planning and structures.[80]

Rather than democratic in any familiar sense, the equalization of things – simultaneously the heterarchical drive of the market applauded by Zaera-Polo – is a mode of power that serves the expansion of neoliberalism and its forms of thought. Interpretation and critique are disenfranchised. The social cannot be prioritized over the commercial. The public cannot be favoured over the private. The subject cannot be afforded more concern than the object. Nothing can be favoured or opposed in a flat ontology. Its powers of equalization can only be witnessed and affirmed. What counts is the operative performance of the system. All things being equal, rendered commensurate, antagonisms can be sublimated as systemically productive. Conflicts between retail-based developments and local populations are resolved – in theory at least – through the hybridized space designed for the new citizen-consumer.[81] The envelope implicates one within the other and underwrites their compact in an appeal to environmental performance. This is the 'move', in Lyotard's terms, with which architecture supplies the system with increased performativity.

Flat Ontology
+
Neoliberalism

Student-entrepreneurs: Formatting the subject of education

In education, too, the systemic equalization of the subject, its mobilization as a thing among other things within architectural environments, has been enthused over. In an essay on the New Academic Building designed for the Cooper Union school in New York by Morphosis, Marikka Trotter writes that 'this building

Figure 18 Morphosis, New Academic Building, Cooper Union, New York City, 2006–9, photo: Manuel Shvartzberg, 2015.

foments human dynamics, strategy, and action ... as a participant harnessing vectors, pulses, and systems ... it reveals itself as part of an agonistic "co-fragile system" that includes each student, visitor, teacher, and administrator, the air it ventilates, the resources it draws up and excretes, and the ecological fabric of Manhattan that evolves and pulses all around it'.[82] The architecture is lauded because it is not about signs, symbols or meanings, it is 'not to be read or decoded', it is to be immediately experienced as a material organization of forces.[83] It is about the 'relationships that humans and human-made things have with each other and with the organic and nonorganic ecology from which they are inseparable'.[84] Rather than its meaning, it is the performance of the architecture that is positively appraised. The New Academic Building 'is a gym for preparing students to act precisely, powerfully, and speculatively in the transforming and unforming and reforming of the dynamic currents of the world'.[85]

The New Academic Building is in fact, though, thoroughly implicated in an economy of signs. Looking to profit from the erection of a building by a signature architect – Morphosis' Thom Mayne the choice for this purpose – the Cooper Union aimed to attract investment from a donor who would pay the school to lend their name to the project. Having borrowed $175 million from MetLife for the building's design and construction no donor could be found to cover these costs. The financial consequences of this venture, in combination with its investments in hedge funds, have been cited as leading to the school's decision to begin charging tuition fees.[86] Having offered free scholarship since 1902, Cooper Union began charging an annual tuition fee of around $20,000 per student in 2014.[87] Failing to perform economically, Morphosis' New Academic Building succeeds, at least, in offering the student a training ground for attuning themselves to the 'dynamic currents of the world', for practising their performance in an environment always shadowed by finance and debt.

Students of Cooper Union responded to the proposals to introduce fees with a series of protests, sit-ins and occupations. At the same time students in the UK were similarly contesting the general introduction of tuition fees of up to £9,000 per year for undergraduates in higher education. The Conservative-led coalition government of David Cameron had based this policy on a study originally commissioned, in 2009, by the previous Labour government. The 'Browne Report' – headed by former chief executive of BP and non-executive director of Goldman Sachs, Lord Browne of Madingley – is a transparently neoliberal screed. 'Our proposals', states the report, titled 'Securing a Sustainable Future for Higher Education', 'are designed to create genuine competition for students

Figure 19 Morphosis, New Academic Building, Cooper Union, New York City, 2006–9, photo: Manuel Shvartzberg, 2015.

between HEIs [Higher Education Institutes], of a kind which cannot take place under the current system. ... This is in our view a surer way to drive up quality than any attempt at central planning.'[88]

The report proposes to place the student at the centre of things – 'we want to put students at the heart of the system. Students are best placed to make the judgment about what they want to get from participating in higher education.'[89] The quality and flexibility of the universities will be improved as they learn to compete, as marketized service providers, for the tuition fees of newly enfranchized consumers of education. Students should receive 'value for money'.[90] Student choice 'will shape the landscape of higher education'.[91] The report sells the idea of tuition fees as affording the student the freedoms of the market. It is equally plain, however, that the remodelling of the student as consumer is designed to serve another purpose. The report notes that the UK, in 2008, 'was rated as only the 12th most competitive nation in the world. … On higher education and training, it ranks as low as 18th. The UK is judged to be "at a competitive disadvantage" due to its "inadequately educated workforce," which is identified … as the 4th most problematic factor for doing business in the UK.'[92] 'Already', the report continues, 'employers in the UK frequently report that some graduates lack communication, entrepreneurial and networking skills, as well as an understanding of how businesses operate.'[93] The thinly concealed logic of the report is that if students are to invest financially in their education to the tune of £27,000, plus living costs, they will be more focused on securing a return on that investment in the form of secure employment. They will exercise their choice in selecting institutions and programmes of education that equip with them marketable skills. This will, in turn, serve the interests of business, which will, in turn, serve to improve the competitive performance of the economy.

The common criticism of the marketization of education – that it turns the student into a consumer and education into a commodity – risks failing to recognize the full implications of this process. It misses the fact that the content of education changes in the process of its mass consumption, that the point of education becomes less and less about the acquisition of knowledge and more and more about the practising of skills – communication skills, business skills, job skills, entrepreneurial skills. This is what Lyotard prognosticated in *The Postmodern Condition*. His reflections on the subsumption of higher education to overall systemic performance, and of the significance attached to skills in this cybernetic turn, resonate strikingly with the contents of the Browne report:

> If the performativity of the supposed social system is taken as the criterion of relevance (that is, when the perspective of systems theory is adopted), higher education becomes a subsystem of the social system. … The desired goal becomes the optimal contribution of higher education to the best performativity of the social system. Accordingly, it will have to create the skills that are indispensable to that system.[94]

Lyotard notes that before the mid-twentieth century, when few attended university, knowledge was sought and transmitted in order to understand and shape the world. Knowledge was 'articulated in terms of the realization of the life of the spirit or the emancipation of humanity' – it served an elite subscribed to the 'grand narrative' of progress.[95] When the university is made more socially accessible, the relationship to knowledge changes. Students, writes Lyotard, become 'users of a complex conceptual and material machinery' over which they have no powers of comprehension or control.[96] The users 'have at their disposal no metalanguage or metanarrative in which to formulate the final goal and correct use of that machinery'.[97] Systemic optimization demands that the subject abandon any 'totalizing' perspective. The role of the university is to 'supply the system with players capable of acceptably fulfilling their roles at the pragmatic posts required by its institutions'.[98]

System theory's optimized user is the complementary counterpart to neoliberalism's necessarily ignorant subject. In both, any aspiration to know or shape the world, beyond what is immediately and systemically performative, is delegitimated. The contemporary burden of debt adds to this the economic disincentive of pursuing knowledge not readily amenable to market valorization. In turn, the university markets itself, above all, whatever the 'content' of particular programmes, as offering a core curriculum of 'transferable skills'.

The university is a base camp for learning and practising these skills. Its gymnasia are the 'hub' spaces – retrofitted to older campuses or purpose built for newly designed facilities – that are now central features of many UK universities. Typically vast, atrial spaces, these are zones for the equalization of multiple activities – drinking coffee, checking emails, having tutorials, having lunch, listening to music, collaborating on projects, posting on Facebook, rehearsing presentations, group work, individual work, essay writing, tweeting – all practised in various combinations, often simultaneously. The hub space is furnished to accommodate these with its desks, work stations, booths, refectory tables, stools, lounge chairs, dining chairs, benches, sofas. Some of the furniture is fixed, some is mobile, its configurations and arrangements to be improvised. This is the spatial equipment with which the student rehearses and becomes practised in locating spaces of relative seclusion, or chances for participation; in communicating in various situations, with varying degrees of formality or informality; in registering opportunities for networking; in signalling availability or unavailability; in combining or moving deftly, and opportunistically, between studying, socializing and working.

Ravensbourne College: The 'learning landscape' and the 'univers-city'

In FOA's design for Ravensbourne College of Design and Communication, relocating from its site in Chislehurst to the Greenwich Peninsula in 2010, the practice conceived a spatial equipment of this type inflected through its own Deleuzian and Latourian conceptual apparatus. Ravensbourne's relocation was designed to facilitate its institutional adoption of a 'flexible learning agenda'.[99] The 'vision' for the college was that 'space, technology and time will work together to create a new and flexible learning landscape that will support ongoing expansion and change, as well as narrowing the gap between an education and industry experience'.[100] Its turn to flexible learning followed broader developments in higher education in Britain, in particular those derived from the recommendations for universities to adopt 'blended learning strategies' made by the Department of Education and Skills and the Higher Education Funding Council for England (HEFCE).[101] Blended learning – 'learning activities that involve a systematic combination of co-present (face-to-face) interactions and technologically-mediated interactions between students, teachers and learning resources'[102] – is better adapted to the needs of contemporary students, runs the argument, since it allows them to 'time-shift' their education to a time and place of their own choosing within the 'virtual learning environment'. It better responds to what are now the real priorities and predispositions of the student, as described by DEGW in their 'User Brief for the New Learning Landscape':

> The ability and motivation of students to learn has changed and will change further as economic pressures compound the effects of new media and new attitudes to learning. Today's students assimilate knowledge vicariously from broadcast and interactive media and through practical application rather than formally from books and many are easily bored by traditional teaching with little visual content. Some lack basic transferable skills in communication, group-working and written English. Most expect time-shifted delivery of learning to accommodate the part-time work that helps them manage student debt. Rapid acquisition of fashionable, marketable skills or commitments to intense personal interests (e.g. bands) can take priority over formal achievements in an academic discipline. Future students are likely to rank educational institutions by their ability to deliver employment and to accommodate diverse approaches to learning.[103]

Figure 20 Foreign Office Architects, Ravensbourne College, London, 2010, photo: the author, 2010.

Blended learning strategies were understood as an opportunity for Ravensbourne College to integrate student practice within market-based forms of enterprise and competition. The college's internal report for its 'Designs on Learning' argues that 'within an academic environment, practice takes place in a vacuum, or, rather, an endlessly self-reflecting hall of mirrors'.[104] Insulated from the 'creative dialectic between creator and client (or public) that exists in the "real world"' students are said to 'overvalue individual artistic or creative input, rather than the negotiated creativity of the marketplace'.[105] As a corrective, students of Ravensbourne are required to adopt 'web 2.0 values', to take to social media to publicize their projects. This will forge 'a renewed connection with the audience, or consumers, of creative products'.[106] The closed circuits of education, its 'hall of mirrors', are opened out to connect with the real world beyond. Creativity is not an end in itself, or something whose value can be adequately assessed within the confines of education. Worth must be gauged in the marketplace, in the economies of systemic performance – comments on blogs, hits, 'likes' – the circulation of feedback modulating output at source.

Not only is the value of creativity calibrated by the market, but it accrues value to the extent that it can be mobilized in processes of economic regeneration. DEGW recommended that Ravensbourne operate as part-college, concerned with teaching and learning, part-lab, focused on experimentation and development, and part-hub, producing new ideas and services for the market.[107] Located on the Greenwich Peninsula, in close proximity to new commercial and business development projects, Ravensbourne was conceived not only as a receptacle for the surrounding environment's enterprise-based values but also as a contributor to the local 'knowledge economy', as a catalyst for 'urban regeneration'.[108]

The circuits, connections and feedback loops on which these relationships between education, creativity and enterprise are forged are not purely 'virtual', operating only through digital media. They also demand an architecture, a space of practice of the kind articulated in DEGW's model of the 'Learning Landscape':

> The Learning Landscape is the total context for students' learning experiences and the diverse landscape of learning settings available today – from specialized to multipurpose, from formal to informal, and from physical to virtual. The goal of the Learning Landscape approach is to acknowledge this richness and maximize encounters among people, places, and ideas, just as a vibrant urban environment does. Applying a learner-centered approach, campuses need to be conceived as 'networks' of places for learning, discovery, and discourse between students, faculty, staff, and the wider community.[109]

In accordance with this model, the architecture of FOA's Ravensbourne College is designed to articulate its interior as an atmosphere inculcating in the student the requisite connective, flexible and informal modes of conduct, at the same time rendering the building permeable to its surrounding environment as a mechanism for the integration of education and business. In plan, Ravensbourne is a chevron-shaped block whose form responds to the outer curvature of the O2 building to which it lies adjacent. The main entrance is situated at the interior junction of the two wings forming this chevron, and opens out onto one of its large atria. This quasi-public space is intended as a bridge between the college and the rest of the Greenwich Peninsula. Having its security barriers recessed deep within the building, rather than placed, conventionally, at its entrance, the threshold between public and institution is deliberately blurred. The visitor, alongside students and staff, enters an informal zone which includes a 'meet and greet' area, a high street chain coffee-outlet and an 'event' space hosting public displays and exhibitions. This is supposed to constitute what DEGW – in their account of 'univer-cities' such as Ravensbourne – describe as a 'third place', existing between home and work, combining 'shopping, learning, meeting, playing, transport, socialising, playing, walking, living'.[110]

From the atrium the successive floors of the college and the bridges spanning its two wings are open to view. Rather than enclosed in stairwells or embedded in corridors, the mesh-sided stairways and passages are exposed to reveal a complex series of crossings and intersections, their structural dynamics animated by the circulation of students and staff. Looking up from the atrium the college appears as a hive of activity, a scene of industrious creativity. The reverse perspective, looking down from the stairs and studio

Figure 21 Foreign Office Architects, Ravensbourne College, London, 2010, photo: the author, 2010.

spaces onto this area, affords the students and staff a motivational image of its field of validation – its audience of clients and consumers – through whom the value of their creative work has always to be negotiated. The market is introjected within the space of the building – student's business ventures are also to be 'incubated' and 'hatched' within its architecture – and the image of this market-negotiated creativity is projected back out into the world of enterprise.[111]

The building's circulatory diagram is designed to avert systemic stagnation. Its ground is not be territorialized by fixed patterns of occupation. Ascent through the building is staggered across its two wings so as to accentuate the idea of fluid movement over stasis. 'The idea is to produce a smoother change of plane', explains Zaera-Polo, 'to liquefy the volume of the building so you don't have this notion of being on the third floor or the fourth floor. You are always in between floors.'[112] The principle of liquefaction is also apparent in the floor plans. Articulated only by mobile partitions, the arrangement of teaching studios and open-access studios zoned within these spaces suggests the integration of programmes within a continuously mobile and flexible whole. Few programmes are assigned to fixed or discrete areas. The interior organization is marked by the application of a principle of deterritorialization consistent with the concepts proposed by DEGW as appropriate to the contemporary 'univers-city': 'Traditional categories of space are becoming less meaningful as space becomes less specialized, [and] boundaries blur. ... Space types [should be] designed primarily around patterns of human interaction rather than specific needs of particular departments, disciplines or technologies.'[113] Lecturers are not provided with private or fixed office space, but required to locate and use available space in open-plan offices on an ad hoc basis. Students are subjected to the same freedoms, having to find for themselves areas in which to study. The negotiation of space is itself an education in creativity, a skill to become practised in. Students are to behave as 'intelligent nomads'.[114]

The diagram of the educational environment replicates its 'virtual' correlate. The online protocols with which students are familiarized, in learning to valorize their creativity, are made those after which their behavioural practices in general should be modelled – circulation within networks, flexible movement across and between activities, self-promotion, receptivity to feedback, opportunistic exchange, engagement in multiple projects, the conduct of the student-entrepreneur.

Neoliberalism and Affect: Architecture and the Patterning of Experience

The protocols of the learning landscape are signalled in the form and appearance of Ravensbourne's architectural envelope.[1] Its apertures are clustered in a honeycomb pattern suggestive of incubation and hatching, of the nurturing of creative enterprise. The fenestration also connotes connectivity, the permeability of the structure to its immediate environment. There are moments of symmetry and repetition, but the impression, overall, is one of spontaneity. The organizational principles of the institution are expressed as freely constituted rather than inflexibly imposed. The Penrose tiling pattern applied across the envelope's outer surface is similarly expressive of organizational concepts. Its close-knit tessellation speaks of some collective intelligence at work in the unification of its surface. The conceptual tropes of self-organization and networked connectivity are affirmed through the geometric expression of their productive capacities, valorized through the visual coherence of the pattern's proliferation. While the external envelope of Hadid's Central Building for BMW appeared as an elevated plan of its organizationally smoothed circuits, that of Ravensbourne reads as a cross section, a revelation of the relations of contiguity through which these circuits are composed. The capacity to produce cohesion while accommodating difference is underlined in the patterning of the envelope.

The ability of the envelope to convey and affirm these organizational principles confirms, for Zaera-Polo, its politics of explicitation, its ability to positively express the 'emergence of a heterarchical order' that joins humans, technology and nature within its flat ontology.[2] This, he argues, has been made possible by recent developments in building technology, relieving the envelope of certain of its traditional features. 'Freed from the technical constraints that previously required cornices, pediments, corners and fenestration,' he writes, the articulation of the envelope 'has become increasingly contingent and indeterminate.'[3] Citing, as exemplary of this new tendency, 'Nouvel's unbuilt, yet influential Tokyo Opera, Gehry's Guggenheim Museum, Future Systems' Selfridges Department Store, OMA's Seattle Public Library and Casa da Musica and Herzog & de Meuron's Prada Tokyo',[4] Zaera-Polo contends that the envelope has now become an 'infinitely pliable' surface.[5] Architectural expression need no longer be channelled through traditionally established modes of articulation, but can operate through supposedly uncoded formal, geometric and tectonic means. The features of the envelope's expressive surface have now, he continues, 'taken over the representational roles that were previously trusted to architectural language and iconographies'.[6] This newly discovered expressive capacity of the envelope coincides historically, claims Zaera-Polo, with a post-linguistic orientation within global capitalism: 'As language becomes politically ineffective in the wake of globalization, and the traditional articulations of the building envelope become technically redundant, the envelope's own physicality, its fabrication and materiality, attract representational roles.'[7] Drawing upon Deleuze and Guattari's concept of 'faciality',[8] he models this shift of the envelope as a movement from 'language and signification' towards a 'differential faciality which resists traditional protocols in which representational mechanisms can be precisely oriented and structured'.[9] Faciality is claimed as a politics of the envelope that operates 'without getting caught in the negative project of the critical tradition or in the use of architecture as a mere representation of politics'.[10] Faciality works, instead, through affect:

> The primary depository of contemporary architectural expression – is now invested in the production of affects, an uncoded, pre-linguistic form of identity that transcends the propositional logic of political rhetorics. These rely on the material organization of the membrane, where the articulation between the parts and the whole is not only a result of technical constraints but also a resonance with the articulation between the individual and the collective, and therefore a mechanism of political expression.[11]

The turn to affect is supposed, in the immediacy of its expression, to have rendered interpretation redundant. Communication is held to be 'prepersonal', 'transmitted by empathy between material organisations'.[12] Affect circulates between one thing and another. There is neither subject nor object of interpretation. The politics of the envelope affirms and reproduces this truth: what exists is good.

Figure 22 Foreign Office Architects, Ravensbourne College, London, 2010, photo: the author, 2010.

Architecture and the affective turn

Affect has also been privileged, following a similar line of argument, by Farshid Moussavi in her *The Function of Form*.[13] Here she argues that the contemporary city is no longer defined by a single culture (in itself a dubious proposition implying that it had, until now, always been so), but is now a space where 'novel subcultures and identities are constantly emerging'.[14] Moussavi asserts that 'architecture can no longer afford to structure itself as an instrument that either reaffirms or resists a single, static idea of culture. Instruments (codes, symbols, languages, etc.) simply repeat without variation. As a function rather than an instrument of contemporary culture, architectural forms need to vary in order to address its plurality and mutability'.[15]

Given that that this supposedly new condition is defined by multiplicity and multiculturalism, runs this argument, the use of language, or any coded form of communication, has been rendered redundant since one can no longer presume the 'universal fluency' of architecture's 'audience': 'Attempts to relate built forms and people through an external medium are therefore destined to remain marginal and ineffectual'.[16] Architectural form is assigned the task, unmediated by any established cultural or historical code, of communicating with the 'molecular' nature of contemporary reality.

As does Zaera-Polo, Moussavi identifies changes within capitalism as key to the development of architectural forms now capable of addressing the 'plurality and mutability' of this reality of product differentiation and mass customization, a reality where capitalism is no longer 'an homogenizing force', but 'contributes to the production of difference and novelty'.[17] Architecture, it follows, should pursue the same path, developing its own novel forms and thereby 'contributing to an environment that connects individuals to multitude [*sic*] of choices'.[18] Moussavi also turns to Deleuzian notions of affect in approaching the question of exactly how it is that these novel architectural forms might 'perform as a multiplicity' adequate to a post-linguistic, mutable and pluralistic social reality:

> The perception of an architectural form involves two stages. First, an affect is transmitted by a form. This affect is then processed by the senses to produce unique affections – thoughts, feelings, emotions and moods. As an affect can unfold into different affections or interpretations in different beings, it embeds a form with ability to be perceived in multiple ways. Through the agency of spatial affects, in each instance an architectural form performs as a singular multiplicity – as a 'function' that connects human beings to their environment as well as each other, albeit in different ways. In order to explore forms as multiplicities, designers need to focus on their affective functions.[19]

Moussavi offers FOA's Yokohama Port Terminal as exemplary of an architecture that performs as a multiplicity. The shifting sectional profile and variable geometry of this complex form are said to result in 'multiple percepts and affects', including those of 'flatness', 'pleating', 'openness', 'axiality', 'efficiency',

Figure 23 AZPML, Birmingham New Street Station, Birmingham, 2010–15, photo: the author, 2015.

'diagonality', 'asymmetry', 'purposefulness', 'landscape', 'valley' and 'mountain'. These (supposed) affects and percepts are held to ensure, in their variety and proliferation, that 'the terminal is not reducible to a single interpretation or meaning'. Since the individual's perception of novel architectural forms – those purported to perform through affect alone – is, she argues, conditioned by his or her particular experience, 'the reception is inevitably different in each case, and therefore multiple'.[20] A later statement by Moussavi suggests the essential incompatibility of practices of interpretation with an architecture of affect: 'Though built forms incorporate different material and intellectual contents, these meld together into novel sensory forms which, once created, are what they are. They have no cognitive content in their actuality. They are just formal and their "meaning" depends on their affects and each individual's perception of them'.[21]

Zaera-Polo and Moussavi's account of affect in architecture originates in a broader affective turn for which Brian Massumi's *Parables for the Virtual: Movement, Affect, Sensation* has become a foundational text.[22] Here he writes:

> There seems to be a growing feeling within media, literary, and art theory that affect is central to an understanding of our information- and image-based late capitalist culture, in which so-called master narratives are perceived to have foundered. Fredric Jameson notwithstanding, belief has waned for many, but not affect. If anything, our condition is characterized by a surfeit of it.[23]

Massumi himself draws on Deleuze, and Deleuze and Guattari, in formulating his conception of affect. In *What is Philosophy?* Deleuze and Guattari identify affect as the modus operandi proper to art, understood as a 'being of sensation' existing apart from the conceptual or the referential in its immediate materiality.[24] Deleuze, in *Francis Bacon: The Logic of Sensation*, affirms sensation as 'that which is transmitted directly, and avoids the detour and boredom of conveying a story'.[25] Art as sensation, the painting of Cezanne or Bacon for instance, is in direct contact with the subject, it 'acts immediately upon the nervous system' bypassing the 'intermediary of the brain'.[26] Massumi, drawing upon these propositions, writes in *Parables for the Virtual* that the work of Deleuze and Guattari, 'could profitably be read together with recent theories of complexity and chaos. It is all a question of *emergence*, which is precisely the focus of the various science-derived theories that converge around the notion of self-organization'.[27] If the allure of Massumi's combination of Deleuze and complexity theory is already obvious, his appeals to affirmation and against criticality only make this more so. The problem with 'critical thinking', writes Massumi, is that 'it sees itself as uncovering something it claims was hidden or as debunking something it desires to subtract from the world'.[28] Rather than subtracting we should be adding. Critical thinking, in the humanities, is 'of limited value'.[29] 'The balance', he argues, 'has to shift to affirmative methods' in order that it be positively productive.[30] 'When you are busy critiquing you are less busy augmenting.'[31]

Addressed to the theory of art, Simon O'Sullivan's essay 'The Aesthetics of Affect', of 2001, adopts a similar line of argument.[32] Affect is conceived as art's fundamental essence. First Marxism, with its 'Social History of Art', and then Derridean deconstruction have caused an 'aesthetic blindness' due to which we fail to recognize this misconstruing art as an 'object of knowledge'.[33] Marxism and deconstruction alike are mistakenly focused on 'negative critique'.[34] Art is not amenable to interpretation or critical reflection because affects are 'extra-discursive and extra-textual'.[35] 'Indeed you cannot read affects', insists O'Sullivan, 'you can only experience them.'[36] In place of any analysis addressing the issue of why art should be understood, exclusively, in terms of affect, O'Sullivan deploys the kind of ontological assertions familiar from the discourse of his counterparts in architectural Deleuzism: 'Affects are moments of intensity, a reaction in/on the body at the level of matter. We might even say that affects are immanent to matter. They are certainly immanent to experience. ... As such, affects are not to do with knowledge or meaning; indeed, they occur on a different, asignifying register.'[37]

Furthermore, the turn to affect will relieve us of the depressive symptoms to which critical thinking has subjected us for too long. 'Adorno', claims O'Sullivan, 'has abandoned the existent (his is a forsaken world). Indeed, this is what gives his work its melancholy tenor.'[38] 'We might want to turn', he continues, 'from Adorno to Deleuze and to a more affirmative notion of the aesthetic impulse.'[39] O'Sullivan does not engage in an analysis of why this should be the case here either. As with Massumi, it seems enough simply to assert that it is better to be positive than to be negative. The historical conditions within which Adorno's conception of aesthetics appeared – the industrialization of culture, the instrumentalization of nature, the rise of Fascism, the Holocaust – are passed over. The possibility that these concerns, rather than Adorno's personal failings, might have imbued his work with its 'melancholy tenor' is left unconsidered. Regardless of context, art and philosophy alike should abandon their utopian pursuits and become pragmatic, functional, productive.

In *Kissing Architecture*, Sylvia Lavin takes the immersive installation art of Pipilotti Rist as her point of access to an affirmation of affect in architecture. Rist's *Pour Your Body Out*, exhibited in the atrium of New York's Museum of Modern

Figure 24 Future Systems, Selfridges Department Store, Birmingham, 2003, photo: the author, 2015.

Art in 2008, is described as a 'multichannel immersive video, twenty-five feet high, that wrapped the museum's traditional white walls with a softly psychedelic garden of Eden populated with a prelapsarian Eve, apples and animalism. The installation also included pink curtains and a gigantic, soft grey, dougnut shaped pouf … where scores of people jostled for comfy spots, blanketed by the oozing pinkish soundtrack.'[40] Rist's concept, notes Lavin, was, in the words of the artist, 'not to try to destroy or be provocative to the architecture, but to melt in, as if I would kiss Taniguchi'. Rather than literally kissing the deceased architect of MOMA, Rist achieved this by 'filling its modernist space with sensuous bodies pouring in and out'.[41] The artist, suggests Lavin, was speaking of a 'new sensibility' that could envelope and suffuse the older ones – 'authority and autonomous intellection' – in the sensory embrace of 'intense affect'.[42]

Intensity, feeling, immediacy, all the usual promises of affect are captured in Rist/Lavin's 'kissing'. So too are the typical renunciations of language and interpretation: 'No one can speak when kissing … kissing interrupts how faces and facades communicate, substituting affect and force for representation and meaning.'[43] Dispensing with the cold and cognitive logics of modernism, and following the lead of Deleuze towards feeling and sensation, architecture should make its newly pliant surfaces 'kissable'. This practice is already exemplified, for Lavin, in projects by FOA, UNStudio, Preston Scott Cohen and Diller Scofidio + Renfro. The 'kissing architectural surface' of such architecture, writes Lavin, 'is neither Kitsch nor avant-garde, neither legible and demanding of focused attention, or simply edible and erotic. It is instead affective and eidetic because it shapes experience through force rather than representation.'[44]

For Lars Spuybroek, 'meaning' is a 'horrible word that lets us believe that the mind can trade aesthetics for textual interpretation.'[45] In his *The Sympathy of Things: Ruskin and the Ecology of Design*, he, like Moussavi, refuses any cognitive component to aesthetics: 'Aesthetics, I argue, is ontology. Things are as they are aesthetically, or, as some would say, because they have an effect; or, as others would say, because they affect each other.'[46] The term preferred by Spuybroek is 'sympathy', the felt relation between things in a world populated, exclusively, by things. Sympathy defines 'the power of things at work, working between all things, and between us as things'.[47] No special privileges are conceded to the subject. 'Humans', says Spuybroek 'are nothing but things among other things.'[48] Ideas, agency and intelligence exist, but these are equalized among things, evenly distributed, rather than centred in any subject exterior to them. There is intelligence in design, but it occurs '*between* things, not behind or above them'.[49] 'Matter', he writes, 'can think perfectly well for itself.'[50]

Drawing upon the nineteenth-century aesthetic philosophies of John Ruskin and Gottfried Semper, Spuybroek imputes to matter autogenetic properties realized through and expressed in its patterning: 'When matter transforms, undergoes a transition, it organizes itself by abstracting into a patterned state.'[51] If 'pattern is the main expression of a self-abstracting capacity of matter', as Spuybroek asserts, then there is no question of mediation, no question of matter's

Figure 25 Mecanoo, Library of Birmingham, Birmingham, 2008–13, photo: the author, 2015.

patterning or design being in any way determined from without, no question of it being in need of, or even amenable to interpretation. If matter does not require us to think on its behalf, or act upon it from without, then we can relinquish our compulsion to master the world, surrender ourselves over to a feeling for things. The twentieth century – 'our true Dark Ages' – can be left behind. Among the horrors that define it as such for Spuybroek, including those of Auschwitz and the H-bomb, special mention is reserved for by now familiar objects of censure. Making it into the twenty-first century, he writes, 'We even survived semiotics and deconstruction. And Criticality too.'[52]

The turn to affect demands the disavowal of critique. A renunciation of interpretation, representation, mediation. The twenty-first century should embrace positive feeling and renounce negative thinking. The argument for this is ontological. Its proofs lie in the immediacy of matter, its sensuous forms and its sympathetic relations. It is also ethical. The horrors of the twentieth century are understood as resulting from a Promethean hubris of which critique is equally culpable. All forms of mastery, whether they be over humanity, nature, or meaning, are expressions of the same cold and unfeeling logic of reason. Operating under the illusion that it exists apart from, and above, the nature of things, the effects of this supposedly faulty logic have been socially, politically and environmentally catastrophic.

This schema makes no discrimination between the traumas of the twentieth century and the forms of critique that have attempted to comprehend their larger causes. In refusing to countenance the possibility of mediation, the way is effectively barred to the possibility of apprehending reality in relation to any larger set of forces beyond immediate impressions, to a 'totality' defined 'not as a collection of separate, unrelated things' but as a whole 'in which everything depends on everything else', as Fredric Jameson wrote in *Marxism and Form*.[53] The attempt to grasp the totality through particular instances of its mediation is delegitimized, both because there is nothing to grasp, it appears, beyond the immediately obvious and its exclusively sensuous existence, and because the attempt to do so, the work of 'totalizing', is in itself understood as implicated in totalitarianism. Things just are as they are, and should be left to be so. This accords, in effect, with the neoliberal truth game by which we are disqualified from making conscious plans for society on the basis of our 'necessary ignorance' of the social order. Its workings are beyond our ken, and any attempt to grasp these, in order to consciously direct them, leads inevitably to totalitarianism.

The turn to affect wants to bring to an end, as if drawing some unfortunate episode to a close, the various practices of critical thought that sought, for

totality

much of the twentieth century, to comprehend the abstract logics and forces of capital through the cultural forms in which they were mediated: Kracauer's mass ornament, Benjamin's flashes of illumination, Adorno's phantasmagoria, Barthes' mythologies, Baudrillard's simulations and Jameson's cognitive mapping. Crucially, these are practices of mastery only to the extent that they aim to master the apprehension of the totality, rather than the totality itself. In seeking to reveal the abstract forces and meanings obscured within naturalized facts, fetishized commodities and aestheticized politics, they attempt to make them amenable to critical reflection.

Jameson, architecture and the totality

Recorded in his *Postmodernism, or, The Cultural Logic of Late Capitalism*, Jameson's encounter with the Bonaventura Hotel, Los Angeles, reflects on the problem of how the totality – here the 'great global multinational and decentered communicational network in which we find ourselves caught as individual subjects' – is mediated through the built environment of the late twentieth century.[54] For Jameson the Bonaventura is exemplary of 'something like a mutation in built space itself', an evolution with which the human subject has 'not kept pace'.[55] There has been no mutation in the subject equivalent to that of the space in which it finds itself immersed. Jameson remarks of the self-segregation of the Bonaventura from the city around it, the strict separation of inside from outside: 'I believe that, with a certain number of other characteristic postmodern buildings, such as the Beaubourg in Paris, or the Eaton Centre in Toronto, the *Bonaventura* aspires to being a total space, a complete world, a kind of miniature city.'[56] The isolation of the hotel from its urban context is reinforced through its appearance, in the mirrored glazing of its exterior:

> One would want … to stress the way in which the glass skin repels the city outside; a repulsion for which we have analogies in those reflector sunglasses which make it impossible for your interlocutor to see your own eyes and thereby achieve a certain aggressivity towards and power over the Other. In a similar way, the glass skin achieves a peculiar and placeless dissociation of the Bonaventura from its neighbourhood: it is not even an exterior, inasmuch as when you seek to look at the hotel's outer walls you cannot see the hotel itself, but only the distorted images of everything that surrounds it.[57]

Inside, Jameson finds the 'suppression of depth' characteristic of postmodern art and cinema realized in architectural form, a 'bewildering immersion' disorientating the visitor.[58] The 'milling confusion' of the space, with its streams of visitors travelling its escalators and elevators, its symmetrical and repeated features, causes the visitor to lose their bearings.[59] For Jameson, 'this latest mutation in space – postmodern hyperspace – has finally succeeded in transcending the capacities of the individual human body to locate itself, to organize its immediate surroundings perceptually, and cognitively to map its position in a mappable external world.'[60] This new spatial condition 'stands as something like an imperative to grow new organs, to expand our sensorium and our body to some new, as yet unimaginable, perhaps ultimately impossible, dimensions.'[61]

Crucially, as David Cunningham has noted, Jameson's reading of the Bonaventura treats it as more than simply 'symptomatic' of a certain 'stage' of capitalism.[62] The critical point is not so much the concern with architecture as a formal mediation of the machinations of globalized capitalism, as it is that 'postmodern hyperspace' calls upon the subject to develop the means to accommodate itself to these new conditions – that the mutation in space demands an equivalent mutation in the subject. As Cunningham observes, the form of the Bonaventura is understood by Jameson as a 'more or less crucial part of … capitalism's own spatial production and reproduction, and of the production of new forms of subjectivity appropriate to it: a kind of education or training, so to speak, in how "to live" in an emergent world constituted through ever-more-transitory and fugitive flows of capital and commodities.'[63] As Cunningham also notes, in this respect, Jameson's analysis has a good deal in common with the work of Tafuri, particularly with that of *Architecture and Utopia*, in its concern with the role of avant-garde architecture in the 'acculturation' of the subject to the abstractions of industrial capitalism and the modern metropolis. In Jameson's reference to the imperatives placed on the 'sensorium', there is also an echo of Benjamin's remarks, in the 'On Some Motifs in Baudelaire' essay, regarding the subjection of the 'human sensorium to a complex kind of training' in its experience of the city.[64]

What sets Jameson apart from Benjamin or Tafuri in this regard, however, are his uncertainties around whether this acculturation is even possible for the subject – the suspicion that this most recent 'imperative to grow new organs' might place an 'ultimately impossible' demand upon the subject's adaptive capacities. Jameson's account of his encounter with the Bonaventura is also, fairly uniquely, critically reflective of the fact that the very indiscernability of its form presents an obstacle to the kind of critique he is attempting to practice. 'I am more at a loss,' he admits, 'when it comes to conveying the thing itself, the experience of space you undergo when you step off such allegorical devices [the elaborate elevators] into the lobby or atrium.'[65] 'I am tempted to say', he continues,

> that such space makes it impossible for us to use the language of volume or volumes any longer, since these last are impossible to seize. Hanging streamers indeed suffuse this empty space in such a way as to distract systematically and deliberately from whatever form it might be supposed to have; while a constant busyness gives the feeling that emptiness is here absolutely packed, that it is an element within which you yourself are immersed, without any of that distance that formerly enabled the perception of perspective or volume.[66]

Jameson's analysis of the Bonaventura records a number of crises, in its form as much as its content. It registers an emergent tendency in architecture to cut itself off from its urban context, a schism between the city and its miniaturized simulations. It questions the ability of the subject to adapt itself to the environments it now finds itself immersed in, suggesting that these might constitute the loci of some irremediable disorientation. It reflects on the obstacles to critique caused by the loss of depth and distance, on the difficulties in even locating a position from which to reflect critically upon experience.

The turn to affect in architecture answers to these crises. The schism between the large-scale architectural interior and its urban context is overcome in the smoothed spaces that fold them into one another, in the 'politics of the envelope' that incorporates public and the private within 'more advanced social structures' signalled and made explicit, as such, through the supposedly affective powers of the envelope.[67] The struggle of the subject to orient itself within the immersive architectural environment, to locate itself within a condition of depthlessness, is overcome in the enjoyment of immediacy, in the subject giving itself over to the sensuous pleasures of immersion. The frustrations of the critic are overcome in the cancellation of both the object and practice of critique – there is nothing beyond appearances. Thinking can be done well enough by things themselves.

Aesthetics, aisthesis and cognition

What the turn to affect demands in order to effect these overcomings, however, is a further and more fundamental schism within the subject: the partition of feeling from knowledge. Its affirmations of a purely sensuous, post-linguistic and unreflective experience of the world return us, in some sense, to an older notion of aesthetics as pure sensation. As Terry Eagleton notes: 'Aesthetics is born as a discourse of the body. In its original formulation by the German philosopher Alexander Baumgarten, the term refers not in the first place to art, but, as the Greek *aisthesis* would suggest, to the whole region of human perception and sensation, in contrast to the more rarified domain of conceptual thought.'[68] While sensation remains uncharted, it threatens power. The terra incognita of subjective experience must be colonized by reason. Aesthetics, mediating between reason and sensation, is instrumental to this process.[69] In addressing itself to the new forms of subjectivity characteristic of this period, power appropriates new modes of control. 'The ultimate binding force of the bourgeois social order', writes Eagleton, 'in contrast to the coercive apparatus of absolutism, will be habits, pieties, sentiments and affections. And this is equivalent to saying that power in such an order has become *aestheticized*. It is at one with the body's spontaneous impulses, entwined with sensibility and the affections, lived out in unreflective custom.'[70]

Power will operate through its investments in the subjective realm newly disclosed to reason. The individual is subject to forms of training that remain unreflected upon precisely because they appear as customary and habitual, as 'given'. Kant's critical philosophy presents a challenge to this in its account of the reflective capacities of the subject. For Hegel, however, Kant's critique is insufficiently critical in the limitations it sets upon the exercise of reason.[71] For Kant, reason is reflective and contemplative, but for Hegel it is a form of praxis. As Seyla Benhabib notes in *Critique, Norm, and Utopia: A Study of the Foundations of Critical Theory*, 'Kantian moral psychology, according to which reason is juxtaposed to inclination and morality to sensuality, does not allow for the view that rationality is not merely a cognitive capacity of abstracting from given content, but primarily one of transforming and reshaping the given.'[72] It is through reason that the world that appears as 'given' is shaped, and through reason that the subject can grasp this fact cognitively. This, in turn, serves as a basis for the subject to act upon the world, to question and transform the given. For Hegel, Benhabib argues, 'we become individuals in that we shape, transform, and reappropriate the given content of our desires, inclinations and needs by reflecting upon them and by developing the capacity to act in accordance with rational principles.'[73]

Figure 26 NOX – Lars Spuybroek, Maison Folie, Lille, France 2001–4, photo: the author, 2004.

In the twentieth century, critical theory builds upon these understandings, and their development in Marx, in order to critique the instrumentalization of reason within industrial capitalism. The alienation of labour, the exploitation of nature and the commodification of culture are subjected to what Benhabib terms a 'defetishizing critique' that originates in Hegel – 'a procedure of analysis whereby the given is shown to be not a natural fact but a socially and historically constituted, and thus changeable, reality'.[74] What appears as *given* is shown to be the product of a praxis in which the subject might also be consciously and actively engaged. Setting out this proposition in the essay 'Traditional and Critical Theory', Max Horkheimer argues that the appearance of the world is to be grasped as historically and socially produced. Not only this, but the forms of perception through which the world is apprehended as such are themselves to be understood as socially and historically produced:

> The world which is given to the individual and which he must accept and take into account is, in its present and continuing form, a product of the activity of society as a whole. The objects we perceive in our surroundings – cities, villages, fields, and woods – bear the mark of having been worked on by man. It is not only in clothing and appearance, in outward form and emotional make-up that men are the product of history. Even the way they see and hear is inseparable from the social life process as it has evolved over the millennia. The facts which our senses present to us are socially preformed in two ways: through the historical character of the object perceived and through the historical character of the perceiving organ. Both are not simply natural; they are shaped by human activity. ...[75]

If the task of critical theory is to reason against reason's own instrumentalization, to defetishize what appears as given within capitalism, then the ways in which the activity of the senses themselves appear as given must also be subject to critique. The sensuous and the sensible are to be amenable to cognitive reflection. Adorno, in his *Aesthetic Theory*, insists on the inseparability of the sensuous and the cognitive in the perception of the artwork: 'Each work, if it is to be experienced, requires thought, however rudimentary it may be, and because this thought does not permit itself to be checked, each work ultimately requires philosophy as the thinking comportment that does not stop short in obedience to the prescriptions stipulated by the division of labor'.[76] All perception, for Adorno, necessarily involves, without being reducible to, cognition. 'Not knowing what one sees or hears', he argues, 'bestows no privileged direct relation to works' but instead makes their perception impossible. Consciousness is not a layer in a hierarchy built over perception; rather all elements of aesthetic experience are reciprocal.'[77] Sensory reception and intellectual reflection, together, afford access to the 'truth content' of the artwork, the historical or 'spiritual' truth sedimented within, but not identical to, what is empirically given in the work.[78] This sedimented truth might also be unearthed from other objects of experience, suggests Adorno: 'Ultimately, perhaps, even carpets, ornaments, all non-figural things longingly await their interpretation.'[79] Grasping the truth content of these, states Adorno, 'postulates critique'.[80]

Architecture's turn to affect refutes critique, denying any place to reflection or reason within the subject's experience of the world. The partition of feeling from knowledge advocated by its proponents, if ever realized, would return the subject to an essentially pre-critical position, to Eagleton's 'aestheticization' of power, 'at one with the body's spontaneous impulses, entwined with sensibility and the affections, lived out in unreflective custom'. Today the totality – the condition in which, as Jameson says, 'everything depends on everything else' – can hardly be said to have disappeared, so that it no longer warrants critical reflection, given, among other things, the intensively networked and electronically mediated conditions of the contemporary world.[81] 'One of the basic lessons of the Frankfurt School', Jameson has noted, 'was indeed that the social totality today is more total than it was – that is to say, that the very logic of late capitalism is an absolutely totalizing one which wishes to penetrate everywhere and to make links with everything.'[82] If this is even more the case today, if things are more connected, more mediated, in the early twenty-first century than they were in the mid-twentieth century, then to insist that experience constrains itself to the immediately sensuous should be understood as a mechanism of the very totality it refuses perception access to. The schism between sensation and cognition is a function of the totality, rather than evidence for its non-existence. On the one side, human perception, affectively responsive to the sensory patterns of the immediate environment, on the other, a machinic perception sifting through vast quantities of information – 'big data' – to glean knowledge of the patterns through which neoliberal capital is able to valorize and secure its operations.[83]

As David Lyon observes, 'Contemporary surveillance expands exponentially – it renders ordinary everyday lives increasingly transparent to large organizations. The corollary, however, is that organizations engaged in surveillance are increasingly invisible to those whose data are garnered and used.'[84] 'Big data', writes Claudia Aradau, 'is the new whole.'[85] As exposed by Edward Snowden's revelations of global surveillance operations, this whole is sustained through the acquisition of information trafficked between commercial organizations and

Figure 27 Crispin Wride, John Lewis Building, Stratford, London 2011, photo: the author, 2015.

governmental departments. In every movement, every communication, every purchase, the subject leaves traces to be reappropriated, mapped out, configured into patterns from which future behaviour can be predicted and acted upon. The ideal of this totality – comprised of corporate, financial, military and governmental agents – is of an unreflective subject, passively and unknowingly productive of the information through which its futures will be shaped. The future tense of this form of managerialism, its orientation towards projection, response and steering, reveals that the maintenance of the market has, in reality, very little to do with spontaneous orders, emergence or self-organization, and everything to do with forms of planning based on absolute knowledge of the kind disavowed in the truth games, but not the practices, of neoliberalism.[86]

Pattern recognition: The 'period eye' of neoliberalism

Patterning is the procedure by which machinic perception deciphers the totality, the means through which the vast quantities of information to which it is party are given intelligible form. From the patterning of data, norms are established, exceptions recognized, trends inferred, events predicted, habits reported and opportunities seized. Patterning, in the world of big data, mediates the totality. It is an instrument of knowledge and planning. In the built environment, however, patterning is a means of absorption. It contains perception within the forms of sensuous experience supposed to be proper to the human. The patterning of the built environment and the patterning of experience within it are the means through which the subject is trained in the part delegated to it within the partition of perception.

In the atrial spaces of the public interior – a shopping mall by Thomas Heatherwick, a library by UNStudio, a port terminal by Reiser + Umemoto – vision is rendered confluent with the circuits marked by the exposed walkways, the strips of lighting, the panels and grilles ribboned around its interior surfaces. The eye is trained in conformity with a condition of elegantly modelled and perpetual mobility. There is no goal or destination for it to fix on. Vanishing points are difficult to discern amid the succession of torqued forms and overlapping arcs. The neoliberal eye does not apprehend, calculate or gauge; it is enjoined to project itself into the play of movement presented to it, to surf the field of vision, revelling in the sensuous freedoms offered up to it.

The patterns are repeated on the outside. The same fluid motions are traced out in the grounds of cultural complexes, transport hubs and mega event masterplans – the West Kowloon Terminus by Aedas, Zaha Hadid Architects' Beko complex in Belgrade, the Rio 2016 Olympic Park by Aecom. Wave-formed paths and platforms ripple out across the terrain or course between buildings. Woven into these are the green spaces, the turfed areas that have come to stand for 'the environment'. Interdigitated with the infrastructure of the ground plane, or patched into the skin of the architectural envelope, the ubiquitous green patterning reassures that nature is consonant and fully compatible with development. Anxieties are appeased through affect.

The envelope carries other patterns. The overtly representational functions of the facade give way to expressions of material performance. Apertures are arrayed across the architectural surface in honeycomb grids, tessellated formations or, seemingly, at random. Energy flows are modulated, light and air are circulated. Envelopes assume the appearance of performative membranes – NOX/Lars Spuybroek's Stockholm Library, MAD's Sinosteel International Plaza in Tianjin, Reiser + Umemoto's O-14 tower in Dubai. Openness, exchange and porosity are signalled. Layers of meshing, glazing and fretwork – FOA's Department Store in Leicester, Morphosis's Cooper Union, the Library of Birmingham by Mecanoo – offer moiré effects and filmy atmospherics. The eye is captivated. These performances are contrived to appear as immanent to matter, the patterning, an emergent property of its operative capacities. Any allusions to anything beyond material immediacy, any representational figures, are eschewed, as if in obedience to some prohibition on graven images. Not in fear of offending some deity, but so as to keep perception trained on what is in front of it, untroubled by questions of meaning or interpretation. There is nothing for the subject to reappropriate from appearances. Scoring the hit on the optic nerve is enough in itself.

An architecture of affect performs as a power of aestheticization. Its work is to absorb the sensorium in an environmental patterning with which the subject can identify, recognizing itself as a thing among other things, a neoliberal subject as operationally agile and efficient as are the forms with which its milieu is increasingly saturated. Where any attempt to critically comprehend the totality is charged with being in itself somehow equivalent to totalitarianism, where the end of language, representation and interpretation are presented as a fait accompli, the subject is robbed of its potential, of what critical theory had, in fact, sought to add to its powers of cognition. It is the affirmation of affect, and not the practice of critique, that subtracts from perception in reducing it to a condition of pure *aisthesis*.

Conclusion: The Necessity of Critique

What is at stake in neoliberalism 'is nothing more, nor less, than the form of our existence – the way in which we are led to conduct ourselves, to relate to others and to ourselves', according to Dardot and Laval.[1] Neoliberalism is, they say, first and foremost a 'rationality' based upon 'the generalization of competition as a behavioural norm and of the enterprise as a model of subjectivation'.[2] For Dardot and Laval this is how we should understand neoliberalism, rather than as an ideology. I think it more accurate to say that it is both ideology and rationality, operating together, that are essential to neoliberalism. In Foucault's terms, neoliberalism is both a truth game and a form of environmental governmentality.

Neoliberalism constructs and disseminates its beliefs about the world in order to have them accepted as commonsensical truths. This is its truth game. Its accounts of the limits of human knowledge and the 'necessary ignorance' of the subject, its equation of planning and welfare with totalitarianism, its universalizing models of evolution, cybernetic systems and spontaneous orders, and its valorization of the market as a kind of super-processor, uniquely able to handle the complexity of the world, legitimate its rationality. It is through these truths that neoliberal thought argues that its rationality – presented simply as the natural way of the world – should govern the conduct and the mentality of the individual.

One of the means through which neoliberalism has been able to achieve the realization of its truths, as forms of environmental control, has been through a tendency in architecture which shares many of its beliefs, and that has been equally committed to establishing these as common-sense truths. The ground on which architecture will later identify itself with neoliberalism is prepared in the 1960s. The promotion of cybernetics, the critique of planning, the affirmations of participation, sensory experience, connectivity and interaction, the denunciations of separation, distance, interpretation and critical reflection, the championing of the enterprising and creative individual, liberated from all constraints and at one with the environment, already mirror the ideals of neoliberalism and the model of the new subjectivity it would like to produce – performative, creative, entrepreneurial. With its more recent turns away from 'negative critique' and towards the affirmative philosophy of Deleuze and Guattari, the sciences of complexity and emergence, and the theory of affect, architecture has legitimated its alignments with and servicing of neoliberal projects for the reorganization of labour, education, culture and public space. Through the projects analysed in this book, I have tried to demonstrate how the truths shared by neoliberalism and the architecture compliant to its agenda have informed projects designed to serve as forms of environmental governmentality.

What both neoliberal thought and the architecture of neoliberalism claim in legitimating the acceptance of their truths accepted is, above all, that in their realization the subject is liberated. The market liberates us from the tyranny of planning, the spontaneous order frees us from predetermined outcomes, participation relieves us from isolation, environmental immersion makes us one with the material world, the experience of affect delivers us from the melancholy essence of critical thought. All such claims, however, are premised on the idea of a given human nature, one whose essence has been distorted or alienated, and is now in the process of being redeemed, at last, through neoliberalism, and its architecture, affording it access to its true potentials. From the perspective of the production of subjectivity – understanding the self, following Foucault, as a historically contingent 'technology' – neoliberalism, and its architecture, is doing no such thing. There is no natural self – creative, communicative, productive – waiting to be restored to its essence. In neoliberalism already existing technologies and techniques of the self are broken down and recomposed – dehumanized and rehumanized, as Lyotard would say – into hybrid figures: the cultural-consumer, the citizen-consumer, the student-entrepreneur. The process appears progressive. It lifts restrictions and transgresses boundaries. It allows for access and participation. It desacralizes. The optimization of the subject's performance within neoliberal systems is affirmed as emancipating. In each case, however, what we actually see is the process of neoliberalization confronting existing technologies of the self and attempting to refashion these for its own operations. The engineer in the former East Germany, the resident of the gecekondu in Istanbul, the office-worker in post-reform China, the student in the UK. There is always a struggle to be overcome or smoothed over in the implementation of neoliberalism, an antagonism to be suppressed or turned into fuel for further systemic optimization.

The architecture of neoliberalism cannot openly acknowledge any such struggles, antagonisms or contradictions. Its rhetoric denounces the very thought of them and its appearance is bent on their dissolution within its smooth surfaces and fluid forms. This is why theory is needed, with all its unproductive negativity and its hateful criticality. The invitation to free ourselves by renouncing any thought of interpreting or acting upon the world, to enjoy our true ontological status as things as among other things, deserves in reply a critical refusal, the act of negation defined by Adorno as 'a revolt against being importuned to bow to every immediate thing'.[3]

Notes

Introduction

1   In a text written in 1982, 'Technologies of the Self', Foucault wrote: 'My objective for more than twenty-five years has been to sketch out a history of the different ways in our culture that humans develop knowledge about themselves: economics, biology, psychiatry, medicine, and penology. The main point is not to accept this knowledge at face value but to analyze these so-called sciences as very specific "truth games" related to specific techniques that human beings use to understand themselves.' He continues, offering an example of his methods and concerns, 'I studied madness not in terms of the criteria of formal sciences but to show what type of management of individuals inside and outside of asylums were made possible by this strange discourse. This encounter between the technologies of domination of others and those of the self I call "governmentality."' *Ethics: Subjectivity and Truth*, ed. Paul Rabinow, trans. Robert Hurley et al. (London: Penguin, 2000), pp. 224, 225.

2   Pierre Dardot and Christian Laval, *The New Way of the World: On Neo-liberal Society*, trans. Gregory Elliot (London and New York: Verso, 2013), p. 314.

3   Philip Mirowski, *Never Let a Serious Crisis Go to Waste: How Neoliberalism Survived the Financial Meltdown* (London: Verso, 2013), pp. 48–9.

4   Foucault uses this term, as a translation of the German *Gesellschaftspolitik*, to describe the governmental ambitions of neoliberalism in a number of lectures recorded in *The Birth of Biopolitics: Lectures at the Collège de France, 1978–79*, trans. Michael Senellart (Basingstoke, UK and New York: Palgrave Macmillan, 2008). He writes, for instance, that 'what the neo-liberals want to construct is a policy of society'. p. 146.

5   Mirowski, *Never Let a Serious Crisis Go to Waste*, pp. 48–9.

6   F. A. Hayek, 'The Intellectuals and Socialism', in *The Intellectuals: A Controversial Portrait*, ed. George B. de Huszar (Glencoe, IL: The Free Press, 1960), p. 371. The phrase 'second-hand dealer' makes plain Hayek's perspective on knowledge itself as a commodity subject to the market for its valorization.

7   Hayek, 'The Intellectuals', p. 372.

8   Mirowski, *Never Let a Serious Crisis Go to Waste*, p. 28.

9   Patrik Schumacher, 'Free Market Urbanism – Urbanism beyond Planning', in *Masterplanning the Adaptive City – Computational Urbanism in the Twenty-First Century*, ed. Tom Verebes (Abingdon, Oxford and New York: Routledge, 2013) p. 120.

10 For a critique of the discourse of metabolism see Douglas Spencer, 'Nature is the Dummy: Circulations of the Metabolic', *New Geographies 6: Ungrounding Metabolism* (2014), pp. 112–17.

11 Jeremy Gilbert, '"Neoliberalism" and "Capitalism" – what's the difference?'. https://jeremygilbertwriting.wordpress.com/2015/07/14/neoliberalism-and-capitalism-whats-the-difference/ [accessed 19 September 2015].

12 Ibid.

13 David Harvey, *A Brief History of Neoliberalism* (Oxford: Oxford University Press, 2005).

14 Mirowski, *Never Let a Serious Crisis Go to Waste*; Dardot and Laval, *The New Way of the World*.

15 Foucault, *Biopolitics*, p. 131.

16 François Cusset, 'Theory (Madness of)', *Radical Philosophy* 167 (May/June, 2011): 24–30.

17 Jean-François Lyotard, *The Postmodern Condition: A Report on Knowledge*, trans. Geoff Bennington and Brian Massumi (Manchester: Manchester University Press, 1984).

18 Alejandro Zaera-Polo, 'The Politics of the Envelope', *Volume #17* (Fall 2008): 76–105.

Chapter 1

1   Harvey, *Neoliberalism*, p. 16.

2   'If the project was to restore class power to the top elites, then neoliberalism was clearly the answer.' Harvey, *Neoliberalism*, p. 90.

3   Harvey, *Neoliberalism*, p. 13.

4   Mirowski, *Never Let a Serious Crisis Go to Waste*, p. 42.

5   Dardot and Laval, *The New Way of the World*, p. 7. See also Daniel Stedman Jones, *Masters of the Universe: Hayek, Friedman, and the Birth of Neoliberal Politics* (Princeton and Oxford: Princeton University Press, 2012), which is similarly critical of approaches to neoliberalism such as those of Harvey: 'It is a mistake to reduce neoliberal ideas to neoclassical economics as these writers tend to do', p. 14.

6   Dardot and Laval, *Way of the World*, p. 7.

7   Ibid., p. 11.

8   Michel Foucault, *Security, Territory, Population: Lectures at the Collège de France, 1977–78*, trans. G. Burchell (Basingstoke, UK and New York: Palgrave Macmillan, 2007); Foucault, *Biopolitics*.

9   Foucault, 'Technologies of the Self', in *Ethics: Subjectivity and Truth*, p. 225.

10 Thomas Lemke, 'Foucault, Governmentality, Critique', *Rethinking Marxism: A Journal of Economics, Culture & Society* 14, no. 3 (2002): 50.

11 Foucault, *Biopolitics*, p. 259.

12 Dardot and Laval, *Way of the World*, p. 11.

13 Ibid.

14 Foucault, *Biopolitics*, p. 131.

15 Milton Friedman, 'Nyliberalismen Og Dens Muligheter' [Neoliberalism and its prospects], trans. Anette Nyqvist and Jamie Peck, *Farmand* (17 February 1951), pp. 91–3, cited in Jamie Peck, *Constructions of Neoliberal Reason* (Oxford: Oxford University Press, 2010), pp. 3–4.

16 Sven-Olov Wallenstein, 'Introduction: Foucault, Biopolitics, and Governmentality', in *Foucault, Biopolitics, and Governmentality*, ed. Sven-Olov Wallenstein and Jakob Nilsson (Stockholm: Södertörn Philosophical Studies, 2013), p. 9.

17 Foucault, 'The Ethics of the Concern of the Self as a Practice of Freedom', *Ethics: Subjectivity and Truth*, p. 282.

18 Foucault, 'Ethics', p. 290.

19 Foucault, *Vol. 2, The History of Sexuality: The Use of Pleasure*, trans. R. Hurley (New York: Vintage Books, 1990); Foucault, *Vol. 3, The History of Sexuality: The Use of Pleasure*, trans. R. Hurley (New York: Vintage Books, 1988).

20 Michel Foucault, *The Government of Self and Others: Lectures at the Collège de France, 1982–83*, trans. G. Burchell (Basingstoke, UK and New York: Palgrave Macmillan, 2011).

21 Foucault, 'Ethics', p. 286. Foucault quotes here from Plutarch: 'You must learn the principles in such a constant way that whenever your desires, appetites, and fears awake like barking dogs, the logos will speak like the voice of the master who silences his dogs with a single cry.'

22 Foucault, 'Ethics', p. 286.

23 Ibid.

24 Ibid., p. 298.

25 Ibid.

26 Foucault, *Biopolitics*, p. 241.

27 I try to grasp the problems through what one might call a practice of the self, a phenomenon which I believe to be very important in our societies since Greek and Roman times, even though it has hardly been studied. In Greek and Roman civilizations these practices of the self had a much greater importance and autonomy than later on, when they were laid siege to, up to a certain point, by institutions: religious, pedagogical or of the medical and psychiatric kind. Foucault, 'Technologies of the Self', p. 282.

28 Foucault, *Biopolitics*, p. 252.

29 Gary S. Becker, 'Human Capital', *The Concise Encyclopedia of Economics*. http://www.econlib.org/library/Enc/HumanCapital.html [accessed 20 April 2014].

30 Foucault, *Biopolitics*, p. 252.

31 Mirowski, *Never Let a Serious Crisis Go to Waste*, pp. 116–17.

32 Margaret Thatcher, 'Margaret Thatcher: The First Two Years', *Sunday Times*, 3 May 1981. http://www.margaretthatcher.org/document/104475 [accessed 17 May 2014].

33 F. A. Hayek, *The Constitution of Liberty* (Abingdon, Oxford and New York: Routledge, 2006), p. 21.

34 F. A. Hayek, *Law, Legislation and Liberty: A New Statement of the Liberal Principles of Justice and Political Economy* (Abingdon, Oxford and New York: Routledge, 2013), p. 13.

35 Hayek, *Law, Legislation and Liberty*, p. 11.

36 Ibid., p. 27.

37 Ibid.

38 F. A. Hayek, 'Kinds of Rationalism', in *Studies in Philosophy, Politics and Economics* (Chicago: The University of Chicago Press, 1967), p. 85.

39 Foucault, *Biopolitics*, p. 110.

40 F. A. Hayek, *The Road to Serfdom* (Abingdon, Oxford and New York: Routledge, 2001), p. 74.

41 Hayek, *Law, Legislation and Liberty*, p. 271.

42 Foucault, *Biopolitics*, p. 282.

43 Immanuel Kant, *Critique of Pure Reason*, trans. J. M. D. Meiklejohn (Mineola and New York: Dover, 2004), p. ix.

44 Hayek, *The Constitution of Liberty*, p. 22.

45 Hayek, *Law, Legislation and Liberty*, p. 141.

46 Michael Polanyi, *The Logic of Liberty: Reflections and Rejoinders* (Abingdon and Oxford: Routledge, 1998), p. 196.

47 Polanyi, *Logic of Liberty*, p. 145.

48 Ibid., p. 195.

49 'In the present essay I have hitherto been concerned with extending the concept of self-coordination – known since Adam Smith to operate within a market – to various other activities in the intellectual field and with clarifying the relationship between the economic and intellectual systems thus brought into analogy to each other.' Polanyi, *Logic of Liberty*, p. 208.

50 Polanyi, *Logic of Liberty*, pp. 42–3.

51 Ibid., p. 191.

52 'A catallaxy', writes Hayek in *Law, Legislation and Liberty*, 'is the special kind of spontaneous order produced by the market through people acting within the rules of the law of property, tort and contract.' p. 269.

53 Hayek, *The Constitution of Liberty*, p. 141.

54 Ibid.

55 Hayek, *Law, Legislation and Liberty*, p. 41.

56 Hayek, 'Degrees of Complexity', in *Studies in Philosophy, Politics and Economics*, pp. 3–21.

57 Hayek, 'Degrees of Complexity', p. 3.

58 Ibid., p. 21.

59 Ibid., p. 18.

60 Hayek writes of the 'supra-conscious rules' by which our thoughts and actions are governed: 'If it should turn out that it is basically impossible to state of communicate all the rules which govern our actions, including our communications and explicit statements, this would imply an inherent limitation of our possible explicit knowledge and, in particular, the impossibility of ever fully explaining a mind of the complexity of our own.' 'Rules, Perception and Intelligibility', in *Studies in Philosophy, Politics and Economics*, p. 60.

61 Hayek, 'Rules', p. 61.

62 Mirowski, *Never Let a Serious Crisis Go to Waste*, p. 54.

63 Hayek, *Law, Legislation and Liberty*, p. 52.

64 Ibid., p. 36.

65 Ibid., p. 283.

66 Norbert Wiener, *The Human Use of Human Beings* (New York: Da Capo Press, 1954), p. 15.

67 Norbert Wiener, *Cybernetics* (Cambridge, MA: MIT Press, 1976), p. 19.

68 Wiener, *The Human Use of Human Beings*, p. 15.

69 Hayek, *The Constitution of Liberty*, p. 66.

70 Mirowski, *Never Let a Serious Crisis Go to Waste*, p. 56.

71 Dardot and Laval, *Way of the World*, p. 3.

Chapter 2

1 D'Arcy Wentworth Thompson, *On Growth and Form*, Cambridge: Cambridge University Press, 1961.

2 Stephen Jay Gould, 'Introduction', *On Growth and Form*, p. xi.

3 Thompson, *On Growth and Form*, p. 8.

4 Ibid., p. 7.

5 Richard Hamilton, 'Growth and Form Exhibition, First Draft Schedule', ICA Papers, Tate Gallery Archive TGA 955.1.12.26, cited in Isabelle Moffat, '"A Horror of Abstract Thought": Postwar Britain and Hamilton's 1951 "Growth and Form" Exhibition', *October*, vol. 94, The Independent Group (Autumn, 2000), p. 100.

6 Moffat, 'Horror of Abstract Thought', p. 100.

7   Michael Weinstock, 'Morphogenesis and the Mathematics of Emergence', in
    Emergence: Morphogenetic Design Strategies, AD (May/June 2004), eds, Michael
    Hensel, Achim Menges and Michael Weinstock, p. 11.

8   Patrik Schumacher, 'Arguing for Elegance', in *Elegance*, AD (January/February
    2007), eds, Ali Rahim and Hina Jamelle, p. 31.

9   See: Brian Massumi, *Parables for the Virtual: Movement, Affect, Sensation* (Durham
    and London: Duke University Press, 2002); Patricia Ticineto Clough with Jean
    Halley, eds, *The Affective Turn: Theorizing the Social* (Durham and London: Duke
    University Press, 2007); Nigel Thrift, *Non-Representational Theory: Space, Politics,
    Affect* (London: Routledge, 2007); Margaret Wetherell, *Affect and Emotion: A
    New Social Science Understanding* (London: Sage, 2012); Farshid Moussavi, *The
    Function of Form* (Barcelona and New York: Actar/Harvard University Graduate
    School of Design, 2009); Farshid Moussavi, *The Function of Style* (Barcelona and
    New York: Actar/Harvard University Graduate School of Design, 2014).

10 Lawrence Alloway, 'Personal Statement', *Ark*, vol. 19 (1957), p. 28, cited in Nigel
    Whiteley, *Pop Design: Modernism to Mod* (London: The Design Council, 1987), p. 49.

11 Fred Turner, *The Democratic Surround: Multimedia & American Liberalism
    from World War II to the Psychedelic Sixties* (Chicago and London: University of
    Chicago Press, 2013).

12 See Nigel Whiteley, *Reyner Banham: Historian of the Immediate Future*
    (Cambridge, MA and London: MIT Press, 2002), p. 85, and Michael Craig-Martin,
    'Richard Hamilton in Conversation with Michael Craig-Martin', *October Files 10*,
    ed. Hal Foster with Alex Bacon (Cambridge, MA and London: MIT Press, 2010),
    pp. 1–13.

13 Craig-Martin, 'In Conversation', p. 6.

14 Hayek, 'Degrees of Complexity', p. 18.

15 Allan Kaprow, 'The Legacy of Jackson Pollock', in *Essays on the Blurring of Art and
    Life* (Berkeley, LA and London: University of California Press, 2003), p. 2.

16 Ibid., p. 6.

17 Ibid.

18 Claire Bishop offers a concise definition of what she terms the 'US-style
    Happenings', as conceived by Kaprow, in her *Artificial Hells: Participatory Art and
    the Politics of Spectatorship* (London and New York: Verso, 2012). These, she writes

        were indebted to the compositional innovations of John Cage, and developed
        in response to the action paintings of Jackson Pollock. The first work to adopt
        the name "Happening" was Kaprow's own *Eighteen Happenings in Six Parts*,
        which took place over several evenings in Autumn 1959 at the Reuben Gallery
        in New York. In his early writings, Kaprow positions Happenings against
        conventional theatre: they deliberately rejected plot, character, narrative
        structure and the audience/performer division in favour of lightly scored

events that injected the everyday with risk, excitement and fear. The audience rarely has a fixed point of observation and, by the mid-1960s, tended to be involved directly as participants in the work's realisation. (p. 94)

19 Kaprow, 'Happenings in the New York Scene', in *Essays on the Blurring of Art and Life*, p. 18.

20 Kaprow, 'Notes on the Creation of a Total Art', in *Essays on the Blurring of Art and Life*, p. 11.

21 Immanuel Kant, *Critique of Pure Reason*, trans. J. M. D. Meiklejohn (Mineola and New York: Dover, 2004), p. 62.

22 Kaprow, 'Pollock', p. 5.

23 Ibid.

24 Ibid.

25 Stewart Brand, 'Notebooks', 14 March 1957, quoted in Fred Turner, *From Counterculture to Cyberculture: Stewart Brand, The Whole Earth Network and the Rise of Digital Utopianism* (Chicago and London: University of Chicago Press, 2008), p. 41.

26 The film made by Lucas as a student at University of Southern California in 1967, on which *THX 1138* is based, is titled *Electronic Labyrinth THX 1138 4EB*.

27 Lucas was probably familiar with Godard's film, given his exposure to the director's work during the 1960s.

28 'Professor Von Braun' was named in reference to the German rocket engineer and former SS officer Wernher von Braun recruited to work for NASA at the end of World War II.

29 Karl Marx, *Grundrisse: Introduction to the Critique of Political Economy*, trans. Martin Nicolaus (London: Penguin, 1973), p. 705.

30 Colin MacCabe, *Godard: A Portrait of the Artist at 70* (London: Bloomsbury, 2003), p. 168.

31 These perspectives featured in films made by Godard around this time, notably *Deux ou trois choses que je sais d'elle* (1967).

32 Henri Lefebvre, *The Urban Revolution*, trans. R. Bononno (Minneapolis and London: University of Minnesota Press, 2003), p. 113.

33 Ibid., p. 48.

34 Guy Debord, *The Society of the Spectacle*, trans. K. Knabb (London: Rebel Press, 2004), p. 95.

35 Jean Meynaud, *Technocracy*, trans. Paul Barnes (New York: Free Press, 1968); Alain Touraine, *The Post-Industrial Society: Tomorrow's Social History: Classes, Conflicts, and Culture in the Programmed Society*, trans. Leonard F. X. Mayhew (New York: Random House, 1971).

36 Gabrielle Hecht, *The Radiance of France: Nuclear Power and National Identity after World War II* (Cambridge, MA and London: The MIT Press, 2009), p. 32.

37 Much of the film was shot on location in suburban projects being constructed
    in Paris at the time, suggesting that *Alphaville* represented not so much another
    world as the contemporary remaking of the French capital.

38 Lucas had earlier immersed himself in the San Francisco arts scene and its
    independent cinema in the early and mid-1960s and the screenwriter and sound
    designer for *THX 1138*, Walter Murch, had staged happenings while a student at
    this time. The film's cinematographer, David Myers, also shot footage for the films
    Woodstock (1970) and *The Grateful Dead Movie* (1977).

39 Attributed to Fred Richardson 'Production in the Desert', *Whole Earth Catalog*,
    1971, cited in Felicity D. Scott, *Living Archive 7: Ant Farm. Allegorical Time Warp:
    The Media Fallout of July 21 1969* (Barcelona and New York: Actar, 2008), p. 81.

40 Turner, *Counterculture*, p. 4.

41 Ibid., p. 73.

42 Steve Jobs, commencement address at Stanford University, 2005, 'Jobs: "Find What
    You Love"', *Wall Street Journal* October 6, 2011, http://online.wsj.com/news/articles/
    SB10001424052970203388804576613572842080228 [accessed 9 April 2014].

43 Herbert Marcuse, 'Social Implications of Technology', in *Readings in the
    Philosophy of Technology*, ed. David M. Kaplan (Oxford: Rowan & Littlefield,
    2004), p. 63.

44 Richard Brautigan, 'All Watched Over by Machines of Loving Grace', quoted in
    Turner, *The Democratic Surround*, pp. 38–9.

45 Scott, *Ant Farm*, p. 32. Original source, Doug Michaels, 'Project Description' c. June
    1969. Attached to Michael's resume. Experiments in Art and Technology Papers
    (94003), Research Library, The Getty Research Institute, Los Angeles, California.

46 Gilbert Simondon, 'Technical Mentality', trans. Arne de Boever, *Parrhesia: A
    Journal of Critical Philosophy*, vol. 7 (2009), Special Issue on the Work of Gilbert
    Simondon, p. 17.

47 Ibid., p. 17.

48 Stewart Brand, *Whole Earth Catalog* (Menlo Park, CA: Portola Institute, Fall
    1968), p. 2.

49 John McHale, 'New Symbiosis', *2000+: Architectural Design* (February 1967), p. 89.

50 Scott, *Ant Farm*, p. 81.

51 Ant Farm, 'The Cowboy from Ant Farm' (Cowboy Nomad manifesto), 1969.
    Reproduced in Scott, *Ant Farm*, p. 21.

52 Gordon Pask, 'The Architectural Relevance of Cybernetics', *Architectural Design*
    (September 1969), p. 494.

53 Ibid.

54 Ibid., p. 496.

55 Ibid. The ideas of Pask's cybernetic models, if not so much his ideas of social
    engineering, were to be highly influential upon Cedric Price, among others, who
    recruited Pask to the team working on his designs for his Fun Palace project to set

up a 'Cybernetics Subcommittee'. See Stanley Matthews, *From Agit-Prop to Free Space: The Architecture of Cedric Price* (London: Black Dog Publishing, 2007), pp. 74–5.

56 Reyner Banham, *The Architecture of the Well-tempered Environment*, 2nd edn (Chicago: University of Chicago Press, 1984), p. 28.

57 Ibid., p. 27.

58 Ibid., p. 21.

59 Ibid., p. 20.

60 Ibid., pp. 19–20.

61 Ibid., p. 20.

62 Reyner Banham, 'People's Palaces', in *A Critic Writes: Essays by Reyner Banham* (Berkeley, LA and London: University of California Press, 1999), p. 108.

63 Reyner Banham, *Scenes in America Deserta* (London: Thames & Hudson, 1982), p. 99.

64 Reyner Banham, *Los Angeles: The Architecture of the Four Ecologies* (Berkeley and Los Angeles, CA: University of California Press, 2001), p. 195.

65 Banham, *Los Angeles*, pp. 196–7.

66 Ibid., p. 198.

67 Ibid., p. 199.

68 Ibid., p. 201.

69 Jean Baudrillard, 'The Ecstasy of Communication', in *The Anti-Aesthetic: Essays on Postmodern Culture*, ed. H. Foster (Washington: Bay Press, 1983), pp. 126–34.

70 Baudrillard, 'Ecstasy', p.127.

71 Ibid.

72 Ibid., p. 128.

73 Marshall McLuhan, 'The Invisible Environment: The Future of an Erosion', *Perspecta*, vol. 11 (1967), pp. 163–7.

74 McLuhan, 'Environment', p. 164.

75 Ibid.

76 Ibid., p. 165.

77 Marshall McLuhan, *Understanding Me: Lectures and Interviews*, ed. Stephanie McLuhan and David (Staines and Toronto: McClelland & Stewart, 2003), pp. 101–2.

78 McLuhan, 'Environment', p. 165.

79 Marshall McLuhan, 'The Playboy Interview: Marshall McLuhan', *Playboy Magazine* (March 1969). http://www.nextnature.net/2009/12/the-playboy-interview-marshall-mcluhan/.

80 Ibid.

81 Marshall McLuhan and Quentin Fiore, *The Medium is the Massage* (London: Penguin, 1967), pp. 84–5.

82 Ibid., p. 92.

83 Marshall McLuhan, 'Notes on Burroughs', *The Nation* (28 December 1964), http://realitystudio.org/criticism/notes-on-burroughs/ [accessed 17 May 2014].

84 Ibid.

85 Oliver Harris, 'Introduction', in *The Soft Machine*, ed. William S. Burroughs (The Restored Text, London: Penguin, 2014), p. xxxiii.

86 William S. Burroughs, *The Ticket that Exploded* (The Restored Text, London: Penguin, 2014), p. 57.

87 William S. Burroughs, *The Soft Machine* (The Restored Text, London: Penguin, 2014), p. 91.

88 Baudrillard, J./The French Group, 'The Environmental Witch-Hunt', in *The Aspen Papers: Twenty Years of Design Theory from the International Design Conference in Aspen*, ed. R. Banham (New York: Praeger, 1974), p. 208.

89 Ibid., p. 210.

90 Nigel Whiteley notes that 'Banham recalled that the conference "was the most bruising experience of my life."', *Reyner Banham: Historian of the Immediate Future* (Cambridge, MA: MIT Press, 2002), p. 264.

91 Theodore Spyropoulos, 'Constructing Adaptive Ecologies: Notes on a Computational Urbanism', in *Adaptive Ecologies: Correlated Systems of Living*, ed. T. Spyropoulos (London: AA Publications, 2013), p. 21.

92 Brett Steele in Spyropoulos, 'Constructing Adaptive Ecologies', p. 13.

Chapter 3

1 '425 Park Ave, competition: OMA', http://www.youtube.com/watch?v=BIyEDuzxYBU [accessed 15 August 2013].

2 Rem Koolhaas, *Delirious New York: A Retroactive Manifesto for Manhattan* (New York: Monacelli Press, 1978).

3 Alejandro Zaera-Polo, 'The Hokusai Wave', *Perspecta* 37 (2005), pp. 78–85.

4 Ibid., p. 79.

5 Ibid., p. 78.

6 Slavoj Žižek, *Revolution at the Gates: Žižek on Lenin–The 1917 Writings* (London: Verso, 2002).

7 Ibid., p. 303.

8 Slavoj Žižek, *The Ticklish Subject: The Absent Centre of Political Ontology*, New Edition (London: Verso, 2009), p. 199.

9 Ibid., p. 199.

10 Ibid.

11 Cusset, 'Theory (Madness of)', p. 25.

12 Ibid.

13 Ibid., p. 24.

14 K. Michael Hays, 'Introduction', *Architecture Theory since 1968*, ed. K. Michael Hays (Cambridge, MA: MIT Press, 1998), p. xi.

15 Michael Speaks, 'Intelligence After Theory', in *Perspecta 38: Architecture After All*, ed. Marcus Carter, Christopher Marcinkowski, Forth Bagley and Ceren Bingol (Cambridge, MA: MIT Press, 2006), p. 103.

16 Luc Boltanski and Eve Chiapello, *The New Spirit of Capitalism*, trans. Gregory Elliot (London and New York: Verso, 2007), p. 460.

17 Michael Speaks, 'Theory Was Interesting … But Now We Have Work', *Architectural Research Quarterly* 6, no. 3 (2002): 209–12.

18 Michael Speaks, 'Design intelligence. Part 1: Introduction', *A + U: Architecture and Urbanism* no. 12 (387) (December 2002): 10–18.

19 See, Zaera-Polo, 'The Hokusai Wave'.

20 See, Patrik Schumacher, *The Autopoiesis of Architecture; Volume I: A New Framework for Architecture* (Chichester: Wiley, 2010), and *The Autopoiesis of Architecture; Volume II: A New Agenda for Architecture* (Chichester: Wiley, 2012).

21 Libero Andreotti, 'Unfaithful Reflections: Re-actualizing Benjamin's aestheticism thesis', in *Architecture Against the Post-Political: Essays in Reclaiming the Critical Project*, ed. Nadir Lahiji (London and New York: Routledge, 2014), p. 41.

22 Ibid. pp. 41–2.

23 Gilles Deleuze, *The Fold: Leibniz and the Baroque*, trans. Tom Conley (London: The Athlone Press, 1993).

24 Gilles Deleuze and Félix Guattari, *A Thousand Plateaus: Capitalism and Schizophrenia*, trans. Brian Massumi (London and New York: Continuum, 1992).

25 Deleuze, *The Fold*, p. 3.

26 Gottfried Wilhelm Leibniz, *Pacidus to Philalethes*, pp. 614–15 cited in Deleuze, *The Fold*, p. 6.

27 Ibid., p. 5.

28 Ibid., p. 4.

29 Ibid.

30 Ibid., p. 5.

31 Ibid.

32 Greg Lynn (ed.), *Folding in Architecture* (Chichester and Hoboken, NJ: Wiley-Academy, 1993/2004, reprinted).

33 John Rajchman, *Constructions* (Cambridge, MA: MIT Press, 1998).

34 Deleuze and Guattari, *A Thousand Plateaus*, p. 480.

35 Ibid., p. 500.

36 Lynn, 'Architectural Curvilinearity: The Folded, the Pliant and the Supple', in *Folding in Architecture*, p. 24.

37 Ibid.

38 Ibid.

39 Jessie Reiser and Nanako Umemoto, 'RUR: Why We Get the Truths We Deserve', in *0-14: Projection and Reception: Reiser + Umemoto*, ed. Brett Steele (London: Architectural Association Publications, 2012), p. 17.

40 Sylvia Lavin, *Kissing Architecture* (Princeton and Oxford: Princeton University Press, 2011).

41 Ibid., p. 15.

42 Lynn, 'Architectural Curvilinearity', p. 25.

43 Ibid.

44 Ibid.

45 Ibid., p. 24.

46 Ibid., p. 28.

47 Ibid.

48 Ibid., p. 30.

49 Ibid., p. 28.

50 Zaha Hadid, in Obrist, Hans Ulrich, *Zaha Hadid and Hans Ulrich Obrist* (The Conversation Series, 8, Cologne: Verlag der Buchhandlung Walther König. 2007), p. 73.

51 Jeffrey Kipnis, 'Towards a New Architecture' in Lynn, *Folding in Architecture*, p. 18.

52 Ibid., p. 18.

53 Ibid.

54 Ibid., p. 337.

55 Jesse Reiser and Nanako Umemoto, *Atlas of Novel Tectonics* (New York: Princeton Architectural Press, 2006), p. 20.

56 See, for example, Robert Somol and Sarah Whiting, 'Notes Around the Doppler Effect and Other Moods of Modernism', *Perspecta*, Vol. 33, *Mining Autonomy* (2002), and 'Okay Here's the Plan', *Log*, (Spring/Summer 2005); George Baird, "Criticality" and its Discontents', *Harvard Design Magazine* 21 (Fall 2004/Winter 2005): 16–21; Jeffrey Kipnis, 'Is Resistance Futile?', *Log* (Spring/Summer 2005); Reinhold Martin, 'Critical of What? Toward a Utopian Realism', *Harvard Design Magazine* 22 (Spring/Summer 2005). 'Post-critical' writings have often taken Koolhaas's well-known reservations about the possibility of a critical architecture as an explicit reference point as well, although the latter has notably declined any direct identification with the label. See Rem Koolhaas and Reinier de Graaf, 'Propaganda Architecture: Interview with David Cunningham and Jon Goodbun', *Radical Philosophy* 154 (March/April 2009): 37–47.

57 Jeffrey Kipnis, 'On the Wild Side', in *Phylogenesis: FOA's Ark*, ed. Farshid Moussavi, Alejandro Zaera-Polo and Sanford Kwinter (Barcelona: Actar, 2004), p. 579.

58 'Educating the Architect: Alejandro Zaera-Polo in conversation with Roemer van Toorn'. http://www.xs4all.nl/~rvtoorn/alejandro.html [accessed 15 December 2008].

59 See Eugene W. Holland, 'Deterritorializing "Deterritorialization": From the "Anti-Oedipus" to "A Thousand Plateaus", *SubStance* 20, no. 3, 66: Special Issue: Deleuze & Guattari (1991): 57.

60 Zaha Hadid, Pritzker Acceptance Speech, 2004. http://www.pritzkerprize.com/laureates/2004/_downloads/2004_Acceptance_Speech.pdf [accessed 22 March 2009].

61 Patrik Schumacher, 'Research Agenda', in *Corporate Fields: New Environments by the AA DRL*, ed. Brett Steele (London: AA Publications, 2005), p. 76.

62 Brett Steele, ed., *Corporate Fields: New Environments by the AA DRL* (London: AA Publications, 2005).

63 Schumacher, 'Research Agenda', p. 75.

64 Ibid.

65 Ibid., p. 76.

66 Ibid., p. 79.

67 Ibid., p. 78.

68 Patrik Schumacher, 'Research Agenda: Spatialising the Complexities of Contemporary Business' (2005). http://www.patrikschumacher.com/Texts/Corporate%20Fields-%20New%20Office%20Environments.html [accessed 8 July 2009]. Note that this sentence, with its strident dismissal of all forms of protest, appears only within the version of the essay which is available online, and does not appear in its published version.

69 Schumacher, 'Research Agenda', p. 77.

70 Ibid., p. 78.

71 Isabelle Stengers and Ilya Prigogine, *Order out of Chaos: Man's New Dialogue with Nature* (Toronto and New York: Bantam Books, 1984).

72 Alejandro Zaera-Polo, 'Order out of chaos: The material organization of advanced capitalism', in *Architectural Design Profile*, vol. 108 (1994), pp. 24–9.

73 Ibid., p. 25.

74 Ibid., p. 26.

75 Ibid., p. 25.

76 Ibid., p. 28.

77 Ibid.

78 Ibid., p. 29.

79 Zaera-Polo, 'The Politics of the Envelope'.

80 Ibid., p. 103.

81 Kipnis, 'On the Wild Side', p. 578.

82 Ibid., pp. 569–70.

83 Ibid., p. 571.

84 Ibid., p. 573.

85 Isabelle Stengers, 'Complexity: A Fad?', in Isabelle Stengers, *Power and Invention: Situating Science*, trans. Paul Bains (Minneapolis and London: University of Minnesota Press, 1997), p. 3.

86   Ibid., p. 4.

87   Stengers and Prigogine, *Order out of Chaos,* p. 38.

88   Stengers, 'Complexity', p. 4.

89   Ibid., p. 2.

90   Ibid.

91   Ibid., p. 4.

92   Moussavi, *The Function of Form*, p. 18.

93   Ibid.

94   Alejandro Zaera-Polo, 'Cheapness: No Frills and Bare Life', *Log* 18 (Winter 2010): 18.

95   Ibid., p. 26.

96   Schumacher, 'Free Market Urbanism – Urbanism beyond Planning', p. 120.

97   Patrik Schumacher and Peter Eisenman, 'I am Trying to Imagine a Radical Free-market Urbanism', *Log* 28 (Summer, 2013): 28.

98   Ibid., p. 25.

99   Zaera-Polo, 'The Politics of the Envelope', p. 103.

100 See, for instance, Manuel DeLanda 'The Nonlinear Development of Cities', in *Eco-Tec: The Architecture of the In-Between*, ed. Amerigo Marras (New York: Princeton Architectural Press, 1999), pp. 22–31; 'Deleuze and the Use of the Genetic Algorithm in Architecture', in *Designing for a Digital World*, ed. Neil Leach (New York: Wiley, 2002), pp. 117–18, and 'Materiality: Anexact and Intense', in *NOX: Machining Architecture*, ed. Lars Spuybroek (London: Thames & Hudson, 2004), pp. 370–7.

101 For a more extensive critique of DeLanda's de-Marxification of Deleuze and Guattari, see Eliot Albert, 'A Thousand Marxes', *Mute* (Autumn 1998). http://www.metamute.org/en/A-Thousand-Marxes [accessed 21 July 2014].

102 Manuel DeLanda, 'Deleuzian Interrogations: A Conversation with Manuel De Landa, John Protevi and Torkild Thanem'. http://www.dif-ferance.org/De Landa-Protevi.pdf [accessed 18 February 2015].

103 Deleuze and Guattari, *Anti-Oedipus*, p. 233.

104 Zaera-Polo, 'The Politics of the Envelope', p. 101.

105 Bruno Latour, 'Why Has Critique Run out of Steam? From Matters of Fact to Matters of Concern', *Critical Inquiry – Special issue on the Future* of Critique 30, no. 2 (2004): 248.

106 Bruno Latour, 'From Realpolitik to DingPolitik: Or How to Make Things Public', in Bruno Latour and Peter Weibel, eds, *Making Things Public: Atmospheres of Democracy* (Cambridge, MA: MIT, 2005).

107 Schumacher, *Autopoiesis I* and *Autopoiesis II*.

108 Schumacher, *Autopoiesis II*, p. 447.

109 Ibid., p. 451.

110 Ibid., p. 472.

111 Schumacher, *Autopoiesis I*, p. 6.

112 Ibid., p. 5.

113 Ibid., p. 29.

114 Rem Koolhaas and Hans Ulrich Obrist, *Project Japan* (Köln: Taschen, 2012).

115 Schumacher, *Autopoiesis II*, p. 458.

116 Ibid.

Chapter 4

1   See, for example, James Riach, 'Zaha Hadid defends Qatar World Cup role following migrant worker deaths', *The Guardian* (25 February 2014). http://www.theguardian.com/world/2014/feb/25/zaha-hadid-qatar-world-cup-migrant-worker-deaths [accessed 2 April 2015].

2   Patrik Schumacher, 'On Parametricism: Georgina Day interviews Patrik Schumacher' (2012). http://www.patrikschumacher.com/Texts/On%20Parametricism_.html [accessed 2 April 2015].

3   Karl Marx, *Capital, Volume I*. trans. Ben Fowkes (London: Penguin, 1976), p. 164.

4   The commodity, writes Marx, 'is nothing but the definite social relation between men themselves which assumes here, for them, the fantastic ["phantasmagorisch" (phantasmagorical) in the original] form of a relation between things'. Marx, *Capital*, p. 165.

5   Theodor Adorno, *In Search of Wagner*, trans. Rodney Livingstone (London and New York: Verso, 2005), p. 74.

6   Moishe Postone, 'Rethinking Marx (in a Post-Marxist World)', in *Reclaiming the Sociological Classics*, ed. Charles Camic (Cambridge, MA: Blackwell Publishers, 1998). http://obeco.no.sapo.pt/mpt.htm [accessed 6 April 2015].

7   Henri Lefebvre, *The Production of Space*, trans. D. Nicholson Smith (Oxford: Blackwell, 2000), pp. 383–4.

8   Ibid., p. 385.

9   Ibid.

10 Postone, 'Rethinking Marx'.

11 Andrew Laing, 'The Future of the Workplace is now' (2004). http://www.degw.com/dnews/ed_5_archive_leader.html [accessed 20 August 2014].

12 Andrew Laing. 'Measuring Workplace Performance' (2005). http://www2.corenetglobal.org/dotCMS/kcoAsset?assetInode=75645 [accessed 20 August 2014].

13 Ibid.

14 Don Tapscott and Anthony D. Williams, *Wikinomics: How Mass Collaboration Changes Everything* (London: Atlantic Books, 2007), p. 1.

15 Ibid.

16 This naturalization of contemporary forms of labour has not, however, gone critically unchallenged. As Jonathan Crary argues, there is in fact a significant

'human cost' in the efforts expended in adapting oneself to such conditions. 'The modeling of one's personal and social identity', he writes, 'has been reorganized to conform to the uninterrupted operation of markets, information networks, and other systems. A 24/7 environment has the semblance of a social world, but it is actually a non-social model of machinic performance and a suspension of living that does not disclose the human cost required to sustain its effectiveness.' Jonathan Crary, *24/7: Late Capitalism and the Ends of Sleep* (London and New York: Verso, 2013), p. 9.

17 Schumacher, 'Research Agenda', p. 78.
18 Boltanski and Chiapello, *The New Spirit of Capitalism*, p. 97.
19 Ibid.
20 Ibid., p. 80.
21 Hayek, *Law, Legislation and Liberty*, p. 52.
22 Don Tapscott, *The Digital Economy: Promise and Peril in the Age of Networked Intelligence* (New York: McGraw-Hill, 1996), p. 53.
23 Ibid.
24 Christopher Meyer and Stan Davis, *It's Alive: The Coming Convergence of Information, Biology, and Business* (New York: Crown Business, 2003), p. 33.
25 Kathleen Melymuka, 'Meeting of the Minds: Technology for business "swarming"'. http://www.computerworld.com/s/article/print/83401/Meeting_of_the_Minds?taxonomyName=Deskto+Applications&taxonomyId=86 [accessed 18 July 2015].
26 Maurizio Lazzarato, 'Immaterial Labour', in *Radical Thought in Italy: A Potential Politics*, ed. Michael Hardt and Paolo Virno (Minneapolis and London: University of Minnesota Press, 1997), p. 132.
27 Ibid.
28 Ibid.
29 Michael Hardt and Antonio Negri, *Empire* (Cambridge, MA: Harvard University Press, 2000), and *Multitude: War and Democracy in the Age of Empire* (London and New York: Penguin, 2004).
30 Hardt and Negri, *Multitude*, p. 108.
31 Ibid.
32 Ibid.
33 Lazzarato, 'Immaterial Labour', p. 137.
34 Ibid., p. 133.
35 Franco "Bifo" Beradi, *The Soul at Work: From Alienation to Autonomy*, trans. Francesca Cadel and Giuseppina Mecchia (Los Angeles, CA: Semiotext(e), 2009), p. 21.
36 Ibid., p. 24.
37 Lazzarato, 'Immaterial Labour', p. 134.
38 Hardt and Negri, *Multitude*, p. 106.

39 Moishe Postone, *Time, Labor and Social Domination: A reinterpretation of Marx's critical theory*, (Cambridge: Cambridge University Press, 1993), p. 16. In 'Rethinking Marx', Postone writes: 'If a critical theory of capitalism is to be adequate to the contemporary world, it must differ in important and basic ways from traditional Marxist critiques of capitalism. And I would argue that Marx's mature social theory provides the point of departure for precisely such a reconceptualized critical theory of capitalism.'

40 Ibid., p. 4.

41 Ibid., p. 16. For Postone, capital is primary as the agent of the production of forms of subjectivity requisite to its production process:

> There is no linear continuum between the demands and conceptions of the working class historically constituting and asserting itself, and the needs, demands, and conceptions that point beyond capitalism. The latter – which might include a need for self-fulfilling activity, for example – would not be limited to the sphere of consumption and to issues of distributive justice, but would call into question the nature of work and the structure of objective constraints that characterize capitalism. This suggests that a critical theory of capitalism and its possible overcoming must entail a theory of the social constitution of such needs and forms of consciousness – one able to address qualitative historical transformations in subjectivity and to understand social movements in these terms. Ibid., p. 37.

42 Postone, 'Rethinking Marx'.

43 Ibid.

44 n.a. *Realisierungswettbewerb BMW Werk Leipzig – Zentralgebäude*, 2001 (translated for the author by Frank Elliot). http://www.bmw-werk-leipzig.de/ [accessed 11 June 2009].

45 Ibid.

46 Ibid.

47 Ibid.

48 Phil Patton, 'Drive-Thru Office', *Metropolis* (July, 2005). http://www. metropolismag.com/story/20050613/drive-thru-office [accessed 29 July 2009].

49 Gail Edmondson, 'BMW Keeps the Home Fires Burning', Businessweek (30 May 2005). http://www.businessweek.com/magazine/content/05_22/b3935087_mz054. htm [accessed 27 July 2009].

50 Peter Drucker used the term 'knowledge work' in reference to increasing demands for communicative interaction between employees, particularly related to the development of Research and Development departments within major corporations, as well as to the rise in office-based work, during the 1960s and 1970s. See, Peter F. Drucker, *Management: Tasks, Responsibilities, Practices* (New York: Harper & Row, 1974).

51 Patton, 'Drive-Thru Office'.

52 The company offers consumers the option to custom-order its vehicles, selecting
    from options such as paint finish, wheels, seating, headlights, dashboards and roof
    type, so as specify the precise configuration of their purchase. Customers can then
    monitor, online, the progress of their order through the factory.

53 Federico Bucci, *Albert Kahn: Architect of Ford* (New York: Princeton Architectural
    Press, 2002), p. 106.

54 Ibid., p. 76.

55 Ibid., p. 52.

56 Edmondson, 'BMW Keeps the Home Fires Burning'.

57 Ludger Pries, 'Cost Competition or Innovation Competition? Lessons from the
    Case of the BMW Plant Location in Leipzig', *Transfer* 1, no. 06 (Spring 2006):
    11–29.

58 Edmondson, 'BMW Keeps the Home Fires Burning'.

59 David Gow, 'From Trabant to BMW: The East Rises Again', *The Guardian*
    (17 May 2005). http://www.theguardian.com/business/2005/may/17/germany.
    internationalnews [accessed 28 July 2009].

60 Pries, 'Cost Competition':

    > Some innovative elements of the Leipzig labour regulation regime are related
    > to the payment system. New output-oriented salary schemes were introduced
    > in certain areas, with a basic salary and bonus payments of up to 21% of
    > the basic salary if production targets are reached. There are also individual
    > bonuses according to performance and goal attainment (with 3% of the basic
    > salary as a general target step, and 6% and 9% as additional steps). The annual
    > bonus payment is oriented around plant seniority – from 25% (less than a year
    > working at BMW) up to 100% (three or more years of BMW service), with the
    > start of production in 2005 as the starting date.

61 In his study of the implementation of the working practices at BMW Ludger, Pries
    notes:

    > From the very beginning, and as a crucial part of the Leipzig offer, the weekly
    > factory running time was designed with a wide range of working hours (from
    > 60 to 140 hours). The possibility of a working scheme with two and three shifts
    > was agreed upon, and even the two-shift scheme allowed for a wide range of
    > working hours (from a model with 8 shifts of 8 hours, or 64 hours weekly;
    > up to a model with 11 shifts of 9 hours, or 135 to 144 hours weekly). Based
    > on different systems of short, medium, and long working time accounts, this
    > system allows the flexible adaptation of the working and factory running
    > rhythms to the market conditions (with up to 30 Saturday shifts per year
    > without additional payments). Pries, 'Cost Competition'.

62   n.a. *Die Zeit* (13 November 2003), cited in Vedrana Miljak and Martin Heidenreich,
     'The Leipzig Economic Region' (June 2004). http://www.cetro.uni-oldenburg.de/
     de/41241.html [accessed 27 July 2009]:

> Flexibility is the key-word in the search for the secret of east German success.
> Never mind the fact that workers in the east work 100 hours more per year
> than their western counterparts: They are also prepared to accept inconvenient
> working hours. In this way BMW negotiated a "BMW-formula for work"
> with the IG-Metall for its Leipzig plant. Their aim was flexible working-hours
> to increase the usage of the factory and thereby higher productivity. There
> are flexible weekly working-hours, which can vary between 38 and 44 hours
> depending on the number of orders, week-ends included. ... In the east
> employees and employers are forming a kind of "community of fate".

63   John Robert Mullin, 'Henry Ford and Field and Factory: An Analysis of the Ford
     Sponsored Village Industries – Experiment in Michigan, 1918-1941'. http://works.
     bepress.com/cgi/viewcontent.cgi?article=1021&context=john_mullin [accessed
     27 April 2010].

64   See, Patrizia Bonifazio and Paolo Scrivano, *Olivetti Builds* (Milan: Skira, 2001).

65   As became evident from the extensive lay-offs resulting from the global
     recession when, in November 2008, 500 temporary workers were dismissed
     from employment at the Leipzig plant. Source: Ludwig Niethammer, 'Germany:
     Temporary Workers are First Victims of Recession', World Socialist Web Site
     (12 January 2009). http://www.wsws.org/articles/2009/jan2009/germ-j12.shtml
     [accessed 28 August 2009].

66   n.a. 'BMW Annual Report 2004'. http://www.bmwgroup.com/e/0_0_www_
     bmwgroup_com/investor_relations/finanzberichte/geschaeftsberichte/2004/pdfs/
     werden_werkes.pdf [accessed 24 August 2009].

67   'Our ambition at BMW was to urbanize the site. As an urban phenomenon, it
     could not remain within the language of the factory sheds and the production
     lines.' Zaha Hadid in Todd Gannon, (ed.), *Zaha Hadid: BMW Central Building,
     Leipzig, Germany* (New York and Princeton Architectural Press, 2006), p. 91.

68   Patrik Schumacher in Patton, 'Drive-Thru Office'.

69   Zaha Hadid in Obrist, *Zaha Hadid and Hans Ulrich Obrist*, p. 84.

70   Ibid., pp. 64–5.

71   Ibid., p. 64.

72   Ibid., pp. 64–5.

73   Ibid., p. 65.

74   Gannon, *Zaha Hadid*, p. 20. 'All of the structure', Schumacher explains, 'was
     oriented to trace the lines of movement through the building, to emphasize these
     linear trajectories ... . You will notice many instances where the steel roof beams
     are curved to follow the flows. These are not the most efficient ways to span these

distances, but as the structure is such a major component of the visual field, we felt it necessary that it work beyond its role as support to become an orienting device within the space.' Ibid., p. 92.

75   Manfredo Tafuri and Francesco Dal Co, *Modern Architecture*, Vol. 1 (London and Milan: Faber and Faber/Electa, 1980), p. 144.

76   Ibid.

77   Schumacher, 'Arguing for Elegance', p. 30.

78   This is not, of course, to say that it will always actually succeed in this work, or that, in this case, workers will necessarily put the interest of the 'community' of BMW before their own, or not wage struggles against it, as recent campaigns against the company's extensive use of temporary contracts have demonstrated. See, for instance, 'BMW Solves Temp Dispute' (2012). http://www.staffingindustry. com/eng/Research-Publications/Daily-News/Germany-BMW-solves-temp-dispute [accessed 6 May 2015].

79   Ole Scheeren, 'Introduction: Made in China', in *CCTV by OMA* (Tokyo: A+U Publishing, 2005), p. 5.

80   Koolhaas, *Delirious New York*, p. 237.

81   Ibid.

82   Ibid., p. 243.

83   Rem Koolhaas, 'Bigness: The Problem of Large', in *S,M,L,XL*, ed. Rem Koolhaas and Bruce Mau (New York: The Monacelli Press, 1995).

84   Ibid., p. 503.

85   Ibid., p. 502.

86   Ibid., p. 501.

87   Ibid., p. 511.

88   Ibid., p. 502.

89   Project description at OMA website. http://www.oma.eu/projects/1996/universal-headquarters [accessed 28 November 2014].

90   Ibid.

91   Ross Exo Adams, 'Natura Urbans, Natura Urbanata: Ecological Urbanism, Circulation, and the Immunization of Nature', *Environment and Planning D: Society and Space* 32, no. 1 (2014): 21.

92   Ibid.

93   Project description at OMA website.

94   Rem Koolhaas, in 'Rem Koolhaas: An Obsessive Compulsion towards the Spectacular', *Der Spiegel* (18 July 2008). http://www.spiegel.de/international/world/0,1518,566655-2,00.html [accessed 28 November 2014].

95   Project description at OMA website.

96   Koolhaas, *Delirious New York*, p. 87.

97   Ibid., p. 91.

98   Koolhaas, *CCTV by OMA*, pp. 10, 12.

99   Ian Buruma, 'Don't be fooled – China is not squeaky clean', *The Guardian*, Tuesday 30 July 2002. http://www.guardian.co.uk/world/2002/jul/30/china.features11 [accessed 28 November 2014].

100   Ibid.

101   Koolhaas *CCTV by OMA*, p. 12.

102   Ibid.

103   Ibid.

104   Ibid., p. 4.

105   Ibid.

106   Ibid., p. 5.

107   Giovanni Arrighi, *Adam Smith in Beijing: Lineages of the Twenty-First Century* (London and New York: Verso, 2007), p. 353.

108   Ibid., p. 355.

109   Wang Hui, *The End of the Revolution: China and the Limits of Modernity* (London and New York: Verso, 2000) p. 19.

110   Ibid.

111   Ibid.

112   Ibid., p. 7.

113   As Yuezhi Zhao has argued in *Communication in China: Political Economy, Power, and Conflict* (Lanham, Maryland, and Plymouth, UK: Rowman & Littlefield, 2008),

> The Hu Jintao leadership, recognizing that social instability had reached the "red line" after it came to power in late 2002 and assumed full control of the Chinese state in late 2004 (when Hu assumed control of the Chinese military), has intensified its attempts to stabilize such a fluid, and indeed potentially explosive, social field for more sustainable development of the Chinese political economy. p. 7.

114   Lisa Rofel, *Desiring China: Experiments in Neoliberalism, Sexuality, and Public Culture* (Durham and London: Duke University Press, 2007), p. 20.

115   Aihwa Ong, *Neoliberalism as Exception: Mutations in Citizenship and Sovereignty* (Durham and London: Duke University Press, 2006), p. 3.

116   Ibid., p. 223.

117   Zhao, *Communication in China*, p. 34.

118   Ole Scheeren, Interview with FeedMeCoolShit (2006). http://www.feedmecoolshit. com/interviews-archive/ole-scheeren/ [accessed 20 November 2014].

119   Scheeren, *CCTV by OMA*, p. 5.

120   Rem Koolhaas, 'Beijing Manifesto', *Wired* 6, no. 11 (2003): 124.

121   Ibid.

122   Zhao, *Communication in China*, p. 7.

123   Ibid., p. 84.

124 Ying Zhu, *Two Billion Eyes: The Story of China Central Television* (New York: The New Press, 2012).

125 Shu Taifeng, 'CCTV Halts Decades-long Practice of "Remuneration though Invoices"', *Caijing* (26 September). http://english.caijing.com.cn/2011-09-26/110874570.htm [accessed 11 December 2014].

126 Ibid.

127 Roberto Gargiani, *Rem Koolhaas/OMA: The Construction of Merveilles* (London and New York: Routledge, 2008), p. 223.

128 Koolhaas, *S,M,L,XL*, p. 336.

129 Ibid., p. 336.

130 Ibid., p 337.

131 Ibid., p. 341.

132 Gargiani, *Rem Koolhaas/OMA*.

133 Koolhaas, *CCTV by OMA*, p. 50.

134 Ibid.

135 Ibid., p. 52.

136 Zhu, *Two Billion Eyes*, p. 54. Indicative of the risk that CCTV might, on the other hand, appear to have too readily embraced the values (or lack thereof) of marketization, is an incident reported Yuezhi Zhao:

> CCTV carried [the] objective of capital accumulation to the extreme during the school hostage crisis in Russia in September 2004. While reporting on the tragedy, CCTV4 concurrently flashed a multiple-choice question at the bottom of the television screen, asking its viewers to guess the correct death toll and to send in their answers as text messages on their mobile phones. Three leading state companies, CCTV, China Mobile, and China Unicorn, shared in the profit collected from mobile phone customers in this business scheme. *Communication in China*, p. 79.

137 Koolhaas, *CCTV by OMA*, p. 86.

138 Ibid.

139 Zhao, *Communication in China*, p. 39.

140 Ibid.

141 Ibid.

Chapter 5

1 n.a. 'History of the Centre Pompidou', official website of the Centre Pompidou. https://www.centrepompidou.fr/en/The-Centre-Pompidou#586 [accessed 5 June 2015].

2   Richard Rogers, competition submission text, cited in Nathan Silver, *The Making of Beaubourg: A Building Biography of the Centre Pompidou, Paris* (Cambridge, MA and London: MIT Press, 1994), p. 33.

3   John Partridge 'Pompodolium', *Architectural Review* (May, 1977): 272.

4   Ibid.

5   Interviewed in 2013, Rogers said of the inspiration for the Pompidou that 'in a sense, it was a "Fun Palace," using a very well know phrase of Cedric Price and Joan Littlewood's'. http://www.dezeen.com/2013/07/26/richard-rogers-centre-pompidou-revolution-1968/ [accessed 7 June 2015].

6   Richard Rogers and Renzo Piano, cited in Rebecca J. DeRoo, *The Museum Establishment and Contemporary Art: The Politics of Artistic Display in France after 1968* (New York: Cambridge University Press, 2006), p. 177.

7   Ibid.

8   Cited in DeRoo, *The Museum Establishment and Contemporary Art*, pp. 177–8.

9   Partridge, 'Pompodolium', p. 286.

10   Cited in DeRoo, *The Museum Establishment and Contemporary Art*, p. 170.

11   Ibid., p. 175.

12   Theodor Adorno, *Aesthetic Theory*, ed. Gretel Adorno and Rolf Tiedermann, trans. R. Hullot-Kentor (London and New York: Continuum, 2002), p. 16.

13   Ibid.

14   Ibid., p. 17.

15   Jean Baudrillard, *Simulacra and Simulation*, trans. Sheila Faria Glaser (Ann Arbor, MI: University of Michigan Press, 1994), p. 69.

16   Ewan Branda, *The Architecture of Information at Plateau Beaubourg*, University of California, Los Angeles, PhD thesis (2012). https://escholarship.org/uc/item/0ww309s3#page-1 [accessed 7 June 2015].

17   Richard Rogers, interviewed by Antoine Picon, 1987, cited in Branda, *Architecture of Information*, p. 82.

18   Adorno, *Aesthetic Theory*, p. 16.

19   Bishop, *Artificial Hells*, pp. 77–104.

20   Ibid., p. 78.

21   Ibid., p. 79.

22   Reyner Banham, 'Enigma of the Rue du Renard', *Architectural Review* (May, 1977): 277.

23   Ibid.

24   Ibid.

25   Alan Colquhoun, 'Plateau Beaubourg', *Architectural Design* 47, no. 2 (1977), reprinted in *Collected Essays in Architectural Criticism* (Cambridge, MA: MIT Press, 1981), p. 110.

26   Ibid., p. 111.

27   Baudrillard, *Simulacra and Simulation*, p. 64. This 'truth' has subsequently become amply evident as a spatial trope of architectural form in numerous projects claiming to be based upon the Möbius strip or loop. See, for instance, Peter Eisenman's Max Reinhardt Haus, 1992–93, or UN Studio's Möbius House Het Gooi, 1993–98.

28   Ibid., p. 74.

29   Ibid., p. 61.

30   Ibid., p. 64.

31   Ibid., p. 61.

32   Ibid., p. 66.

33   Ibid.

34   Ibid., p. 71.

35   Lyotard, *The Postmodern Condition*, p. 15.

36   Jean Baudrillard, *In the Shadow of the Silent Majorities*, trans P. Foss, P. Patton and J. Johnston (New York, NY: Semiotext(e), 1983), p. 25.

37   Ibid., p. 30.

38   Ibid., p. 31.

39   Lyotard, *The Postmodern Condition*, p. 4.

40   Ibid., p. 11.

41   Ibid., p. 62.

42   Lyotard writes that 'one's mobility in relation to these language game effects (language games, of course, are what this is all about) is tolerable … it is even solicited by regulatory mechanisms, and in particular by the self-adjustments the system undertakes in order to improve its performance. It may even be said that the system can and must encourage such movement to the extent that it combats its own entropy; the novelty of an unexpected "move"… can supply the system with that increased performativity it forever demands and consumes.' Ibid., p. 57.

43   Ibid., p. xxiv.

44   Ibid.

45   Ibid., p. 63.

46   Ibid.

47   Patrik Schumacher, 'The Historical Pertinence of Parametricism and the Prospect of a Free Market Urban Order', in *The Politics of Parametricism: Digital Technologies in Architecture*, ed. Matthew Poole and Manuel Shvartzberg (London, New Delhi, New York and Sydney: Bloomsbury, 2015), p. 35.

48   Ibid., pp. 40–1.

49   Ibid., p. 31.

50   Lyotard, *The Postmodern Condition*, pp. 11–12.

51   Debord, *The Society of the Spectacle*.

52 n.a. 'Istanbul in Numbers'. http://www.greatistanbul.com/numbers.htm [accessed 3 July 2015].

53 Cihan Tug˘al, 'The Greening of Istanbul', *New Left Review* 51 (May/June 2008): 65.

54 The nature and extent of these polarities, and of popular feeling against the commercial development of land in Turkey, became amply evident in 2013, during the protests against the destruction of Istanbul's Gezi Park in order to build a shopping mall. For an account of the meaning and significance of these protests see Bülent Gökay and Ilia Xypolia, eds, *Reflections on Taksim – Gezi Park: Protests in Turkey* (2013). http://www.keele.ac.uk/journal-globalfaultlines/publications/geziReflections.pdf [accessed 30 September 2015].

55 'Meydan – New Shopping Square in Istanbul'. http://www.meydan.metro-mam.com/servlet/PB/menu/1025929_l2_yno/1281705334186.html [accessed 12 August 2010].

56 This broad strategy is evident, for instance, in the group's investment in the building and provision of a day-care centre for the children of its workers in the garment district of Dhaka, Bangladesh. This was lauded by the German ambassador there as 'a most welcome display of social responsibility'. 'Germany's Metro Group opens child day care centre in Bangladesh'. http://www.german-info.com/gsa_shownews.php?pid=595 [accessed 12 August 2010].

57 Tuğal, 'The Greening of Istanbul', p. 78.

58 Zaera-Polo, 'The Politics of the Envelope', pp. 76–105.

59 Ibid., p. 84.

60 Ibid.

61 Ibid.

62 Alejandro Zaera-Polo and Farshid Moussavi, 'Foreign Office Architects: A Conversation', in *Meydan Shopping Square: A New Prototype by FOA*, ed. Michael Cesarz and Manina Ferreira-Erlenbach (Berlin: Jovis, 2007), p. 57.

63 Ibid., p. 11.

64 Ibid., p. 15.

65 Ibid., p. 44.

66 Ibid., p. 59.

67 Zaera-Polo, 'The Politics of the Envelope', p. 76.

68 Ibid., p. 77.

69 Ibid., p. 82.

> As public infrastructures become increasingly procured by the private sector, and the private sector becomes increasingly concerned with the public nature of retail developments, the degree of engagement between the flat-horizontal envelopes and the surrounding urban fabric intensifies. As flat-horizontal envelopes keep getting larger to provide for a burgeoning urban population

and the consequent growth of consumers, goods and transient populations, an interesting dynamic powered by the contradiction between permeability and energy-efficiency emerges.

70 'Making Things Public: Atmospheres of Democracy' is the name of an exhibition curated by Bruno Latour and Peter Weibel at ZKM Karlsruhe in March 2005. It is also the title of the book of the exhibition edited by Latour and Weibel, Cambridge, MA: MIT, 2005.

71 Latour, 'From Realpolitik to DingPolitik: Or How to Make Things Public', p. 4.

72 Ibid., p. 5.

73 Zaera-Polo, 'The Politics of the Envelope', p. 101. Zaera-Polo defines Sloterdijk's 'explicitation' in the same essay as follows:

> Explicitation is the term used by Sloterdijk as an alternative process to revolution and emancipation. The history of explicitation is made increasingly intelligible in the spheres and objects to which we are attached. The categories of the French revolution and left and right, both with their particular techniques of classification and of positioning, no longer correspond to the order of things that is no longer hierarchical but heterarchical. Whether we talk about carbon footprints, deregulation, genetically modified foods, congestion pricing or public transport, these issues give rise to a variety of political configurations that exceed the left/right distinction. The left/right divide still exists, but has been diluted by a multitude of alternative attitudes. p. 79.

74 Ibid.

75 Ibid., p. 104.

76 Ibid., p. 103.

77 Ibid., p. 104.

78 Ibid., p. 103.

79 Thompson, *On Growth and Form*, p. 7.

80 Benjamin Noys, 'The Discreet Charm of Bruno Latour', in *(Mis)readings of Marx in Continental Philosophy*, ed. Jernej Habjan and Jessica Whyte (Basingstoke: Palgrave, 2014), p. 199.

81 As David Keuning reported in an essay published in *Mark*, in 2008, 'Shopping Permitted: Meydan shopping mall in Istanbul, Turkey': 'The complex may look like a carefully designed public space, yet nothing could be further from the truth. I notice this again as I attempt to climb one of the green hills and a guard call tells me off for the second time.' 'It is definitely the idea that visitors can walk on the grass roofs,' Moussavi replies when I tell her about this, 'and it's strange that you were called back when climbing them. The same happened in Yokohama though. The undulating roof was intended to walk on, but soon after completion

fences and notice boards appeared, saying that people were not allowed on some parts of the roof because of their personal safety. But people ignored them, even in Japan, and over time the notice boards disappeared again. Now anyone can go anywhere they want.' 'Shopping Permitted: Meydan shopping mall in Istanbul, Turkey (Foreign Office Architects)' *Mark*, (February/March 2008). http://www. davidkeuning.com/article.php?$lang=en&$w=i&$t=1371&$a=25 [accessed 10 August 2010].

82   Marikka Trotter, 'Get Fit: Morphosis's New Academic Building for the Cooper Union', *Harvard Design Magazine* (Fall/Winter 2009/10, Number 31). http:// www.harvarddesignmagazine.org/issues/31/get-fit-morphosiss-new-academic-building-for-the-cooper-union [accessed 11 July 2015].

83   Ibid.

84   Ibid.

85   Ibid.

86   Joel Rose, 'Cooper Union Students Fight For Freedom From Tuition', NPR (10 June 2013). http://www.npr.org/2013/06/10/190427334/cooper-union-students-fight-for-freedom-from-tuition; James B. Stewart, 10 May 2013, 'How Cooper Union's Endowment Failed in Its Mission'. http://www.nytimes.com/2013/05/11/business/how-cooper-unions-endowment-failed-in-its-mission.html?_r=0 [accessed 16 July 2015].

87   A fact of which all mention has been removed from the school's website. The Cooper Union, 'Tuition & Student Fees'. http://cooper.edu/about/finance-and-administration/financial-faq/tuition-student-fees#1 [accessed 16 July 2015].

88   John Browne, et al., 'Securing a Sustainable Future for Higher Education' (2010), p. 8. https://www.gov.uk/government/uploads/system/uploads/attachment_data/file/422565/bis-10-1208-securing-sustainable-higher-education-browne-report.pdf [accessed 16 July 2015].

89   Ibid., p. 25.

90   Ibid.

91   Ibid., p. 4.

92   Ibid., p. 16.

93   Ibid.

94   Lyotard, *The Postmodern Condition*, p. 48.

95   Ibid., p. 52.

96   Ibid.

97   Ibid.

98   Ibid., p. 48.

99   Jeanette Johansson-Young, 'The BIG picture: A case for a flexible learning agenda at Ravensbourne', internal publication of Ravensbourne College (2006). http://intranet.rave.ac.uk/quality/docs/LTR060203-flexlearn_4.pdf [accessed 21 July 2015].

100 Ibid.

101 Department of Education and Skills, 'The future of higher education' (2003). www.
     dfes.gov.uk/hegateway/strategy/hestrategy/pdfs/DfES-Higher
     Education.pdf; HEFCE, 'HEFCE strategy for e-learning', 2005. www.hefce.ac.uk/
     pubs/hefce/2005/ [Accessed 21 July 2015].

102 A. M. Bliuc, P. Goodyear and R. A. Ellis, 'Research Focus and Methodological
     Choices in Studies into Students' Experiences of Blended Learning in Higher
     Education', *The Internet and Higher Education* 10, no. 4 (2007): 231–44, cited in
     Paul Harris, John Connolly and Luke Feeney, 'Blended Learning: Overview and
     Recommendations for Successful Implementation', *Industrial and Commercial
     Training* 41, no. 3 (2009): 156.

103 DEGW, 'User Brief for the New Learning Landscape', 2004, cited in Johansson-
     Young, 'The BIG picture'.

104 Miles Metcalfe, Ruth Carlow, Remmert de Vroorne, and Roger Rees, 'Final Report
     for the Designs on Learning Project', internal publication of Ravensbourne College
     (2008), p. 3.

105 Ibid.

106 Ibid. The report recommends that this practice 'should become "a normative
     component of creative education"'.

107 John Worthington/DEGW, 'Univer-Cities in their Cities: Conflict and
     Collaboration', paper presented at OECD Education Management Infrastructure
     Division, Higher Education Spaces & Places for Learning, Education and
     Knowledge Exchange, University of Latvia, Riga: 6–8 December, 2009. http://
     www.oecd.lu.lv/materials/john-worthington.pdf [accessed 21 July 2015].

108 Ibid.

109 Shirley Dugdale, 'Space Strategies for the New Learning Landscape',
     EDUCAUSE Review 44, no. 2 (March/April 2009). http://www.educause.
     edu/EDUCAUSE+Review/EDUCAUSEReviewMagazineVolume44/
     SpaceStrategiesfortheNewLearni/163820 [accessed 21 July 2015].

110 Worthington/DEGW, 'Univer-Cities', p. 14.

111 Lucy Hodges, 'Ravensbourne college gets ready to move in to eye-catching new
     premises', *The Independent* (Thursday, 15 July 2010). http://www.independent.
     co.uk/news/education/higher/ravensbourne-college-gets-ready-to-move-in-to-
     eyecatching-new-premises-2026802.html [accessed 21 July 2015].

112 Alejandro Zaera-Polo, quoted in Graham Bizley, 'FOA's peninsula patterns for
     Ravensbourne College', *BD Online* (29 July 2009). http://www.bdonline.co.uk/
     practice-and-it/foa's-peninsula-patterns-for-ravensbourne-college/3144928.article
     [accessed 21 July 2015].

113 Worthington/DEGW, 'Univer-Cities', p. 16.

114 Layton Reid, Ravensbourne college's head of architecture, as recorded at
     Ravensbourne's media briefing by the author, 9 September 2010.

Chapter 6

1 The publicity brochure for the college states that

> the new building has a unique tessellated outer skin, inspired by the Penrose
> tiling pattern: a multidirectional surface free of conventional symmetry, or
> any obvious reference to what's happening inside. The ambiguity is more than
> superficial; the radical style far more than a gesture. Both signal the equally
> innovative approach within. Because here, we've removed the walls between
> departments. Literally. Instead, our interior space has been designed to
> encourage flow and interaction between disciplines.

   n.a., 'We Are the Future', 2010, unpaginated.
2 Zaera-Polo, 'The Politics of the Envelope', p. 104.
3 Ibid., p. 89.
4 Ibid.
5 Ibid.
6 Alejandro Zaera-Polo, 'Patterns, Fabrics, Prototypes, Tessellations', *Architectural
   Design, Special Issue: Patterns of Architecture* 79, no. 6 (November/December
   2009): 18–27, 22.
7 Zaera-Polo, 'The Politics of the Envelope', p. 88.
8 See Deleuze and Guattari, 'Year Zero: Faciality', in *A Thousand Plateaus:
   Capitalism and Schizophrenia*, p. 198.
9 Zaera-Polo, 'The Politics of the Envelope', p. 89.
10 Ibid., p. 90.
11 Ibid., p. 89.
12 Ibid., p. 27.
13 Moussavi, *The Function of Form*.
14 Ibid., p. 7.
15 Ibid., p. 9.
16 Ibid., p. 13.
17 Ibid., p. 16.
18 Ibid., p. 18.
19 Ibid., pp. 19–20.
20 Ibid., p. 34.
21 Farshid Moussavi, in Nico Saieh, 'Venice Biennale 2012: Architecture and its
   Affects/Farshid Moussavi', *ArchDaily* (4 September 2012). http://www.archdaily.
   com/269585/venice-biennale-2012-farshid-moussavi/ [accessed 4 August 2015].
22 Massumi, *Parables for the Virtual*.
23 Ibid., p. 27.
24 'We paint, sculpt, compose and write sensations. As percepts, sensations are not
   perceptions referring to an object (reference): if they resemble something it is with

a resemblance produced with their own methods; and the smile on the canvas is made solely with colors, lines, shadow, and light. ... Sensation refers only to its material: it is the percept of affect of the material itself.' Gilles Deleuze and Félix Guattari, *What is Philosophy?* trans. Graham Burchell and Hugh Tomlinson (London and New York: Verso, 1994), p. 166.

25 Gilles Deleuze, *Francis Bacon: The Logic of Sensation*, trans. Daniel W. Smith (London and New York: Continuum, 2003), p. 36.

26 Ibid.

27 Ibid.

28 Ibid., p. 12.

29 Ibid.

30 Ibid.

31 Ibid.

32 Simon O'Sullivan, 'The Aesthetics of Affect: Thinking art Beyond Representation', *Angelaki* 6, no. 3 (December 2001): 125–35.

33 Ibid., p. 125.

34 Ibid.

35 Ibid.

36 Ibid., p. 126.

37 Ibid.

38 Ibid., p. 129.

39 Ibid.

40 Lavin, *Kissing Architecture*, p. 1.

41 Ibid., p. 4.

42 Ibid.

43 Ibid., p. 14.

44 Ibid., p. 30.

45 Lars Spuybroek, *The Sympathy of Things: Ruskin and the Ecology of Design* (Rotterdam: V2_Publishing, 2011), p. 174.

46 Ibid., p. 209.

47 Ibid., p. 74.

48 Ibid.

49 Ibid., p. 67.

50 Ibid., p. 96.

51 Ibid., p. 97.

52 Ibid., p. 264.

53 Fredric Jameson, *Marxism and Form: Twentieth-Century Dialectical Theories of Literature* (Princeton, NJ: Princeton University Press, 1971), p. 188.

54 Fredric Jameson, *Postmodernism, or The Cultural Logic of Late Capitalism* (London and New York: Verso, 1991), p. 83.

55 Ibid., p. 80.

56 Ibid., p. 81.

57 Ibid., p. 82.

58 Ibid., p. 83.

59 Ibid.

60 Ibid.

61 Ibid., p. 80.

62 David Cunningham, 'The Architecture of Money: Jameson, Abstraction and Form', in *The Political Unconscious of Architecture: Re-opening Jameson's Narrative*, ed. Nadir Lahiji (Farnham, England and Burlington, USA: Ashgate, 2012), pp. 37–55.

63 Ibid., p. 47.

64 At dangerous intersections, nervous impulses flow through him in rapid succession, like the energy from a battery. Baudelaire speaks of a man who plunges into the crowd as into a reservoir of electric energy. Circumscribing the experience of the shock, he calls this man "a kaleidoscope endowed with consciousness." Whereas Poe's passers-by cast glances in all directions, seemingly without cause, today's pedestrians are obliged to look about them so that they can be aware of traffic signals. Thus, technology has subjected the human sensorium to a complex kind of training. Walter Benjamin, 'On Some Motifs in Baudelaire', in *Illuminations*, ed. Hannah Arendt, trans. Harry Zorn (London: Pimlico, 1999), p. 171.

65 Jameson, *Postmodernism*, p. 82.

66 Ibid.

67 Zaera-Polo 'The Politics of the Envelope', p. 79.

68 Terry Eagleton, *The Ideology of the Aesthetic* (Malden and Oxford: Blackwell, 1990), p. 13.

69 Ibid., p. 15.

70 Ibid., p. 20.

71 The schemata of the *Critique of Pure Reason* posits 'an art concealed in the depths of the human soul, whose true modes of action we shall only ever with difficulty discover and unveil.' Kant, *Critique of Pure Reason*, p. 103.

72 Seyla Benhabib, *Critique, Norm, and Utopia: A Study of the Foundations of Critical Theory* (New York: Columbia University Press, 1986), p. 82.

73 Benhabib, *Critique, Norm, and Utopia*, p. 81–2.

74 Ibid., p. 47.

75 Max Horkheimer, 'Traditional and Critical Theory', in *Critical Theory: Selected Essays*, trans. Matthew J. O'Conell et al. (New York: Continuum, 2002), p. 200.

76 Adorno, *Aesthetic Theory*, p. 462.

77 Ibid., p. 338.

78 Ibid., p. 129. Adorno writes,

> What transcends the factual in the artwork, its spiritual content, cannot be pinned down to what is individually, sensually given but is, rather, constituted by way of this empirical givenness. This defines the mediatedness of the

truth content. The spiritual content does not hover above the work's facture; rather, artworks transcend their factuality through their facture, through the consistency of their elaboration.

79 Ibid., p. 128.

80 Ibid.

81 Jameson, *Marxism and Form*, p. 188.

82 Fredric Jameson, *Jameson on Jameson: Conversations on Cultural Marxism*, ed. Ian Buchanan (Durham and London: Duke University Press, 2007), p. 105.

83 By 'machinic perception' I refer to the automated operations through which information – gathered and appropriated from personalized mobile technologies, surveillance cameras, web-browsing histories, social media, RFID tracking devices, biometric scanning, banking and shopping activity etc – is recorded, processed and ordered for the various corporate and governmental agents making use of this data. John Johnston uses the term 'machinic vision', in his essay of the same name, which he defines as 'not only an environment of interacting machines and human-machine systems but a field of decoded perceptions that, whether or not produced by or issuing from these machines, assume their full intelligibility only in relation to them'. I am drawing on, but adapting Johnston's term to refer to the subsequent further developments in the autonomization of perception from humans, and to the fact that vision is only one mode through which this perception 'senses' the informatic environment in which it is embedded. John Johnston, 'Machinic Vision', *Critical Enquiry* 26 (Autumn 1999): 27.

84 David Lyon, 'Surveillance, Snowden, and Big Data: Capacities, Consequences, Critique', *Big Data & Society* (July to December, 2014): 4.

85 Claudia Aradau, 'The Signature of Security: Big Data, Anticipation, Surveillance', *Radical Philosophy* (May/June 2015): 25.

86 As David Cunningham has recently cautioned, there have been significant errors in 'misrecognising the degree to which neo-liberalism does not in fact "negate" forms of planning to anything like the extent that its rhetoric suggests. What else, after all, is "logistics"?', 'Architecture, the Built and the Idea of Socialism' in Nadir Lahiji, (ed.), *Can Architecture be an Emancipatory Project?: Dialogues on the Left* (Winchester, UK, Washington, USA: Zero Books), forthcoming.

Conclusion

1 Dardot and Laval, *The New Way of the World*, p. 3.

2 Ibid., p. 4.

3 Theodor Adorno, *Negative Dialectics*, trans. E. B. Ashton (London: Routledge, 1973), p. 19.

Bibliography

Adams, R. E., 'Natura Urbans, Natura Urbanata: Ecological Urbanism, Circulation, and the Immunization of Nature', *Environment and Planning D: Society and Space*, vol. 32, no. 1 (2014), pp. 12–29.

Adorno, T., *Negative Dialectics*, trans. E. B. Ashton, London: Routledge, 1973.

Adorno, T., *In Search of Wagner*, trans. Rodney Livingstone, London and New York: Verso, 2005.

Adorno, T., *Aesthetic Theory*, trans. R. Hullot-Kentor, London and New York: Continuum, 2002.

Adorno, T. and M. Horkheimer, *Dialectic of Enlightenment*, trans. J. Cumming, London: Verso, 1979.

Amnesty International, *The Dark Side of Migration: Spotlight on Qatar's Construction Sector Ahead of the World Cup*, London: Amnesty International Publications, 2013.

Andreotti, L., 'Unfaithful Reflections: Re-actualizing Benjamin's aestheticism thesis', in N. Lahiji (ed.), *Architecture Against the Post-Political: Essays in Reclaiming the Critical Project*, London and New York: Routledge, 2014, pp. 41–52.

Aradau, C., 'The Signature of Security: Big Data, Anticipation, Surveillance', *Radical Philosophy* 191 (May/June 2015), pp. 21–8.

Arrighi, G., *Adam Smith in Beijing: Lineages of the Twenty-First Century*, London and New York: Verso, 2007.

Baird, G., ' "Criticality" and its Discontents', *Harvard Design Magazine* 21 (Fall 2004/ Winter 2005), pp. 16–21.

Banham, R., 'Enigma of the Rue du Renard', *Architectural Review* (May 1977), pp. 277–8.

Banham, R., *Scenes in America Deserta*, London: Thames & Hudson, 1982.

Banham, R., *The Architecture of the Well-tempered Environment*, 2nd edn, Chicago: University of Chicago Press, 1984.

Banham, R., *A Critic Writes: Essays by Reyner Banham*, Berkeley and Los Angeles, CA: University of California Press, 1999.

Banham, R., *Los Angeles: The Architecture of the Four Ecologies*, Berkeley and Los Angeles, CA: University of California Press, 2001.

Barry, N., 'The Tradition of Spontaneous Order', *Literature of Liberty*, vol. 5, no. 2 (Summer 1982), pp. 7–58.

Baudrillard, J. / The French Group, 'The Environmental Witch-Hunt', in R. Banham (ed.), *The Aspen Papers: Twenty Years of Design Theory from the International Design Conference in Aspen*, New York: Praeger, 1974, pp. 208–10.

Baudrillard, J., *In the Shadow of the Silent Majorities*, trans P. Foss, P. Patton and J. Johnston, New York, NY: Semiotext(e), 1983.

Baudrillard, J., 'The Ecstasy of Communication', in H. Foster (ed.), *The Anti-Aesthetic: Essays on Postmodern Culture*, Washington: Bay Press, 1983, pp. 126–34.

Baudrillard, J., *America*, trans. G. Dyer, London and New York: Verso, 1988.

Baudrillard, J., *Symbolic Exchange and Death*, trans. I. H. Grant, London: Sage, 1993.

Baudrillard, J., *Simulacra and Simulation*, trans. Sheila Faria Glaser, Ann Arbor, MI: University of Michigan Press, 1994.

Becker, G. S., 'Human Capital', *The Concise Encyclopaedia of Economics*, http://www.econlib.org/library/Enc/HumanCapital.html [accessed 20 April 2014].

Beckmann, J., ed. *The Virtual Dimension: Architecture, Representation and Crash Culture*, New York: Princeton Architectural Press, 1998.

Benhabib, S., *Critique, Norm, and Utopia: A Study of the Foundations of Critical Theory*, New York: Columbia University Press, 1986.

Benjamin, W., *Illuminations*, ed. H. Arendt, trans. H. Zorn, London: Pimlico, 1999.

Beradi, F., *The Soul at Work: From Alienation to Autonomy*, trans. Francesca Cadel and Giuseppina Mecchia, Los Angeles, CA: Semiotext(e), 2009.

Bishop, C., *Artificial Hells: Participatory Art and the Politics of Spectatorship*, London and New York: Verso, 2012.

Bizley, G., 'FOA's peninsula patterns for Ravensbourne College', *BD Online*, 29 July 2009, http://www.bdonline.co.uk/practice-and-it/foa's-peninsula-patterns-for-ravensbourne-college/3144928.article [accessed 21 July 2015].

Bladel, J. P., 'Against Polanyi-Centrism: Hayek and the Re-emergence of "Spontaneous Order"', *The Quarterly Journal of Austrian Economics*, vol. 8, no. 4 (Winter 2005), pp. 15–30.

Bliuc, A. M., Goodyear, P. and Ellis R. A., 'Research Focus and Methodological Choices in Studies into Students' Experiences of Blended Learning in Higher Education', *The Internet and Higher Education*, vol. 10, no. 4 (2007), pp. 231–44.

Bonifazio, P., and Scrivano P., *Olivetti Builds*, Milan: Skira, 2001.

Borch, C., *Niklas Luhmann*, London and New York: Routledge, 2011.

Bourdieu, P., *The Field of Cultural Production: Essays on Art and Literature*, Columbia Cambridge: Polity Press, 1993.

Boltanski, L. and Chiapello E., *The New Spirit of Capitalism*, trans. G. Elliot, London and New York: Verso, 2007.

Brand, S., ed., *Whole Earth Catalog*, Menlo Park, CA, Portola Institute, Fall 1968.

Branda, E., *The Architecture of Information at Plateau Beaubourg*, University of California, Los Angeles, PhD thesis, 2012, https://escholarship.org/uc/item/0ww309s3#page-1 [accessed 7 June 2015].

Browne, J., 'Securing a Sustainable Future for Higher Education', 2010, p. 8, https://www.gov.uk/government/uploads/system/uploads/attachment_data/file/422565/bis-10-1208-securing-sustainable-higher-education-browne-report.pdf [accessed 16 July 2015].

Bucci, F., *Albert Kahn: Architect of Ford*, New York: Princeton Architectural Press, 2002.

Buchloh, B. H. D. and Rodenbeck, J. F., eds *Experiments in the Everyday: Allan Kaprow and Robert Watts – Events, Objects, Documents*, New York: Miriam and Ira D. Wallach Art Gallery, Columbia University in the City of New York, 1999.

Buckley, C. and Violeau, J., eds, *Utopie: Texts and Projects, 1967-1978*, Los Angeles, CA: Semiotext(e), 2011.

Bunz, M., 'Facing Our New Monster: On Critique in the Era of Affirmation', *Academia. edu*, https://www.academia.edu/2309534/Facing_Our_New_Monster_On_ Critique_in_the_Era_of_Affirmation [accessed 25 January 2014].

Burroughs, W. S., *The Soft Machine*, The Restored Text, London: Penguin, 2014.

Burroughs, W. S., *The Ticket That Exploded*, The Restored Text, London: Penguin, 2014.

Buruma, I., 'Don't be fooled – China is not squeaky clean', *The Guardian*, Tuesday 30 July 2002, http://www.guardian.co.uk/world/2002/jul/30/china.features11 [accessed 28 November 2014].

Caldwell, B., *Hayek's Challenge: An Intellectual Biography of F.A. Hayek*, Chicago and London: University of Chicago Press, 2004.

Cesarz, M., and Ferreira-Erlenbach, M., eds, *Meydan Shopping Square: A New Prototype by FOA*, Berlin: Jovis, 2007.

Chabot, P., *The Philosophy of Simondon: Between Technology and Individuation*, trans. A. Krefetz, London and New York: Bloomsbury, 2013.

Clough, P. T., with Halley, J., eds, *The Affective Turn: Theorizing the Social*, Durham and London: Duke University Press, 2007.

Cohen, M., 'Walter Benjamin's Phantasmagoria', *New German Critique*, vol. 48 (Autumn 1989), pp. 87–107.

Colquhoun, A., 'Plateau Beaubourg', *Architectural Design*, vol. 47, no. 2 (1977), reprinted in *Collected Essays in Architectural Criticism*, Cambridge, MA: MIT Press, 1981.

Craig-Martin, M, 'Richard Hamilton in Conversation with Michael Craig-Martin', in H. Foster with A. Bacon (eds), *October Files 10*, Cambridge, MA and London: MIT, 2010, pp. 1–13.

Crary, J., *24/7: Late Capitalism and the Ends of Sleep*, London and New York: Verso, 2013.

Cunningham, D., 'The Architecture of Money: Jameson, Abstraction and Form', in Nadir Lahiji (ed.), *The Political Unconscious of Architecture: Re-opening Jameson's Narrative*, Farnham, England, and Burlington, USA: Ashgate, 2012, pp. 37–55.

Cusset, F., 'Theory (Madness of)', *Radical Philosophy* 167 (May/June 2011), pp. 24–30.

Dardot, P. and Laval, C., *The New Way of the World: On Neo-liberal Society*, trans. G. Elliot, London and New York: Verso, 2013.

Dean, J., *Democracy and Other Neoliberal Fantasies: Communicative Capitalism & Left Politics*, Durham and London: Duke University Press, 2012.

Dean, J., 'Complexity as Capture – Neoliberalism and the Loop of Drive', in J. Gilbert (ed.), *New Formations 80-81: Neoliberal Culture*, London: Lawrence and Wishart, 2013, pp. 138–54.

De Boever, A., Murray, A., Roffe, J., and Woodward, A., eds, *Gilbert Simondon: Being and Technology*, Edinburgh: Edinburgh University Press, 2012.

Debord, G., *The Society of the Spectacle*, trans. K. Knabb, London: Rebel Press, 2004.

DeLanda, M., 'The Nonlinear Development of Cities', in *Eco-Tec: The Architecture of the In-Between*, ed. A. Marras, New York: Princeton Architectural Press, 1999, pp. 22–31.

DeLanda, M., 'Deleuze and the Use of the Genetic Algorithm in Architecture', in *Designing for a Digital World*, ed. N. Leach, New York: Wiley, 2002, pp. 117–18.

DeLanda, M., 'Materiality: Anexact and Intense', in *NOX: Machining Architecture*, ed. L. Spuybroek, London: Thames & Hudson, 2004, pp. 370–7.

Deleuze, G., *The Fold: Leibniz and the Baroque*, trans. Tom Conley, London: The Athlone Press, 1993.

Deleuze, G., 'Postscript on Control Societies', in *Negotiations, 1972-1990*, trans. Martin Joughin, New York and Chichester: Columbia University Press, 1995. pp. 177–82.

Deleuze, G., *Francis Bacon: The Logic of Sensation*, trans. D. W. Smith, London and New York: Continuum, 2003.

Deleuze, G. and Guattari, F., *A Thousand Plateaus: Capitalism and Schizophrenia*, trans. Brian Massumi, London and New York: Continuum, 1992.

Deleuze, G. and Guattari, F., *What is Philosophy?*, trans. Graham Burchell and Hugh Tomlinson, London and New York: Verso, 1994.

Department of Education and Skills, 'The future of higher education', 2003, www.dfes.gov.uk/hegateway/strategy/hestrategy/pdfs/DfES-HigherEducation.pdf; www.hefce.ac.uk/pubs/hefce/2005/ [accessed 21 July 2015].

DeRoo, R. J., *The Museum Establishment and Contemporary Art: The Politics of Artistic Display in France after 1968*, New York: Cambridge University Press, 2006.

Derrida, J., 'Psyché: Invention of the Other', in Derek Attridge (ed.), *Acts of Literature*, London and New York: Routledge, 1992, pp. 335–6.

Drucker, P. F., *Management: Tasks, Responsibilities, Practices*, New York: Harper & Row, 1974.

Dugdale, S., 'Space Strategies for the New Learning Landscape', *EDUCAUSE Review*, vol. 44, no. 2 (March/April 2009), http://www.educause.edu/EDUCAUSE+Review/EDUCAUSEReviewMagazineVolume44/SpaceStrategiesfortheNewLearni/163820 [accessed 21 July 2015].

Duménil, G. and Lévy, D., *Capital Resurgent: Roots of the Neoliberal Revolution*, trans. D. Jeffers, Cambridge, MA and London: Harvard University Press, 2004.

Eagleton, T., *The Ideology of the Aesthetic*, Malden and Oxford: Blackwell, 1990.

Edmondson, G., 'BMW Keeps the Home Fires Burning', Businessweek, 30 May 2005, http://www.businessweek.com/magazine/content/05_22/b3935087_mz054.htm [accessed 27 July 2009].

Fezer, J., *Design In & Against the Neoliberal City*, London: Bedford Press, 2013.

Flew, T., 'Six Theories of Neoliberalism' (2012), http://terryflew.com/2012/11/six-theories-of-neoliberalism.html [accessed 22 March 2014].

Foucault, M., *Vol. 3, The History of Sexuality: The Use of Pleasure*, trans. R. Hurley, New York: Vintage Books, 1988.

Foucault, M., *Vol. 2, The History of Sexuality: The Use of Pleasure*, trans. R. Hurley, New York: Vintage Books, 1990.

Foucault, M., *Ethics: Subjectivity and Truth*, ed. P. Rabinow, trans. R. Hurley, London: Penguin, 2000.

Foucault, M., *Security, Territory, Population: Lectures at the Collège de France, 1977-78*, trans. G. Burchell, Basingstoke, UK and New York: Palgrave Macmillan, 2007.

Foucault, M., *The Birth of Biopolitics: Lectures at the Collège de France, 1978-79*, trans. M. Senellart, Basingstoke, UK and New York: Palgrave Macmillan, 2008.

Foucault, M., *The Government of Self and Others: Lectures at the Collège de France, 1982-83*, trans. G. Burchell, Basingstoke, UK and New York: Palgrave Macmillan, 2011.

Frank, T., *The Conquest of Cool: Business Culture, Counterculture, and the Rise of Hip Consumerism*, Chicago and London: University of Chicago Press, 1997.

Frank, T., *One Market Under God: Extreme Capitalism, Market Populism, and the End of Economic Democracy*, New York: Doubleday, 2000.

French, S., Leyshon, A., and Wainwright, T., 'Financializing space, spacing financialization', *Progress in Human Geography*, vol. 35, no. 6 (December 2011), pp. 798–819.

Fuller, R. B., *Operating Manual for Spaceship Earth*, Baden, Switzerland: Lars Müller, 2008.

Furuhata, Y., 'Multimedia Environments and Security Operations: Expo '70 as a Laboratory of Governance', *Grey Room*, vol. 54 (Winter 2014), pp. 56–79.

Gannon, T., ed., *Zaha Hadid: BMW Central Building, Leipzig, Germany*, New York: Princeton Architectural Press, 2006.

Gargiani, R., *Rem Koolhaas/OMA: The Construction of Merveilles*, London and New York: Routledge, 2008.

Gibson, O, 'More than 500 Indian workers have died in Qatar since 2012, figures show', *The Guardian*, 18 February 2014, http://www.theguardian.com/world/2014/feb/18/qatar-world-cup-india-migrant-worker-deaths [accessed 2 April 2015].

Giedion, S., *Space, Time and Architecture: The Growth of a New Tradition*, fifth edition, Cambridge, MA: Harvard University Press, 2008 (1941).

Gilbert, J., '"Neoliberalism" and "Capitalism" – what's the difference?', https://jeremygilbertwriting.wordpress.com/2015/07/14/neoliberalism-and-capitalism-whats-the-difference/ [accessed 19 September 2015].

Godard, J. L., *Alphaville – Screenplay*, trans. P. Whitehead, London: Faber and Faber, 2000.

Gökay, B., and Xypolia, I., eds, *Reflections on Taksim – Gezi Park: Protests in Turkey*, 2013, http://www.keele.ac.uk/journal-globalfaultlines/publications/geziReflections.pdf [accessed 30 September 2015].

Gow, D., 'From Trabant to BMW: The east rises again', *The Guardian*, 17 May 2005, http://www.theguardian.com/business/2005/may/17/germany.internationalnews [accessed 28 July 2009].

Haiven, M., 'The Financial Crisis as a Crisis of Imagination', *Cultural Logic: Marxist Theory and Practice*, Special Issue: Culture and Crisis (2010), http://clogic.eserver.org/2010/Haiven.pdf [accessed 28 June 2014].

Hardt, M., and Negri, A., *Empire*, Cambridge, MA: Harvard University Press, 2000.

Hardt, M., and Negri, A., *Multitude: War and Democracy in the Age of Empire*, London and New York: Penguin, 2004.

Harris, P., Connolly, J., and Feeney, L., 'Blended Learning: Overview and Recommendations for Successful Implementation', *Industrial and Commercial Training*, vol. 41, no. 3 (2009), pp. 155–63.

Harvey, D., *A Brief History of Neoliberalism*, Oxford: Oxford University Press, 2005.

Hays, K. M., ed., *Architecture Theory since 1968*, Cambridge, MA and London: MIT Press, 1998.

Hayek, F. A., *The Sensory Order: An Inquiry into the Foundations of Theoretical Psychology*, Chicago and London: University of Chicago Press, 1952.

Hayek, F. A., 'The Intellectuals and Socialism', in George B. de Huszar (ed.), *The Intellectuals: A Controversial Portrait*, Glencoe, IL: The Free Press, 1960, pp. 371–84.

Hayek, F. A., *Studies in Philosophy, Politics and Economics*, Chicago: The University of Chicago Press, 1967.

Hayek, F. A., *The Road to Serfdom*, Abingdon, Oxon and New York: Routledge, 2001.

Hayek, F. A., *The Constitution of Liberty*, Abingdon, Oxon and New York: Routledge, 2006.

Hayek, F. A., *Law, Legislation and Liberty: A New Statement of the Liberal Principles of Justice and Political Economy*, Abingdon, Oxon and New York: Routledge, 2013.

Hayek, F. A., *The Market and Other Orders*, Collected Works of F. A. Hayek, Vol. 15, ed. Caldwell, B., Chicago: University of Chicago Press, 2014.

Hecht, G., *The Radiance of France: Nuclear Power and National Identity after World War II*, Cambridge, MA and London: The MIT Press, 2009.

HEFCE, 'HEFCE strategy for e-learning', 2005, www.hefce.ac.uk/pubs/hefce/2005/ [accessed 21 July 2015].

Helmling, S., *Adorno's Poetics of Critique*, London and New York: Continuum, 2009.

Hodges, L., 'Ravensbourne college gets ready to move in to eye-catching new premises' in *The Independent*, Thursday, 15 July 2010, http://www.independent.co.uk/news/ education/higher/ravensbourne-college-gets-ready-to-move-in-to-eyecatching-new-premises-2026802.html [accessed 21 July 2015].

Holland, E. W., 'Deterritorializing "Deterritorialization": From the "Anti-Oedipus" to "A Thousand Plateaus"', *SubStance*, vol. 20, no. 3, Issue 66: Special Issue: Deleuze & Guattari (1991), pp. 55–65.

Horkheimer, M., *Critical Theory: Selected Essays*, trans. Matthew J. O'Conell, New York: Continuum, 2002.

Hughes, J., and Sadler, S., eds, *Non-Plan: Essays on Freedom, Participation and Change in Modern Architecture and Urbanism*, Oxford: Architectural Press, 2000.

Hui, W., *The End of the Revolution: China and the Limits of Modernity*, London and New York: Verso, 2007.

Jacobs, J., *The Death and Life of Great American Cities*, New York: Vintage Books, 1992.

Jameson, F., *Marxism and Form: Twentieth-Century Dialectical Theories of Literature*, Princeton: Princeton University Press, 1971.

Jameson, F., *Postmodernism, or The Cultural Logic of Late Capitalism*, London and New York: Verso, 1991.

Jameson, F., *Jameson on Jameson: Conversations on Cultural Marxism*, ed. Ian Buchanan, Durham and London: Duke University Press, 2007.

Jencks, C., *The Language of Post-Modern Architecture*, 4th edn, New York: Rizzoli, 1984.

Jobs, S., 'Find What You Love', *Wall Street Journal*, 6 October 2011, http://online.wsj.com/news/articles/SB10001424052970203388804576613572842080228 [accessed 18 July 2015].

Johansson-Young, J., 'The BIG picture: A case for a flexible learning agenda at Ravensbourne', internal publication of Ravensbourne College, 2006, http://intranet.rave.ac.uk/quality/docs/LTR060203-flexlearn_4.pdf [accessed 21 July 2015].

Johnston, J., 'Machinic Vision', *Critical Enquiry*, vol. 26 (Autumn 1999), pp. 27–48.

Jones, D. S., *Masters of the Universe: Hayek, Friedman, and the Birth of Neoliberal Politics*, Princeton and Oxford: Princeton University Press, 2012.

Kant, I., *Critique of Pure Reason*, trans. J. M. D. Meiklejohn, Mineola, New York: Dover, 2004.

Kaprow, A., *Essays on the Blurring of Art and Life*, Berkeley, LA and London, University of California Press, 2003.

Keuning, D., 'Shopping Permitted: Meydan shopping mall in Istanbul, Turkey (Foreign Office Architects)' *Mark*, February/March 2008, http://www.davidkeuning.com/article.php?$lang=en&$w=i&$t=1371&$a=25 [accessed 10 July 2015].

Kipnis, J., 'On the Wild Side', in Farshid Moussavi, Alejandro Zaera-Polo and Sanford Kwinter (eds), *Phylogenesis: FOA's Ark*, Barcelona: Actar, 2004, pp. 566–80.

Knabb, K., ed. and trans. *Situationist International Anthology*, Berkeley, CA: Bureau of Public Secrets, 1989.

Koolhaas, R., *Delirious New York: A Retroactive Manifesto for Manhattan*, New York: Monacelli Press, 1978.

Koolhaas, R., 'Beijing Manifesto', *Wired*, vol. 6, no. 11 (2003), pp. 120–9.

Koolhaas, R., and Mau, B., *S,M,L,XL*, New York: The Monacelli Press, 1995.

Koolhaas, R., and Scheeren, O., *CCTV by OMA, A + U (Architecture and Urbanism): CCTV by OMA* (July 2005).

Koolhaas, R., and *Der Spiegel*, 'Rem Koolhaas: An obsessive compulsion towards the spectacular', *Der Spiegel*, July 18, 2008, http://www.spiegel.de/international/world/0,1518,566655-2,00.html [accessed 28 November 2014].

Koolhaas, R. and Obrist, H. U., *Project Japan*, Köln: Taschen, 2012.

Lahiji, N., ed., *Can Architecture be an Emancipatory Project?: Dialogues on the Left*, Winchester, UK, Washington, USA: Zero Books, forthcoming.

Laing, A., 'The Future of the Workplace is now', 2004, http://www.degw.com/dnews/ed_5_archive_leader.html [accessed 20 August 2014].

Laing, A., 'Measuring Workplace Performance', 2005, http://www2.corenetglobal.org/dotCMS/kcoAsset?assetInode=75645 [accessed 21 August 2014].

Latour, B., 'Why has critique run out of steam? From matters of fact to matters of concern', *Critical Inquiry*, vol. 30, no. 2 (2004), pp. 225–48.

Latour, B., and Weibel, P., eds, *Making Things Public: Atmospheres of Democracy*, Cambridge, MA: MIT, 2005.

Lavin, S., *Kissing Architecture,* Princeton and Oxford: Princeton University Press, 2011.

Lazzarato, M., 'Immaterial Labour', in M. Hardt and P. Virno (eds), *Radical Thought in Italy: A Potential Politics*, Minneapolis and London: University of Minnesota Press, 1997.

Lazzarato, M., *Signs and Machines: Capitalism and the Production of Subjectivity*, trans. J. D. Jordan, Los Angeles, CA: Semiotext(e), 2014.

Lefebvre, H., *The Production of Space*, trans. D. Nicholson Smith, Oxford: Blackwell, 2000.

Lefebvre, H., *The Urban Revolution*, trans. R. Bononno, Minneapolis and London: University of Minnesota Press, 2003.

Lemke, T., 'Foucault, Governmentality, Critique', *Rethinking Marxism: A Journal of Economics, Culture & Society*, vol. 14, no. 3 (2002), pp. 49–64.

Lynn, G., ed., *Folding in Architecture*, Chichester and Hoboken, NJ: Wiley-Academy, 1993/2004 (reprinted).

Lyon, D., 'Surveillance, Snowden, and Big Data: Capacities, Consequences, Critique', *Big Data & Society* (July to December 2014), pp. 1–13.

Lyotard, J., *The Postmodern Condition: A Report on Knowledge*, trans. Geoff Bennington and Brian Massumi, Manchester: Manchester University Press, 1984.

MacCabe, C., *Godard: A Portrait of the Artist at 70*, London: Bloomsbury, 2003.

Marcuse, H., *One Dimensional Man: Studies in the Ideology of Advanced Industrial Society*, London and New York: Routledge, 2002.

Marcuse, H., 'Social Implications of Technology', in D. M. Kaplan (ed.), *Readings in the Philosophy of Technology*, Oxford: Rowan & Littlefield, 2004, pp. 63–80.

Martin, R., *Utopia's Ghost: Architecture and Postmodernism, Again*, Minneapolis and London: University of Minnesota Press, 2010.

Marx, K., *Grundrisse: Introduction to the Critique of Political Economy*, trans. M. Nicolaus, London: Penguin, 1973.

Marx, K., *Capital, Volume I*, trans. B. Fowkes, London: Penguin, 1976.

Massumi, B., *Parables for the Virtual: Movement, Affect, Sensation*, Durham and London: Duke University Press, 2002.

Matthews, S., *From Agit-Prop to Free Space: The Architecture of Cedric Price*, London: Black Dog Publishing, 2007.

McHale, J., 'New Symbiosis', *Architectural Design*, vol. 37 (February 1967), pp. 89–92.

McHale, J., *The Ecological Context*, London: Studio Vista, 1971.

McLuhan, M., 'The Invisible Environment: The Future of an Erosion', *Perspecta*, vol. 11 (1967), pp. 163–7.

McLuhan, M., 'The Playboy Interview: Marshall McLuhan', *Playboy Magazine*, March 1969, http://www.nextnature.net/2009/12/the-playboy-interview-marshall-mcluhan/ [accessed March 2014].

McLuhan, M., and Fiore, Q., *The Medium is the Massage*, London: Penguin, 1967.

Metcalfe, M., Carlow, R., de Vroorne, R., and Rees, R., 'Final Report for the Designs on Learning Project', internal publication of Ravensbourne College, 2008.

Meyer, C., and Davis, S., *It's Alive: The Coming Convergence of Information, Biology, and Business*, New York: Crown Business, 2003.

Meynaud, J., *Technocracy*, trans. P. Barnes, New York: Free Press, 1968.

Mitropoulos, A., *Contract and Contagion: From Biopolitics to Oikonomia*, Brooklyn, NY: Minor Compositions/Autonomedia, 2012.

Mirowski, P., *Machine Dreams: Economics Becomes a Cyborg Science*, Cambridge: Cambridge University Press, 2002.

Mirowski, P., *Never Let a Serious Crisis Go to Waste: How Neoliberalism Survived the Financial Meltdown*, London: Verso, 2013.

Mirowski, P. and Plehwe, D., eds, *The Road from Mont Pèlerin: The Making of the Neoliberal Thought Collective*, Cambridge, MA and London: Harvard University Press, 2009.

Moffat, I., '"A Horror of Abstract Thought": Postwar Britain and Hamilton's 1951 "Growth and Form" Exhibition', *October*, vol. 94, The Independent Group (Autumn 2000), pp. 89–112.

Moussavi, F., *The Function of Form*, Barcelona and New York: Actar/Harvard University Graduate School of Design, 2009.

Moussavi, F., *The Function of Style*, Barcelona and New York: Actar/Harvard University Graduate School of Design, 2014.

Mullin, J. R., 'Henry Ford and Field and Factory: An Analysis of the Ford Sponsored Village Industries – Experiment in Michigan, 1918-1941', http://works.bepress.com/ cgi/viewcontent.cgi?article=1021&context=john_mullin [accessed 27 April 2010].

n.a. 'Istanbul in Numbers', http://www.greatistanbul.com/numbers.htm [accessed 3 July 2015].

n.a. *Realisierungswettbewerb BMW Werk Leipzig – Zentralgebäude*, 2001, translated for the author by Frank Elliot, http://www.bmw-werk-leipzig.de/ [accessed 11 June 2009].

Negroponte, N., 'Toward a Theory of Architecture Machines', *Journal of Architectural Education*, vol. 23, no. 2 (March 1969), pp. 9–12.

Niethammer, L., 'Germany: Temporary workers are first victims of recession', World Socialist Web Site, 12 January 2009, http://www.wsws.org/articles/2009/jan2009/ germ-j12.shtml [accessed 28 August 2009].

Nilsson, J. and Wallenstein, S., eds, *Foucault, Biopolitics, and Governmentality*, Stockholm: Södertörn Philosophical Studies, 2013.

Noys, B., 'The Discreet Charm of Bruno Latour', in Jernej Habjan and Jessica Whyte (eds), *(Mis)readings of Marx in Continental Philosophy*, Basingstoke: Palgrave, 2014, pp. 195–210.

Obrist, H. U., *Zaha Hadid and Hans Ulrich Obrist* (The Conversation Series, 8), Cologne: Verlag der Buchhandlung Walther König. 2007.

Ong, A., *Neoliberalism as Exception: Mutations in Citizenship and Sovereignty*, Durham and London: Duke University Press, 2006.

O'Sullivan, S., 'The Aesthetics of Affect: Thinking art Beyond Representation', *Angelaki*, vol. 6, no. 3 (December 2001), pp. 125–35.

Partridge, J., 'Pompodolium', *Architectural Review* (May 1977), pp. 271–2.

Pask, G., 'The Architectural Relevance of Cybernetics', *Architectural Design* (September 1969), pp. 494–6.

Patton, P., 'Drive-Thru Office', *Metropolis* July, 2005, http://www.metropolismag.com/story/20050613/drive-thru-office [accessed 29 July 2009].

Patton, P. and Protevi, J., eds, *Between Deleuze and Derrida*, London and New York: Continuum, 2003.

Peck, J., *Constructions of Neoliberal Reason*, Oxford and New York: Oxford University Press, 2010.

Picon, A., *Ornament: The Politics of Architecture and Subjectivity*, Chichester, West Sussex: Wiley, 2013.

Pitts-Taylor, V., 'The Plastic Brain: Neoliberalism and the Neuronal Self', *Health*, vol. 14, no. 6 (November 2010), pp. 635–52.

Polanyi, M., *The Logic of Liberty: Reflections and Rejoinders*, Abingdon, Oxon: Routledge, 1998.

Poole, M., and Shvartzberg, M., eds, *The Politics of Parametricism: Digital Technologies in Architecture*, London, New Dehli, New York and Sydney: Bloomsbury, 2015.

Postone, M., *Time, Labor and Social Domination: A reinterpretation of Marx's critical theory*, Cambridge: Cambridge University Press, 1993.

Postone, M., 'Rethinking Marx (in a Post-Marxist World)', in C. Camic (ed.), *Reclaiming the Sociological Classics*, Cambridge, MA: Blackwell Publishers, 1998.

Pries, L., 'Cost competition or innovation competition? Lessons from the case of the BMW plant location in Leipzig', *Transfer* 1/06 (Spring 2006), pp. 11–29.

Rajchman, J., *Constructions*, Cambridge, MA: MIT Press, 1998.

Raunig, G., *A Thousand Machines: A Concise Philosophy of the Machine as Social Movement*, trans. A. Derieg, Los Angeles, CA: Semiotext(e), 2010.

Read, J., 'The Production of Subjectivity: From Transindividuality To The Commons', *New Formations*, vol. 70 (Winter 2011), pp. 113–31.

Reiser, J. and Umemoto, N., *Atlas of Novel Tectonics*, New York: Princeton Architectural Press, 2006

Riach, J., 'Zaha Hadid defends Qatar World Cup role following migrant worker deaths', *The Guardian*, 25 February 2014, http://www.theguardian.com/world/2014/feb/25/zaha-hadid-qatar-world-cup-migrant-worker-deaths [accessed 2 April 2015].

Rofel, L., *Desiring China: Experiments in Neoliberalism, Sexuality, and Public Culture*, Durham and London: Duke University Press, 2007.

Rogers, R., *Cities for a Small Planet*, London: Faber and Faber, 1997.

Rose, J. 'Cooper Union Students Fight For Freedom From Tuition', NPR, 10 June 2013, http://www.npr.org/2013/06/10/190427334/cooper-union-students-fight-for-freedom-from-tuition [accessed 16 July 2015].

Ross, A., *Nice Work If You Can Get It: Life and Labor in Precarious Times*, New York: New York University Press, 2009.

Ross, K., *Fast Cars, Clean Bodies: Decolonization and the Reordering of French Culture*, Cambridge, MA and London: The MIT Press, 1996.

Rosser, J. B., 'How complex are the Austrians?', in R. Koppl, S. Horwitz and P. Desrochers (eds), *Advances in Austrian Economics, Volume 14: What is so Austrian about Austrian Economics?* Bingley: Emerald Group Publishing, 2010, pp. 165–79.

Roy, A., and Ong, A., eds, *Worlding Cities: Asian Experiments and the Art of Being Global*, Oxford: Blackwell, 2011.

Saieh, N., 'Venice Biennale 2012: Architecture and its Affects / Farshid Moussavi', 4 September 2012. *ArchDaily*, http://www.archdaily.com/269585/venice-biennale-2012-farshid-moussavi/ [accessed 4 August 2015].

Scheeren, O., Interview with FeedMeCoolShit, 2006, http://www.feedmecoolshit.com/interviews-archive/ole-scheeren/ [accessed 20 November 2014].

Schumacher, P., *Digital Hadid: Landscapes in Motion*, Basel: Birkhäuser, 2003.

Schumacher, P., 'Arguing for Elegance', in A. Rahim and H. Jamelle (eds), *Elegance*, AD, New York: Wiley, January/February 2007, pp. 29–37.

Schumacher, P., *The Autopoiesis of Architecture; Volume I: A New Framework for Architecture.* Chichester: Wiley, 2010.

Schumacher, P., *The Autopoiesis of Architecture; Volume II: A New Agenda for Architecture.* Chichester: Wiley, 2012.

Schumacher, P., 'On Parametricism: Georgina Day interviews Patrik Schumacher', 2012, http://www.patrikschumacher.com/Texts/On%20Parametricism_.html [accessed 2 April 2015].

Schumacher, P., 'Free Market Urbanism – Urbanism beyond Planning', in Tom Verebes (ed.), *Masterplanning the Adaptive City – Computational Urbanism in the Twenty-First Century*, Abingdon, Oxford and New York: Routledge, 2013, pp. 118–22.

Schumacher, P., 'The Historical Pertinence of Parametricism and the Prospect of a Free Market Urban Order', in Poole, M., and Shvartzberg, M. (eds), *The Politics of Parametricism: Digital Technologies in Architecture*, London, New Delhi, New York and Sydney: Bloomsbury, 2015, pp. 19–44.

Schumacher, P., and Eisenman, P., 'I am Trying to Imagine a Radical Free-market Urbanism', *Log* 28 (Summer 2013), pp. 39–52.

Schütz, A., 'Imperatives Without *Imperator*', *Law and Critique*, vol. 20, no. 3 (November 2009), pp. 233–43.

Scott, F. D., *Living Archive 7: Ant Farm. Allegorical Time Warp: The Media Fallout of July 21 1969*, Barcelona and New York: Actar, 2008.

Silberman, S., 'Life After Darth', *Wired*, no. 13, 5 May 2005, http://archive.wired.com/wired/archive/13.05/lucas.html?pg=2&topic=lucas&topic_set= [accessed 2 May 2014].

Silver, N., *The Making of Beaubourg: A Building Biography of the Centre Pompidou, Paris*, Cambridge, MA and London: MIT Press, 1994.

Simondon, G., 'Technical Mentality', trans. A. de Boever, *Parrhesia: A Journal of Critical Philosophy*, Vol. 7 (2009), Special Issue on the Work of Gilbert Simondon.

Speaks, M., 'Design intelligence. Part 1: Introduction', *A+U: Architecture and Urbanism*, no. 12 (December 2002), pp.10–18.

Speaks, M., 'Theory Was Interesting ... But Now We Have Work', *Architectural Research Quarterly*, vol. 6, no. 3 (2002), pp. 209–12.

Speaks, M., 'Intelligence After Theory', in M. Carter, C. Marcinkowski, F. Bagley and C. Bingo (eds), *Perspecta 38: Architecture After All*, Cambridge, MA: MIT, 2006, p.103.

Spectacular Times, *Buffo! Amazing Tales of Political Pranks and Anarchic Buffoonery*, London, n.d.

Spencer, D., 'Alphaville: A Strange Case of Urbanism and Genre', *Genre*, vol. 24 (2004), pp. 151–64.

Spencer, D., 'Nature is the Dummy: Circulations of the Metabolic', *New Geographies 6: Ungrounding Metabolism* (2014), pp. 112–17.

Spuybroek, L., *The Sympathy of Things: Ruskin and the Ecology of Design*, Rotterdam: V2_Publishing, 2011.

Spyropoulos, T., ed., *Adaptive Ecologies: Correlated Systems of Living*, London: AA Publications, 2013.

Steele, B., ed., *Corporate Fields: New Environments by the AA DRL*, London: AA Publications, 2005.

Steele, B., ed., *0-14: Projection and Reception: Reiser + Umemoto*, London: Architectural Association Publications, 2012.

Stengers, I., and Prigogine, I., *Order out of Chaos: Man's New Dialogue with Nature*, Toronto and New York: Bantam Books, 1984.

Stengers, I., *Power and Invention: Situating Science*, trans. Paul Bains, Minneapolis and London: University of Minnesota Press, 1997.

Stewart, J. B., 'How Cooper Union's Endowment Failed in Its Mission'. 10 May 2013, http://www.nytimes.com/2013/05/11/business/how-cooper-unions-endowment-failed-in-its-mission.html?_r=0 [accessed 16 July 2015].

Tafuri, M., *Interpreting the Renaissance: Princes, Cities, Architects*, trans. Daniel Sherer, New Haven and London: Yale University Press, in association with Cambridge, MA: Harvard University Graduate School of Design, 2006.

Tafuri, M. and Dal Co, F., *Modern Architecture*, Vol. 1, London and Milan: Faber and Faber/Electa, 1980.

Taifeng, S., 'CCTV Halts Decades-long Practice of "Remuneration though Invoices"', *Caijing*, 26 September, http://english.caijing.com.cn/2011-09-26/110874570.html [accessed 11 December 2014].

Tapscott, D., *The Digital Economy: Promise and Peril in the Age of Networked Intelligence*, New York: McGraw-Hill, 1996.

Tapscott, D., and Williams, A. D., *Wikinomics: How Mass Collaboration Changes Everything*, London: Atlantic Books, 2007.

Thatcher, M., 'Margaret Thatcher: The First Two Years', *Sunday Times*, 3 May 1981, http://www.margaretthatcher.org/document/104475 [accessed 11 May 2014].

Thompson, D. W., *On Growth and Form*, Cambridge: Cambridge University Press, 1945.

Thrift, N., *Non-Representational Theory: Space, Politics, Affect*, London: Routledge, 2007.

Toscano, A., 'Vital Strategies: Maurizio Lazzarato and the Metaphysics of Contemporary Capitalism', *Theory, Culture & Society*, vol. 24, no. 6 (2007), pp. 71–91.

Touraine, A., *The Post-Industrial Society: Tomorrow's Social History: Classes, Conflicts, and Culture in the Programmed Society*, trans. L. F. X. Mayhew, New York: Random House, 1971.

Tovar-Restrepo, M., *Castoriadis, Foucault, and Autonomy: New Approaches to Subjectivity, Society, and Social Change*, London and New York: Bloomsbury, 2013.

Trotter, M., 'Get Fit: Morphosis's New Academic Building for the Cooper Union', *Harvard Design Magazine* (Fall/Winter 2009/10), no. 31, http://www.harvarddesignmagazine.org/issues/31/get-fit-morphosiss-new-academic-building-for-the-cooper-union [accessed 11 July 2015].

Tuğal, C., 'The Greening of Istanbul', *New Left Review*, vol. 51 (May/June 2008), pp. 65–80.

Turner, F., *From Counterculture to Cyberculture: Stewart Brand, The Whole Earth Network and the Rise of Digital Utopianism*, Chicago and London: University of Chicago Press, 2008.

Turner, F., *The Democratic Surround: Multimedia & American Liberalism from World War II to the Psychedelic Sixties*, Chicago and London: University of Chicago Press, 2013.

Wacquant, L., 'Critical Thought as Solvent of *Doxa*', *Constellations*, vol. 11, no. 1 (2004), pp. 97–101.

Wacquant, L., 'Three Steps to a Historical Anthropology of Actually Existing Neoliberalism', *SocialAnthropology/AnthropologieSociale*, vol. 20, no. 1 (2012), pp. 166–79.

Wallenstein, S. O. and Nilsson, J., eds, *Foucault, Biopolitics, and Governmentality*, Stockholm: Södertörn Philosophical Studies, 2013.

Weinstock, M., 'Morphogenesis and the Mathematics of Emergence', in M. Hensel, A. Menges and M. Weinstock (eds), *Emergence: Morphogenetic Design Strategies*, AD, New York: Wiley, May/June 2004, pp. 10–7.

Wetherell, M., *Affect and Emotion: A New Social Science* Understanding, London: Sage, 2012.

Whiteley, N., *Pop Design: Modernism to Mod*, London: The Design Council, 1987.

Whiteley, N., *Reyner Banham: Historian of the Immediate Future*, Cambridge, MA and London: MIT Press, 2002.

Wiener, N., *The Human Use of Human Beings*, New York: Da Capo Press, 1954.

Wiener, N., *Cybernetics*, Cambridge, MA: MIT Press, 1976.

Worthington, J., and DEGW, 'Univer-Cities in their Cities: Conflict and Collaboration', paper presented at OECD Education Management Infrastructure Division, Higher Education Spaces & Places for Learning, Education and Knowledge Exchange,

University of Latvia, Riga: 6–8 December 2009, http://www.oecd.lu.lv/materials/ john-worthington.pdf [accessed 21 July 2015].

Zaera-Polo, A., 'Order out of Chaos: The Material Organization of Advanced Capitalism', *Architectural Design Profile*, vol. 108 (1994), pp. 24–9.

Zaera-Polo, A., 'The Hokusai Wave', *Perspecta*, vol. 37 (2005), pp. 78–85.

Zaera-Polo, A., 'The Politics of the Envelope', *Volume*, vol. 17 (Fall 2008), pp. 76–105.

Zaera-Polo, A., 'Patterns, Fabrics, Prototypes, Tessellations', *Architectural Design, Special Issue: Patterns of Architecture*, vol. 79, no. 6 (November/December 2009), pp. 18–27.

Zaera-Polo, A., 'Cheapnesss: No Frills and Bare Life', *Log*, vol. 18 (Winter 2010), pp. 15–27.

Zaera-Polo, A., *The Sniper's Log: Architectural Chronicles of Generation X*, Barcelona and New York: Actar, 2012.

Zhao, Y., *Communication in China: Political Economy, Power, and Conflict*, Lanham, MD, and Plymouth, UK: Rowman & Littlefield, 2008.

Zhu, Y., *Two Billion Eyes: The Story of China Central Television*, New York: The New Press, 2012.

Žižek, S., *Revolution at the Gates: Žižek on Lenin – The 1917 Writings*, London: Verso, 2002.

Žižek, S., *Organs Without Bodies: On Deleuze and Consequences*, London and New York: Routledge, 2004.

Žižek, S., *The Ticklish Subject: The Absent Centre of Political Ontology*, New Edition, London: Verso, 2009.

Index